———

True
Peace
Work

———

ESSENTIAL
WRITINGS
ON ENGAGED
BUDDHISM

True
Peace
Work

Edited by
Parallax Press

PARALLAX
PRESS

BERKELEY, CALIFORNIA

Parallax Press
P.O. Box 7355
Berkeley, California 94707
parallax.org

Parallax Press is the publishing division of Plum Village
Community of Engaged Buddhism, Inc.

First edition copyright © 1996 by Parallax Press
Second edition copyright © 2019 by Parallax Press

First edition, titled *Engaged Buddhist Reader*,
edited by Arnold Kotler
Second edition, titled *True Peace Work*,
edited by Parallax Press

Cover art ©Katie Eberle
Cover and text design by Debbie Berne

"Toward a Worldwide Culture of Love" by bell hooks,
"I Vow Not to Burn Out" by Mushim Patricia Ikeda, and
"Be Peace Embodied" by Charles Johnson reprinted
courtesy of *Lion's Roar*.

"Enoughness" by Bill McKibben was first published
in *Resurgence & Ecologist Magazine*, issue 299, March/
April 2005. All rights to this article are reserved to The
Resurgence Trust.

"Reflections on the Fire Sermon," by Bhikkhu Bodhi was
originally published in *Parabola* (parabola.org).

"In the Moments of Non-Awakening," by Larry Yang was
originally published in *Buddhadharma*, Spring 2019.

"Where the Heart Lives," by Zenju Earthlyn Manuel is
excerpted from *Sanctuary* and reprinted with permission
from Wisdom Publications.

ISBN: 978-1-946764-45-4

Library of Congress Cataloging-in-Publication Data
is available upon request.

1 2 3 4 5 / 23 22 21 20 19

"True peace is always possible. Yet it requires strength and practice, particularly in times of great difficulty. To some, peace and nonviolence are synonymous with passivity and weakness. In truth, practicing peace and nonviolence is far from passive. To practice peace, to make peace alive in us, is to actively cultivate understanding, love, and compassion, even in the face of misperception and conflict. Practicing peace, especially in times of war, requires courage."

—Thich Nhat Hanh

CONTENTS

Part VI : For a Future to Be Possible

INTRODUCTION TO THE SECOND EDITION

True Peace Work is a revised edition of *Engaged Buddhist Reader*, originally published in 1996 and edited by Arnold Kotler, then publisher of Parallax Press. The *Reader* was a celebration of ten years of publishing at Parallax Press, which was founded in 1986 with Vietnamese Zen teacher Thich Nhat Hanh's *Being Peace*. Each piece in the *Reader* was collected from books published by Parallax in that ten-year span, and the book included authors such as His Holiness the Dalai Lama, Robert Thurman, Peter Matthiessen, and Gary Snyder.

With *True Peace Work*, we have tried to remain true to the first edition, and have kept many of the essays in their original form. Of course, in publishing the second edition twenty-three years after the first, some updates have been needed, and we have taken the opportunity to include additional contributors as well. There are eleven new contributors to this edition: bell hooks, Bhikkhu Bodhi, Bill McKibben, Charles Johnson, Cheri Maples, Joan Halifax, Larry Yang, Matthieu Ricard, Mushim Patricia Ikeda, Brother Phap Dung, and Zenju Earthlyn Manuel. A sincere thank you to each of these profound teachers and thinkers for allowing their work to be included in this collection.

The term "Engaged Buddhism" was first used by Thich Nhat Hanh when he was talking about the response of Buddhist monks, nuns, and lay practitioners to the suffering of war in the 1960s. He writes: "What was going on around us was the suffering of many people and the destruction of life. So we were motivated by the desire to do something to relieve the suffering in us and around us." Thich Nhat Hanh and his disciples went out of the temple to help the wounded, and while they helped, they practiced mindful walking and mindful breathing.

Buddhism in its essence is Engaged Buddhism. Buddhism's Noble Eightfold Path is a path of right action and right livelihood. Wherever the Noble Eightfold Path is practiced, Engaged Buddhism is also practiced. The pieces collected here reflect the practice of the Noble Eightfold Path, which Thich Nhat Hanh talks about as the Buddhist contribution to a global ethic, something very practical which does not belong to the rituals of religion. Although readers will learn some of the history of Engaged Buddhism by reading this collection, it is not primarily historical or informational. This is a teaching collection, with insights and practices from some of the most widely respected spiritual leaders of our time.

Parallax Press Editors
Berkeley, California
January 2019

Cß

PART I

———

BEING PEACE

THICH NHAT HANH

Suffering Is Not Enough
1986

L IFE IS FILLED with suffering, but it is also filled with many wonders, like the blue sky, the sunshine, the eyes of a baby. To suffer is not enough. We must also be in touch with the wonders of life. They are within us and all around us, everywhere, any time.

If we are not happy, if we are not peaceful, we cannot share peace and happiness with others, even those we love, those who live under the same roof. If we are peaceful, if we are happy, we can smile and blossom like a flower, and everyone in our family, our entire society, will benefit from our peace. Do we need to make a special effort to enjoy the beauty of the blue sky? Do we have to practice to be able to enjoy it? No, we just enjoy it. Each second, each minute of our lives can be like this. Wherever we are, at any time, we have the capacity to enjoy the sunshine, the presence of each other, even the sensation of our breathing. We don't need to go to China to enjoy the blue sky. We don't have to travel into the future to enjoy our breathing. We can be in touch with these things right now. It would be a pity if we are only aware of suffering.

Meditation is to be aware of what is going on—in our bodies, our feelings, our minds, and the world. Each day 10,000 children die of hunger. The former superpowers still have 10,000 nuclear warheads, enough to destroy the Earth many times. Yet the sunrise is beautiful, and the rose that bloomed this morning along the wall is a miracle. Life is both dreadful and wonderful. To practice meditation is to be in touch with both aspects. Don't think you have to be solemn in order to meditate. To meditate well, you have to smile a lot.

Recently I was sitting with a group of children, and a boy named Tim was smiling beautifully. I said, "Tim, you have a beautiful smile," and he said, "Thank you." I told him, "You don't have to thank me, I have to thank you. Because of your smile, you make life more beautiful. Instead of saying, 'Thank you,' you should say 'You're welcome.'"

If a child smiles, if an adult smiles, that is very important. If in our daily life we can smile, if we can be peaceful and happy, not only we, but everyone will profit from it. This is the most basic kind of peace work. When I see Tim smiling, I am so happy. If he is aware that he is making other people happy, he can say, "You are welcome."

Even though life is hard, even though it is sometimes difficult to smile, we have to try. When we wish each other, "Good morning," it must be a real "Good morning." One friend asked me, "How can I force myself to smile when I am filled with sorrow?" I told her to smile to her sorrow. We are more than our sorrow. A human being is like a television set with millions of channels. If we turn the Buddha on, we are the Buddha. If we turn sorrow on, we are sorrow. If we turn a smile on, we are really the smile. We must not let just one channel dominate us. We have the seeds of everything in us, so we have to seize the situation at hand and recover our sovereignty.

We are so busy we hardly have time to look at the people we love, even in our own household, and to look at ourselves. Society is organized in a way that even when we have some leisure time, we don't know how to use it to get back in touch with ourselves. We have millions of ways to lose this precious time—we turn on the TV or pick up the telephone, or start the car and go somewhere. We are not used to being with ourselves, and we act as if we don't like ourselves and are trying to escape from ourselves.

When we sit down peacefully, breathing and smiling, with awareness, we are our true selves. When we open ourselves up to a TV program, we let ourselves be invaded by the program. Sometimes it is a good program, but often it is just noisy. Because we want something other than ourselves to enter us, we sit there and let a noisy television program invade us, assail us, destroy us. Even if our nervous system suffers, we don't have the courage to stand up and turn it off, because if we do that, we will have to return to our self.

Meditation is the opposite. It helps us return to our true self. Practicing meditation in this kind of society is very difficult. Everything seems to work in concert to try to take us away from our true self. We have thousands of things, like movies, the Internet, and music, that help us be away from ourselves. Practicing meditation is to be aware, to smile, to breathe. These are on the opposite side. We go back to ourselves in order to see what is going on, because to meditate means to be aware of what is going on. What is going on is very important.

Children understand very well that in each woman, in each man, there is a capacity of waking up, of understanding, and of loving. Many children have told me that they cannot show me anyone who does not have this capacity. Some people allow it to develop and some do not, but everyone has it. This capacity of waking up, of being aware of what is going on in our feelings, our body, our perceptions, and the world is called Buddha nature, the capacity of understanding and loving. We must give the baby of the Buddha in us a chance. Smiling is very important. It is not by going out for a demonstration that we can bring about peace. It is with our capacity of smiling, breathing, and being peace that we make peace.

THE DALAI LAMA

Cultivating Altruism
1992

T HE BASIC SOURCES of happiness are a good heart, compassion, and love. If we have these, even if we are surrounded by hostility, we will feel little disturbance. On the other hand, if we lack compassion and our mental state is filled with anger or hatred, no matter what the situation, we will not have peace. We will feel insecure and, eventually, afraid and lacking in self-confidence. Then even something small can destabilize our inner world. But if we are calm, even if we are confronted by a serious problem, we will know how to handle it.

To utilize our human intelligence fully, we need calmness. If we become unstable through anger, it is difficult for us to use our intelligence well. When we are overly influenced by negative thoughts, our intelligence becomes tarnished. Looking at human history over the last few thousand years, and particularly in this century, we see that human tragedies like the Holocaust arise from negative emotions such as hatred, anger, fear, and suspicion. And we also see that the many positive developments of human history have all come from good mental states, such as compassion.

In economics today, every nation is dependent on every other nation. Even hostile nations have to cooperate in the use of the world's resources. In both the global community and in the family, human beings need harmony and cooperation, which comes through mutual respect. Altruism is the most crucial factor.

If an individual has a sense of responsibility for humanity, he or she will naturally take care of the environment, including slowing down industrial growth and population growth. If we think narrow-mindedly and see only our own surroundings, we will not create a positive future. In the past, when we neglected the long-term effects of our actions, it was less consequential. But today, through science and technology, we can create far greater benefits or much more serious damage. The threat of nuclear weapons and the ability to damage our environment through, for example, deforestation, pollution, and ozone layer depletion, are quite alarming. We can all see the dangers of potential tragedies here. But other, barely noticeable changes, such as the loss of natural resources like topsoil, may be even more dangerous because, by the time they begin to affect us, it will be too late. In all respects, we see that genuine cooperation, the real sense of responsibility based on compassion and altruism, requires not only that we respect human beings, but also that we respect, take care of, and refrain from interfering with other species and the environment. On every level of work concerning the happiness or satisfaction of the individual, the family, the nation, and the international community, the key is our altruistic mind.

As I travel around the world and meet people from various walks of life, I see that many are now showing real concern about these matters and agree with these views. The fundamental question is how to develop and maintain compassion. Certain religious beliefs, if you have them, can be very helpful, but if you do not have them, you can also survive quite well. Compassion, love, and forgiveness, however, are not luxuries. They are fundamental for our survival.

Whenever I speak about the importance of compassion and love, people ask me what is the method for developing them? It is not easy. There is no particular package or method that enables you to develop these qualities instantaneously. You cannot just press a button and wait for them to appear. I know that many people expect things like this from a Dalai Lama, but, really, all I have to offer is my own experience. If you find something useful in this, please use it. But if you don't find much of interest, I don't mind if you just leave it.

We must begin by investigating our own daily experience and reading stories about others to see the consequences of anger and the consequences of love and compassion. If we make a comparative study of these two attitudes, we will develop a deeper understanding of the negative results of anger and the positive results of compassion. Once we are convinced of the benefits of compassion and the negative consequences of anger and hatred—that they always cause unhappiness within us—we will make greater efforts to have less anger. We usually think our anger is protecting us from something, but that is a deception. Most important is to realize the negative consequences of anger and hatred. Negative emotions do not help at all.

Sometimes people feel that when there is a natural disaster or a tragedy brought about by human beings, they will have more energy and boldness to fight back if they are angry. But, in my experience, even though anger gives us energy to act or to speak out, it is blind energy and difficult to control. During that moment, we may not care, but, after a few minutes, we will feel much regret. When we are angry, we use nasty or harsh words, which, once spoken, cannot be withdrawn. Afterward, when our anger has disappeared and we see the other person again, we feel terrible. During that moment, we lost our judgment and became half-mad. There are many different levels and forces of anger. When a small anger is about to arise, it is easy to control. But if a stronger, more forceful anger comes, we have to try different techniques to handle it. Once we see negative mental states as negative, that alone will reduce their strength. Through my own experience, I am convinced that as a result of less anger, we become happier and healthier, smile and laugh more, and have more friends. Mental tranquility, or calmness, is a very important source of happiness. An external enemy, no matter how powerful, cannot strike directly at our mental calmness, because calmness is formless. Our happiness or joy can only be destroyed by our own anger. The real enemy of joy is anger.

There are many different states of mind, and each directly affects our happiness. When we examine different states of mind within ourselves, we can cultivate and develop those that are positive and beneficial and avoid and eliminate those that are negative and destructive. The basic difference between the investigation of external matter and the investigation of mind is that the former requires large laboratories and a huge budget. In the internal world, you just investigate which thoughts are useful and which ones are harmful, and you keep and develop the ones you like, making constant effort. Over time, your mental state will become much better balanced, and you will find that you are happier and more stable. This is a kind of yoga for the mind.

Each day when we wake up, we can say to ourselves, "Altruistic attitude." If we have an altruistic attitude, many favorable things will come. I practice these things and I know they are helpful. I try to be sincere to everyone, even the Chinese. If I develop some kind of ill will, anger, or hatred, who will lose? I will lose my happiness, my sleep, and my appetite, but my ill feelings won't hurt the Chinese at all. If I am agitated, my physical condition will become weak, and some people I could make happy will not become happy.

Some people may criticize me, but I try to remain joyful. If we want to work effectively for freedom and justice, it is best to do so without anger or ill will. If we feel calm and have a sincere motivation, we can work hard for thirty or forty years. I believe that because of my firm commitment to nonviolence, based on a genuine sense of brotherhood and sisterhood, some positive results have been produced.

Letting Go of Suffering
1992

T HE BUDDHA SAID, "I teach only two things—suffering and the end of suffering."

What is the cause of suffering? Suffering arises from clinging. As long as the mind clings, it suffers. When the mind is silent, it becomes peaceful and free.

How can we be free from suffering? The road to peace is called the Middle Path. It is beyond all duality and opposites. Sometimes it is called equanimity. Equanimity harmonizes extremes, like the string of a finely-tuned instrument. Neither too tight nor too loose, it vibrates perfectly and makes beautiful music.

Don't pick or choose. Opposites are endless, and in fact, they produce each other. Day becomes night, light becomes darkness, good luck and bad luck are an endless cycle.

There was once a farmer who lost his mare. When the mare disappeared, the people of the village said, "Bad luck!" But when the mare came home the very next day followed by a good strong horse, the people of the village said, "Good luck!" Yesterday they thought "bad luck," today they think "good luck." Yesterday they said "loss," but today they say "gain." Which is true? Gain and loss are opposites.

When the farmer's son rode the beautiful horse, he fell and broke his leg. Then all of the people said, "Bad luck!" War came, and all of the strong men were drafted. Many men fought and died on the battlefield. Because the farmer's son had broken his leg, he could not go to war. Was this loss or gain? Good luck or bad luck? Who can say?

Life is filled with eating and drinking through our senses, and life is also keeping from being eaten. What eats us? Time! What is time? Time is living in the past or living in the future, feeding on the emotions. Beings who have been truly mentally healthy for even one minute are rare. Most of us suffer from clinging to pleasant, unpleasant, and neutral feelings, and from hunger and thirst. We eat and drink every second through our eyes, ears, nose, tongue, skin, and nerves, twenty-four hours a day without stopping! We crave food for the body, food for feeling, food for volitional action, and food for rebirth. We are the world, and we eat the world.

When he saw the endless cycle of suffering, the Buddha cried. The fly eats the flower; the frog eats the fly; the snake eats the frog; the bird eats the snake; the tiger eats the bird; the hunter kills the tiger; the tiger's body becomes swollen; flies come and eat the tiger's corpse; the flies lay eggs in the corpse; the eggs become more flies; and the flies eat the flowers . . . .

The Dharma is good in the beginning, good in the middle, and good in the end. Good in the beginning is the goodness of the moral precepts—not to kill, steal, commit adultery, tell lies, or take intoxicants. Good in the middle is concentration. Good in the end is wisdom and nirvana. The Dharma is visible here and now. It is always in the present, the omnipresent. The Dharma is timeless. It offers results at once.

In Buddhism, there are three *yanas*, or vehicles, and none is higher or better than any other. All three carry the same Dharma. There is a fourth vehicle that is even more complete, called

Dharmayana. It is the universe itself, and it includes every way that leads to peace and loving kindness. Dharmayana can never be sectarian. It can never divide us from any of our brothers or sisters. Come and experience it for yourself. The Dharma vehicle will bring you to peace right here and now. Step by step, moment by moment, it is comprehensible and can be understood by anyone. This is the kind of Buddhism I love.

JACK KORNFIELD

Spiritual Practice and Social Action
1988

H OW CAN WE reconcile the question of service and responsibility in the world with the Buddhist concepts of nonattachment, emptiness of self, and non-self? First we must learn to distinguish love, compassion, and equanimity from what might be called their "near-enemies."

The near-enemy of love is attachment. It masquerades as love: "I love this person, I love this thing," which usually means, "I want to hold it, I want to keep it, I don't want to let it be." This is not love at all; it is attachment, and they are different. There is a big difference between love, which allows and honors and appreciates, and attachment, which grasps and holds and aims to possess.

The near-enemy of compassion is pity. Instead of feeling the openness of compassion, pity says, "Oh, that poor person! They're suffering; they're different from me," and this sets up separation and duality. "That is outside me. I want it. I need it to be complete." I and it are seen as different.

The near enemy of equanimity is indifference. It feels very equanimous to say, "I don't care, I'm not really attached to it," and in a way it is a very peaceful feeling, a great relief. Why is that? Because it is a withdrawal. It is a removal from world and from life. Can you see the difference? Equanimity, like love and compassion, is not a removal. It is being in the middle of the world and opening to it with balance, seeing the unity in things. Compassion is a sense of our shared suffering. Equanimity is a balanced engagement with life. The "near-enemies"—attachment, pity, and indifference—all are ways of backing away or removing ourselves from the things that cause fear. Meditation does not lead to a departure from the world. It leads to a deeper vision of it, one which is not self-centered, which moves from a dualistic way of viewing ("I and other") to a more spontaneous, whole, unified way.

Vimala Thakar has been a meditation teacher in India and Europe for many years. In many ways, she is a Dharma heir to Krishnamurti. After she had been working in rural development for many years, Krishnamurti asked her to begin to teach, and she became a powerful and much-loved meditation teacher. Then she returned to her rural development work, teaching meditation considerably less. I asked her, "Why did you go back to rural development and helping the hungry and homeless after teaching meditation?" and she was insulted by my question. She said, "Sir, I am a lover of life, and I make no distinction between serving people who are starving and have no dignity in their physical lives and serving people who are fearful and closed and have no dignity in their mental lives. I love all of life."

What a wonderful response! There is a Sufi or Islamic phrase that says, "Praise Allah, and tie your camel to the post." It expresses both sides: pray, yes, but also make sure you do what is necessary in the world. It is what Don Juan called "a balance between controlled folly and impeccability." Controlled folly means seeing that all of life is a show of light and sound and that this tiny blue-green planet hangs in space with millions and billions of stars and galaxies, and that people have only been here for one second of world-time compared with millions of years of other changes.

This context helps us to laugh more often, to enter into life with joy. The quality of impeccability entails realizing how precious life is, even though it is transient and ephemeral, and how, in fact, each of our actions and words do count; each affects all the beings around us in a very profound way.

If I wanted, I could make a very convincing case for just practicing sitting meditation and doing nothing else; and an equally convincing case for going out and serving the world. Looking at it from the first side, does the world need more oil and energy and food? Actually, no. There are enough resources for all of us. There is starvation, poverty, and disease because of ignorance, prejudice, and fear, because we hoard and create wars over imaginary geographic boundaries and act as if one group of people is different from another. What the world needs is not more oil, but more love and generosity, kindness and understanding. Until those are attained, the other levels will never work. So you really have to sit and meditate and get that understanding in yourself first. Only when you have actually done it yourself can you have the insight to effectively help change the greed in the world and to love. It is not a privilege to meditate, but a responsibility. I will not go any further with this argument, but it is very convincing.

As for the other side, I only have to mention Cambodia or Somalia and the starvation in Central Africa and India, where the enormity of the suffering is beyond comprehension. In India alone, 350 million people live in such poverty that they have to work that day to get enough food to feed themselves that night, when they are lucky. I once interviewed a sixty-four-year-old man in Calcutta who pulled a rickshaw for a living. He had been pulling it for forty years and had ten people dependent on him for income. He had gotten sick once the year before for ten days, and after a week they ran out of money and had nothing to eat. How can we let this happen? Forty deaths per minute from starvation in the world; $714,000 a minute spent on machines to kill people. We must do something!

Both arguments are totally convincing. The question is how to choose what to do, what path to take, where to put our life energy, even which spiritual path to follow. Spirituality in the West has blossomed and it is exquisite! It is also kind of confusing. There are so many ways to go—how can we choose what to do? For me the answer has been to simply follow the heart. Sometimes it is clear that we must take time to meditate and simplify—to do our inner work. Sometimes it is clear that we must begin to act and give and serve.

I can share my own experience. Ordinarily I spend my year teaching meditation retreats. Some years ago, when war began raging in Cambodia, something in me said, "I'm going." I went, not for very long but long enough to be of some assistance. The following year, feeling a real need to bring a greater marriage of service and formal meditation, I went to India with some friends to collect tapes for radio and television on the relationship between spiritual practice and social responsibility. And now I am back teaching meditation.

I did not think about it much. It just had to be done, and I went and did it. It was immediate and personal. There is not some simple solution, some easy formula for everyone to follow. It is not a matter of imitation. You have to be yourself. That means listening to your heart and knowing the right thing to do, and then doing it in the spirit of growing in awareness and service.

In the face of the tremendous suffering of the world, there is a joy that comes not from denying the pain, but from sitting in meditation, even when it is difficult, and letting our hearts open to the experience. It is the nitty-gritty work of practice to sit here and feel your sadness and my sadness and our fear, desperation, and rest-lessness, to open to them and begin to learn that to love is to die to how we wanted it to be, and to open more to its truth. To love is to accept. It is not a weakness. It is the most extraordinary power.

True love is really the same as awareness. True love is to see the divine goodness, the Buddha nature, the truth of each moment, and to say, "Yes," to allow ourselves to open, to accept. That is our practice every moment, whether in sitting meditation or action meditation. To be aware, to see the truth, frees us. It opens us to what is now, to what is here, and we see it as it is.

The forces of injustice in the world loom large, and some-times we feel so tiny. How are we to have an impact? I will leave you with the words of Don Juan: "Only if one loves this Earth with unbending passion can one release one's sadness. A warrior is always joyful because his love is unalterable and his beloved, the Earth, bestows upon him inconceivable gifts . . . . Only the love for this splendorous being can give freedom to a warrior's spirit; and freedom is joy, efficiency, and abandon in the face of any odds."[1]

---

1 Carlos Castañeda, *Tales of Power* (Cutchogue, NY: Buccaneer Books, 1991).

BILL MCKIBBEN

Enoughness
2004

L AST EVENING, ON the longest day of the year, I took a walk in a meadow near my home.

At the edge of the meadow a path opened into the woods, and I followed it perhaps a hundred yards to the bank of a small stream where I rested on a rock and watched the brook flow. Then I walked back.

Nothing spectacular happened. No large animal jumped out to demonstrate its majesty. The flora was beautiful but unremarkable: buttercups, Queen Anne's lace, daisies, lupins. The sky didn't crackle with summer lightning; the sunset was only streaks of purple, some rosy glow on the underbellies of the clouds. A few mosquitoes made their presence known. It was simply a lovely night.

And simply the sort of scene that we have evolved with for hundreds of thousands of years, that has made us who we are, that we can't be fully human, or at least fully sane, without. The sort of scene whose absence in our lives is now making us slowly crazy. If there is a pertinent modern question, it is "How much is enough?" The consumer societies we have created posit that the only possible answer is "More." And so in pursuit of more we have turned ourselves into tubby folk, raised the temperature of the planet one degree with a further five degrees in prospect, countenanced the ever deeper gulfs between rich and poor, and so on. And in the process made ourselves . . . happy?

But say you're in a meadow, surrounded by wildflowers. Do you find yourself thinking, "They could do with some more wildflowers over there"? Do you glance up at the mountains on the horizon and think, "Some more mountains would be nice"? Do you lie on the rock by the brook thinking, "This brook needs more rocks"? Does the robin in that tree chide herself for not tripling the size of her nest? I think not. Nature schools us in sufficiency—its aesthetic and its economy demonstrate "enoughness" at every turn. Time moves circularly through the natural world—next spring there will be wildflowers again. Not more wildflowers: second quarter output for 2005 will show no year-on-year gain. Growth only replaces, since the planet is already accomplishing all the photosynthesis that's possible. It offers the great lesson of being simultaneously abundant and finite.

Interdependent, too. The emergent science of ecology is easily summed up: everything's connected. Field biologists using sensitive detectors have discovered that the needles of trees near Alaskan rivers owe their nitrogen to the carcasses of salmon that die along the banks, the same salmon that feed the bears whose pawing aerates the soil that . . .

We know now that this is true, but interconnection is anathema to a consumer notion of the world, where each of us is useful precisely to the degree that we consider ourselves the center of everything. We believe that pleasure comes from being big, outsized, immortal; now our zealots imagine genetically engineering us for greater greatness. But the testimony of the rest of creation is that there's something to be said for fitting in.

And because of that, the natural world offers us a way to think about dying, the chief craziness for the only species that can anticipate its own demise. If one is a small part of something large, if that something goes on forever, and if it is full of beauty and meaning, then dying seems less shocking. Which undermines about half the reason for being a dutiful consumer, for holding ageing forever at bay. Six months from now, on the shortest night of the year, this field will be under two feet of snow. Most of what I can see will be dead or dormant. And six months after that it will be here again as it is tonight.

Advertising, hyperconsumerism, ultra-individualism—these are designed to make you crazy. Nature, like close-knit human community, is designed to help you stay sane. You needn't be in the wilderness to feel in balm: a park, a container garden on the patio, a pet dog, a night sky, a rainstorm will do. For free.

PART II

———

TOUCHING PEACE

THICH NHAT HANH

Life Is a Miracle
1992

I N VIETNAM WHEN I was a young monk, each village temple had a big bell, like those in Christian churches in Europe and America. Whenever the bell was invited to sound, all the villagers would stop what they were doing and pause for a few moments to breathe in and out in mindfulness. At Plum Village, the community where I live in France, we do the same. Every time we hear the bell, we go back to ourselves and enjoy our breathing. When we breathe in, we say, silently, "Listen, listen," and when we breathe out, we say, "This wonderful sound brings me back to my true home."

Our true home is in the present moment. To live in the present moment is a miracle. The miracle is not to walk on water. The miracle is to walk on the green Earth in the present moment, to appreciate the peace and beauty that are available now. Peace is all around us—in the world and in nature and within us—in our bodies and our spirits. Once we learn to touch this peace, we will be healed and transformed. It is not a matter of faith; it is a matter of practice. We need only to find ways to bring our body and mind back to the present moment so we can touch what is refreshing, healing, and wondrous.

Once in New York City, I rode in a taxi, and I saw that the driver was not at all happy. He was not in the present moment.

There was no peace or joy in him, no capacity of being alive while doing the work of driving, and he expressed it in the way he drove.

Many of us do the same. We rush about, but we are not at one with what we are doing; we are not at peace. Our body is here, but our mind is somewhere else—in the past or the future, possessed by anger, frustration, hopes, or dreams. We are not really alive; we are like ghosts. If our beautiful child were to come up to us and offer us a smile, we would miss him completely, and he would miss us. What a pity!

In *The Stranger,* Albert Camus described a man who was going to be executed in a few days. Sitting alone in his cell, he noticed a small patch of blue sky through the skylight, and suddenly he felt deeply in touch with life, deeply in the present moment. He vowed to live his remaining days in mindfulness, in full appreciation of each moment, and he did so for several days. Then, just three hours before the time of his execution, a priest came into the cell to receive a confession and administer the last rites. But the man wanted only to be alone. He tried many ways to get the priest to leave, and when he finally succeeded, he said to himself that that priest lived like a dead man. "*Il vit comme un mort.*" He saw that the one who was trying to save him was less alive than he, the one who was about to be executed.

Many of us, although alive, are not really alive, because we are not able to touch life in the present moment. We are like dead people, as Camus says. I would like to share with you a few simple exercises we can practice that can help us reunify our body and mind and get back in touch with life in the present moment. The first is called conscious breathing, and human beings like us have been practicing this for more than three thousand years. As we breathe in, we know we are breathing in, and as we breathe out, we know we are breathing out. As we do this, we observe many elements of happiness inside us and around us. We can really enjoy touching our breathing and our being alive.

Life is found only in the present moment. I think we should have a holiday to celebrate this fact. We have holidays for so many important occasions—Christmas, New Year's, Mother's Day, Father's Day, even Earth Day—why not celebrate a day when we can live happily in the present moment all day long. I would like to declare today "Today's Day," a day dedicated to touching the Earth, touching the sky, touching the trees, and touching the peace that is available in the present moment.

Some time ago, I planted three beautiful Himalayan cedars outside my hermitage, and now, whenever I walk by one of them, I bow, touch its bark with my cheek, and hug it. As I breathe in and out mindfully, I look up at its branches and beautiful leaves. I receive a lot of peace and sustenance from hugging trees. Touching a tree gives both you and the tree great pleasure. Trees are beautiful, refreshing, and solid. When you want to hug a tree, it will never refuse. You can rely on trees. I have even taught my students the practice of tree-hugging.

At Plum Village, we have a beautiful linden tree that provides shade and joy to hundreds of people every summer. A few years ago during a big storm, many of its branches were broken off, and the tree almost died. When I saw the linden tree after the storm, I wanted to cry. I felt the need to touch it, but I did not get much pleasure from that touching. I saw that the tree was suffering, and I resolved to find ways to help it. Fortunately, our friend Scott Mayer is a doctor for trees, and he took such good care of the linden tree that now it is even stronger and more beautiful than before. Plum Village would not be the same without that tree. Whenever I can, I touch its bark and feel it deeply.

In the same way that we touch trees, we can touch ourselves

and others, with compassion. Sometimes, when we try to hammer a nail into a piece of wood, instead of pounding the nail, we pound our finger. Right away we put down the hammer and take care of our wounded finger. We do everything possible to help it, giving first aid and also compassion and concern. We may need a doctor or nurse to help, but we also need compassion and joy for the wound to heal quickly. Whenever we have some pain, it is wonderful to touch it with compassion. Even if the pain is inside—in our liver, our heart, or our lungs—we can touch it with mindfulness.

Our right hand has touched our left hand many times, but it may not have done so with compassion. Let us practice together. Breathing in and out three times, touch your left hand with your right hand and, at the same time, with your compassion. Do you notice that while your left hand is receiving comfort and love, your right hand is also receiving comfort and love? This practice is for both parties, not just one. When we see someone suffering, if we touch her with compassion, she will receive our comfort and love, and we will also receive comfort and love. We can do the same when we ourselves are suffering. Touching in this way, everyone benefits.

The best way to touch is with mindfulness. You know, it is possible to touch without mindfulness. When you wash your face in the morning, you might touch your eyes without being aware that you are touching them. You might be thinking about other things. But if you wash your face in mindfulness, aware that you have eyes that can see, that the water comes from distant sources to make washing your face possible, your washing will be much deeper. As you touch your eyes, you can say, "Breathing in, I am aware of my eyes. Breathing out, I smile to my eyes."

Our eyes are refreshing, healing, and peaceful elements that are available to us. We pay so much attention to what is wrong, why not notice what is wonderful and refreshing? We rarely take the time to appreciate our eyes. When we touch our eyes with our hands and our mindfulness, we notice that our eyes are precious jewels that are fundamental for our happiness. Those who have lost their sight feel that if they could see as well as we do, they would be in paradise. We only need to open our eyes, and we see every kind of form and color—the blue sky, the beautiful hills, the trees, the clouds, the rivers, the children, the butterflies. Just sitting here and enjoying these colors and shapes, we can be extremely happy. Seeing is a miracle, a condition for our happiness, yet most of the time we take it for granted. We don't act as if we are in paradise. When we practice breathing in and becoming aware of our eyes, breathing out and smiling to our eyes, we touch real peace and joy.

We can do the same with our heart. "Breathing in, I am aware of my heart. Breathing out, I smile to my heart." If we practice this a few times, we will realize that our heart has been working hard, day and night, for many years to keep us alive. Our heart pumps thousands of gallons of blood every day, without stopping. Even while we sleep, our heart continues its work to bring us peace and well-being. Our heart is an element of peace and joy, but we don't touch or appreciate it. We only touch the things that make us suffer, and because of that, we give our heart a hard time by our worries and strong emotions, and by what we eat and drink. Doing so, we undermine our own peace and joy. When we practice breathing in and becoming aware of our heart, breathing out and smiling to our heart, we become enlightened. We see our heart so clearly. When we smile to our heart, we are massaging it with our compassion. When we know what to eat and what not to eat, what to drink and what not to drink, what worries and despair we should avoid, we will keep our heart safe.

The same practice can be applied to other organs in our body, for instance our liver. "Breathing in, I know that my liver has been working hard to keep me well. Breathing out, I vow not to harm my liver by drinking too much alcohol." This is love meditation. Our eyes are us. Our heart is us. Our liver is us. If we cannot love our own heart and our own liver, how can we love another person? To practice love is, first of all, to practice love directed toward ourselves taking care of our body, taking care of our heart, taking care of our liver. We are touching ourselves with love and compassion.

When we have a toothache, we know that not having a toothache is a wonderful thing. "Breathing in, I am aware of my non-toothache. Breathing out, I smile at my non-toothache." We can touch our non-toothache with our mindfulness, and even with our hands. When we have asthma and can hardly breathe, we realize that breathing freely is a wonderful thing. Even when we have just a stuffed nose, we know that breathing freely is a wonderful thing.

Every day we touch what is wrong, and, as a result, we are becoming less and less healthy. That is why we have to learn to practice touching what is not wrong—inside us and around us. When we get in touch with our eyes, our heart, our liver, our breathing, and our non-toothache and really enjoy them, we see that the conditions for peace and happiness are already present. When we walk mindfully and touch the Earth with our feet, when we drink tea with friends and touch the tea and our friendship, we get healed, and we can bring this healing to society. The more we have suffered in the past, the stronger a healer we can become. We can learn to transform our suffering into the kind of insight that will help our friends and society.

We do not have to die to enter the Kingdom of Heaven. In fact, we have to be fully alive. When we breathe in and out and hug a beautiful tree, we are in Heaven. When we take one conscious breath, aware of our eyes, our heart, our liver, and our non-toothache, we are transported to Paradise right away. Peace is available. We only have to touch it. When we are truly alive, we can see that the tree is part of Heaven, and we are also part of Heaven. The whole universe is conspiring to reveal this to us, but we are so out of touch that we invest our resources in cutting down the trees. If we want to enter Heaven on Earth, we need only one conscious step and one conscious breath. When we touch peace, everything becomes real. We become ourselves, fully alive in the present moment, and the tree, our child, and everything else reveal themselves to us in their full splendor.

"The miracle is to walk on Earth." This statement was made by Zen Master Lin Chi. The miracle is not to walk on thin air or water, but to walk on Earth. The Earth is so beautiful. We are beautiful also. We can allow ourselves to walk mindfully, touching the Earth, our wonderful mother, with each step. We don't need to wish our friends, "Peace be with you." Peace is already with them. We only need to help them cultivate the habit of touching peace in each moment.

ROBERT AITKEN

The Dragon Who Never Sleeps
1992

T HE POEMS THAT follow set forth occasions for religious practice. Though I made them for modern students, I was inspired by antique antecedents, back to the historical Buddha. My purpose in this essay is to present the ideas and forms of those antecedents. The Buddha's original teaching is essentially a matter of four points—the Four Noble Truths:

1. Anguish is everywhere.

2. We desire permanent existence for ourselves and for our loved ones, and we desire to prove ourselves independent of others and superior to them. These desires conflict with the way things are: nothing abides, and everything and everyone depends upon everything and everyone else. This conflict causes our anguish, and we project this anguish on those we meet.

3. Release from anguish comes with the personal acknowledgment and resolve: we are here together very briefly, so let us accept reality fully and take care of one another while we can.

4.   This acknowledgment and resolve are realized by following
     the Eightfold Path: Right Views, Right Thinking, Right
     Speech, Right Conduct, Right Livelihood, Right Effort,
     Right Recollection, and Right Meditation. Here "Right"
     means "correct" or "accurate"—in keeping with the reality of
     impermanence and interdependence.[1]

The Four Noble Truths are called "noble" because they present
the vocation of wisdom and compassion. They are the foundation
of all Buddhism, and form the heart of modern-day Theravada,
the Buddhism of South and Southeast Asia. Mahayana, a later tradition that became the Buddhism of East Asia, produced quite
radical changes in the way those basic ideas were interpreted and
expressed. For example, early emphasis was upon demonstrating
the insubstantial nature of the self but in the Mahayana that insubstantial essence itself is given attention:

> It shines everywhere in the daily activities of everyone,
> appearing in everything. Though you try to grasp it you
> cannot get it; though you try to abandon it, it always
> remains. It is vast and unobstructed, utterly empty.[2]

As to interdependence, the Mahayana Buddhist finds that
relationships are not just the ordinary activity of giving and
receiving support, but in every situation the other person, animal, plant, or thing is experienced as oneself. This is "interbeing," to use Thich Nhat Hanh's felicitous term, and is presented

---

1   Walpola Rahula, *What the Buddha Taught* (New York: Grove Press, 1974),
16–50.
2   Christopher Cleary, trans., *Swampland Flowers: The Letters and Lectures of the Zen
Master Ta Hui* (New York: Grove Press, 1977), 34.

vividly in a multitude of expansive and profound metaphors in The Avatamsaka Sutra, translated into Chinese as the Hua-yen Ching, the last great chronicle of the Mahayana. Central among these metaphors is "The Net of Indra": a multidimensional net of all beings (including inanimate things), with each point, each knot, a jewel that perfectly reflects, and indeed contains, all other points.[3] This cosmic, yet intimate perspective is offered again and again throughout the sutra. Thomas Cleary, scholar of Hua-yen philosophy, writes:

> All things [are interdependent, and] therefore imply
> in their individual being the simultaneous being of all
> other things. Thus it is said that the existence of each
> element of the universe includes the existence of the
> whole universe and hence is as extensive as the universe
> itself.[4]

This is philosophy at its grandest, and the Buddhist is left with the task of making it personal. Religions with Near Eastern antecedents permit a personal relationship with God, and while many of the metaphorical figures in the Hua-yen Ching could be called deities, there is no single God ruling all. The Buddha's followers cannot pray, "Thy kingdom come, Thy will be done" but instead they have made such formal promises as, "I will awaken my mind to the teachings of the Buddha for the benefit of all beings." Such vows are found in the very earliest Buddhist writings, and continue to be of primary importance as a way of personalizing

---

3 Thomas Cleary, *Entry into the Inconceivable: An Introduction to Hua-yen Buddhism* (Honolulu: University of Hawaii Press, 1983), 37.
4 Ibid., 7.

the practice in all forms of the religion today.[1] In addition to vows, another way to personalize the Buddha's teaching has been to repeat *gathas*, four-line verses that sum up important points. Gathas too are found in the earliest Buddhist writings, and commonly have been memorized and used for Right Recollection— guideposts on the Buddha's path. The Dhammapada, an anthology drawn from early Buddhist texts, consists entirely of gathas, some of them probably dating from the Buddha's own time. Here is one that is known throughout the various streams of Buddhism today:

> Renounce all evil;
> practice all good;
> keep your mind pure;
> thus all the Buddhas taught.[2]

As Buddhism evolved, we find gathas and vows evolving as well. Early followers vowed to practice wisdom and compassion so that everyone and everything could thereby be freed from anguish. Their successors also vow to engage in wisdom and compassion, but *with,* rather than for, everyone and everything. This is called the way of the Bodhisattva, "The Enlightening Being."[3]

Certain traditional Bodhisattvas like Kuan-yin are venerated and even worshipped for the power of the vows they have taken to save everyone and everything. However, Mahayana teachers are clear that the Bodhisattva is an archetype rather than a deity.

---

1 Har Dayal, *The Bodhisattva Doctrine in Buddhist Sanskrit Literature* (London: Kegan Paul, 1931), 65.

2 Cf. Irving Babbitt, trans., *The Dhammapada* (New York: New Directions, 1965), 30.

3 Thomas Cleary, trans., *The Flower Ornament Scripture: A Translation of the Avatamsaka Sutra,* 3 vols. (Boulder, CO: Shambhala, 1984–87), II: 16–17.

When I take the noble path of the Buddha, the Bodhisattva is no other than my selfless self. The Bodhisattva-vows are my own.[4]

In the Mahayana the two forms of vows and gathas often converge. The Hua-yen Ching includes a chapter called "Purifying Practice," consisting of 139 gatha-vows, and I have followed their form in composing the poems in this chapter. The first line establishes the occasion, the second line presents the act of vowing, and the last two lines follow through with the specific conduct that one promises to undertake in these circumstances.

For example, here is a gatha from the "Purifying Practice" chapter:

> When I see flowing water
> I vow with all beings
> to develop a wholesome will
> and wash away the stains of delusion.[5]

As always, translation is problematic. Word-for-word the Chinese original reads:

> If see flow water
> then vow all beings
> gain good intention desire
> cleanse dispel delusion dirt.[6]

---

4 The monk Nyogen Senzaki used to address his American students, "Bodhisattvas," the way speakers of his time would begin their talks, "Ladies and Gentlemen." See also ibid., 312–313.

5 Cf. ibid., 1: 321.

6 For the original Chinese see *Flower Adornment Sutra,* ed. by Hsüan Hua, multiple vols. in process, *Chapter II: Pure Conduct,* trans. by Heng Tsai et al. (Talmage, Calif.: Dharma Realm Buddhist University, 1982), 171.

The second line is the same in all the Hua-yen gathas, and its wording is crucial. The translator must choose a pronoun to indicate who is vowing, and also a word to connect "vow" with the rest of the poem. Cleary translates the line, "They should wish that all beings."[1] "They" are Bodhisattvas, a reference back to the introductory part of the chapter, where Manjushri is asked an elaborate, lengthy question about how Bodhisattvas can attain to wisdom and compassion. He replies with the 139 gathas that set forth occasions to follow the Buddha Way.[2]

We ourselves are Bodhisattvas, so we make these gathas our own. The translation, "They should vow that all beings / develop a wholesome will" becomes "I vow with all beings to develop a wholesome will." I myself follow the Eightfold Path and I join everyone and everything in turning the wheel of the Dharma toward universal understanding. I vow to use the many events of my day as opportunities to fulfill the task I share with all people, animals, plants, and things. Such vows take *ahimsa,* or non-harming, to the most profound level of personal responsibility. I might not realize them completely, but I do the best I can.

Making the vows my own is in keeping with the innermost purpose of Mahayana practice, especially Zen practice. I make the reality of the Buddha's teaching my own. We are here only briefly and we depend on each other—this reality is my own. Even more personally: "This very body is the Buddha," as Hakuin Zenji declared.[3] This is my truth, told of my own body, spoken for me. Everything is affected each time I make a move, here in the grand net of the universe, and as I rediscover my own Buddha nature,

---

1 Cleary, *The Flower Ornament Scripture* 1, 321.

2 Ibid., I: 313–329.

3 Hakuin Ekaku, *Zazen Wasan* (Song of Zazen), Robert Aitken, trans., *Taking the Path of Zen* (San Francisco: North Point Press, 1982), 113.

my vows are naturally the vows of the Buddha that all beings be freed from their anguish.

"I vow with all beings" is my compassionate vow: "I vow, and I yearn that all beings might vow with me." It is my invitation that we enter the noble way together. It is also my affirmation of the Buddha's wise teaching of harmony: "I vow, and with universal affinities uniting everyone and everything, all beings are joining me as I vow." Compassion and wisdom thus blend and are one as I repeat, "I vow with all beings."

It is a noble, yet everyday-life practice. Events set forth in *Hua-yen* gathas follow the routine of T'ang period monks and nuns. Each act in the monastery: washing up, putting on clothes, entering the Buddha hall, sitting down for meditation, getting up from meditation, receives its Dharma poem. Events on pilgrimage: encountering a tree, a river, a bridge, a dignitary, a mendicant— likewise offer entries into the truth. My purpose in this chapter is similar: to show how ordinary occurrences in our modern lay life are in fact the Buddha's own teachings, and also to show how we can involve ourselves accordingly in the practice of wisdom and compassion with family and friends—with everyone and everything.

Of course, monks and nuns of the T'ang period had no gathas for noticing a billboard advertising Jim Beam Kentucky Sour Mash Whiskey. As lay Western Buddhists, however, we pick our way daily through an agglomeration of compelling reminders to pamper ourselves and serve no one else. Our task is harder, it seems, than the one that faced our ancestors. Somehow we must cultivate methods, perhaps including gathas, to follow the noble path of the Buddha as fellow citizens of Jim Beam and his acquisitive cohorts.

Formal meditation for twenty-five minutes or so per day, meditation meetings once or twice a week, and periodic retreats—

all are helpful methods. Most of us do not, however, live in temples, with their moment-to-moment invitations to religious practice. We are caught up in the accelerating tempo of earning a living, and Right Recollection tends to disappear except during times of formal meditation.

Moreover, we in the modern Western world are children of Freud as well as of the Buddha. Classical gathas do not deal with human relationships or emotions, just as the Japanese haiku form of poetry leaves that side of life alone. I find myself wanting gathas that show the way to practice and realize interbeing when I am angry with someone. I want gathas of impermanence when my plans don't work out.

What do I do if I am made to wait for someone? How should I respond to an offer of meaningless sex?

Accordingly, I find that many of my gathas are rather like *senryu,* the Japanese poetical form that uses the same syllabic count and line arrangement as haiku. Senryu verses deal with parents, spouses, children, in-laws, neighbors, work supervisors, economies, and politics. The metaphors are as complex as the situations, full of irony and satire.[1] This is human life, which I want my gathas to address.

Finally, gathas must be reckoned as poetry, and in this respect the classical gathas are rather thin. I don't find much ambiguity, irony, paradox, doubt, humor, playfulness, chance, absurdity, frustration, or mystery in them. However, they inspire my practice (including my writing), and for the devotional occasions of stepping into the meditation hall, bowing, reciting sutras, and settling down for zazen, I hope that my gathas will tend for the most part to be as straightforward and simple-hearted as my models.

---

1 R. H. Blyth, "Haiku and Senryu" in *Senryu: Japanese Satirical Verses* (Tokyo: Hokuseido Press, 1949), 12–47.

Waking up in the morning
I vow with all beings
to be ready for sparks of the Dharma
from flowers or children or birds.

Sounding a bell at the temple
I vow with all beings
to ring as true in each moment:
mellow, steady, and clear.

When I bow at the end of zazen
I vow with all beings
to practice this intimate lightness
with family and friends and myself.

When people show anger and malice
I vow with all beings
to listen for truth in the message,
ignoring the way it is said.

Facing my imminent death
I vow with all beings
to go with the natural process,
at peace with whatever comes.

When my efforts are clearly outclassed
I vow with all beings
to face my own limitations
and bring forth my original self.

When things fall apart on the job
I vow with all beings
to use this regretful energy
and pick up the pieces with care.

When thoughts form an endless procession,
I vow with all beings
to notice the spaces between them
and give the thrushes a chance.

In agony over my koan
I vow with all beings
to give up and refer it along
to the dragon who never sleeps.

When anger or sadness arises
I vow with all beings
to accept my emotional nature—
it's how I embody the Tao.

When I'm left with nothing to say
I vow with all beings
to rest content in the knowledge
there is really nothing to say.

Hearing the crickets at night
I vow with all beings
to find my place in the harmony
crickets enjoy with the stars.

On the shore of the ocean at sunrise
I vow with all beings
to rejoin this enormous power
that rises and falls in great peace.

When green leaves turn in the wind
I vow with all beings
to enjoy the forces that turn me
face up, face down on my stem.

When a train rattles by at the crossing
I vow with all beings
to remember my mother and father
and imagine their thoughts in the night.

When the table is spread for a meal
I vow with all beings
to accept each dish as an offering
that honors my ancient path.

When someone is late for a meeting
I vow with all beings
to give up the past and the future
and relax where nothing begins.

When offered meaningless sex
I vow with all beings
to draw on my store of affection
and grace as I turn it down.

With resources scarcer and scarcer
I vow with all beings
to consider the law of proportion:
my have is another's have-not.

Watching the stars after midnight
I vow with all beings
to remember the point of existence
has no dimension at all.

When roosters crow before dawn
I vow with all beings
to acknowledge each voice in the chorus,
there you are, there you are, friend.

THICH NHAT HANH

Walking Meditation
1996

WALKING MEDITATION IS meditation while walking. We walk slowly, in a relaxed way, keeping a light smile on our lips. When we practice this way, we feel deeply at ease, and our steps are those of the most secure person on Earth. All our sorrows and anxieties drop away, and peace and joy fill our hearts. Anyone can do it. It takes only a little time, a little mindfulness, and the wish to be happy.

Most of the time, we are lost in the past or carried away by the future. When we are mindful, deeply in touch with the present moment, our understanding of what is going on deepens, and we begin to be filled with acceptance, joy, peace, and love. The seed of mindfulness is in each of us, but we usually forget to water it. We struggle in our mind and body, and we don't touch the peace and joy that are available right now—the blue sky, the green leaves, the eyes of our beloved. To have peace, we can begin by walking peacefully. Everything depends on our steps.

In Buddhism, the word *apranihita* means wishlessness or aimlessness. We do not put anything ahead of ourselves and run after it. We practice walking meditation in this spirit. We just enjoy the walking, with no particular aim or destination. We walk for the sake of walking, and it brings us peace and joy. Why rush? Our final destination will only be the graveyard.

In daily life, there is so much to do and so little time. We feel pressured to run all the time. Just stop! Touch the ground of the present moment deeply, and you will touch real peace and joy.

While walking, practice conscious breathing by counting steps. Notice each breath and the number of steps you take as you breathe in and as you breathe out. If you take three steps during an in-breath, say, silently, "One, two, three," or "In, in, in," one word with each step. As you breathe out, if you take three steps, say, "Out, out, out," with each step. If you take three steps as you breathe in and four steps as you breathe out, you say, "In, in, in. Out, out, out, out," or "One, two, three. One, two, three, four."

Don't try to control your breathing. Allow your lungs as much time and air as they need, and simply notice how many steps you take as your lungs fill up and how many you take as they empty, mindful of both your breath and your steps. The link is the counting. When you walk uphill or downhill, the number of steps per breath will change. Always follow the needs of your lungs. Do not try to control your breathing or your walking. Just observe them deeply.

If you see something along the way that you want to touch with your mindfulness—the blue sky, the hills, a tree, or a bird— just stop, but while you do, continue breathing mindfully. You can keep the object of your contemplation alive by means of mindful breathing. If you don't breathe consciously, sooner or later your thinking will settle back in, and the bird or the tree will disappear. Always stay with your breathing.

You can also practice walking meditation using the lines of a poem, such as the one that follows. In Zen Buddhism, poetry and practice always go together.

I have arrived, I am home
In the here, in the now.
I am solid, I am free.
In the ultimate I dwell.

When the baby Buddha was born, he took seven steps, and a lotus flower appeared under each step. When you practice walking meditation, you can do the same. Visualize a lotus, a tulip, or a gardenia blooming under each step the moment your foot touches the ground. If you practice beautifully like this, your friends will see fields of flowers everywhere you walk.

LARRY YANG

In the Moments of Non-Awakening 2019

A S BUDDHISTS, WE spend so much of our time talking about awakening, about developing a compassionate heart and an enlightened mind, about freedom and liberation. While the centrality of those experiences can't be disputed, neither should they become an excuse for denying the reality of our situation right now. We give short shrift to the places where we get caught, where we are not inspired or really not living up to our vision of who we aspire to be. From my perspective, spending our time longing for some idealized state of mind is not genuine Buddhist practice but merely spiritual bypassing. If we focus only on awakening, we miss most of the spiritual practice. I'm much more interested in how we practice with *not* awakening, with *not* being enlightened, because, frankly, those states of being are more present in my life than not.

Lately, as I strive to promote diversity and anti-racism both inside and outside of dharma communities, I'm finding new depths of disappointment and disillusionment at the limitations of my own capacities, at the imperfections of our communities, and at the harm occurring in our larger culture. We don't live in an enlightened world—have you noticed? As a dharma teacher, I was trained to teach the insights and kindnesses that I have felt. However, these days I feel propelled to teach from where I am—to be real and authentic in the moment, in the midst of places where I do not have answers, and from the limitations of my own flaws.

Beyond an occasional mention of the five hindrances, which are numerically contained, and therefore perhaps conceptually manageable, acknowledgement of the opposite of freedom and awakening is largely absent in many dharma teachings. In more than thirty years of Buddhist practice, I have rarely encountered any discussion about what happens when enlightenment doesn't happen—*really, positively* doesn't happen. Or about what occurs in that potential crisis of faith, that edge of practice, when awakening is no longer a sufficient motivation for practice.

Vedana practice (the second foundation of mindfulness, the awareness of feelings) teaches that each moment of our lives is experienced as pleasant, unpleasant, or neutral; the unconscious mind tends to lean toward pleasant experiences and push away the unpleasant ones. And this happens even in our practice of awakening. We do not like to turn to the unpleasant reality of not awakening, so we often push it away and hide our imperfections behind a facade of serenity.

Dharma teachers aren't immune to this. A close friend was the primary caregiver for a family member who was struggling with a debilitating illness. They were as close as two human beings could be, and when that family member finally died, my friend's grief felt inconsolable and interminable. In response to the depth of that grief, a well-meaning dharma teacher told my friend, "Arahants (enlightened beings) do not need to grieve." My friend was shocked at this remark, as was I. How can we ignore, deny, or repress the reality of our lives and still say we are living mindfully?

Is the point of practice to negate and deny our very tender, human experiences? Even if we are encouraged to "go through" them rather than go around them, the value is placed on the getting through, rather than on being in and with. What happens when we're stuck in the quicksand of life's circumstances with no foreseeable resolution? What if the limitations in our lives prevent us from seeing a path out of despair—whether existential (in the form of disillusionment), psychological (in the form of loss or depression), or sociocultural (in the form of racism, misogyny, heterosexism, transphobia, ableism, and other outgrowths of oppressive cultural unconsciousness that are certain to last well beyond any single human lifetime)?

When we become aware of our disillusionment or disappointment, our next impulse is often to try and fix whatever it is we think is broken so we don't have to deal with our feelings of despair. But what if nothing is actually broken and yet the disappointment and hopelessness remain? The world is imperfect and flawed with the reality of the First Noble Truth. It is what it is, and often there is nothing we can do. No wonder we feel despair.

If we don't look deeply into these states of non-enlightenment, we deny the authentic reality arising in the moment. That contradiction can create a crisis of faith in the dharma itself. So how do we turn toward that despair, even immerse ourselves in it, as part of our spiritual practice?

We must dig deep into our practice in order to navigate the extremes of despair and disillusionment. We must listen to what is underneath it all, to where freedom is calling from, by asking: Can I open to this? Can I turn toward this as well? Or in the inadequate language with which we must communicate, can I love this too? Can we incline toward the despair and imperfections of this life with the same diligence we give other objects of mindfulness? Can we practice presence when life feels impossible?

It may seem counterintuitive, but when we practice awareness and offer kindness to the uncooked, imperfect aspects of our lives, we actually strengthen our mindfulness. We don't need to attach to either awakening or non-awakening; neither is anything more than an experience to hold with tender awareness.

Awakening and not awakening are two sides of the same coin. They are the same experience. We can't experience awakening without experiencing not awakening. We can't experience insight without becoming intimately familiar with our conditioned patterns.

Thus, in exploring the full range of our life and practice, I wonder what the space between the seven factors of awakening (mindfulness, investigation, effort/energy, joy/rapture, tranquility, concentration, equanimity) and the seven factors of non-awakening (unconsciousness, boredom, lethargy, depression, agitation, distraction, reactivity) might look like. What is the range of experience between unconsciousness and mindfulness? Life is not dual. Mindfulness and unconsciousness are not light switches to be simply turned on or off. What are the subtle levels of gray in between the extremes of these factors? Where does unconsciousness bleed into consciousness? If I can feel that relationship, then I can stay connected to mindfulness even in my lapse of mindfulness. I can stay in alignment with awakening even in my failure to be awake.

Likewise, what is the incremental set of sensations, thoughts, and feelings between boredom and investigation? Where is the transition between lethargy and energy? How does despair connect to joy and rapture? What are the nuances between the extremes of agitation and tranquility? Where is the breadth of landscape bounded by distraction and concentration? And what happens between the states of reactivity and equanimity?

The nuanced spectrum of experience between despair and joy might look something like:

Despair—Hopelessness—Depression—Grief—Pain—
Sadness—Regret—Distress—Dejection—Worry—
Heavy-heartedness—Gloominess—Apprehension—
Confusion—Irritation—Questioning—Dullness—
Indifference—Neutrality—Nonchalance—
Stillness—Coolness—Calm—Ease—Relaxation—
Contentment—Replenishment—Comfort—
Gladness—Cheer—Mirth—Wonder—Delight—
Excitement—Rapture—Collective Joy

In the Western Vipassana tradition, there is a popular acronym, RAIN, which encourages us to R̲ecognize the moment, in order to have A̲cceptance of the moment, so that we can I̲nvestigate the moment's true nature, in order to realize our N̲on-identification with that moment arising—the last of which is a state of insight and awakening. All the factors of RAIN are actions of incremental progress toward awakening. But this acronym belies the messiness of our painful and complicated lives. In a similar parallel, Dr. Elizabeth Kübler-Ross outlined five stages of grief—denial, anger, bargaining, depression, and acceptance—that the human psyche experiences when coming to terms with loss and trauma. That is, we must pass through denial, anger, bargaining, and depression before acceptance is possible. When these five stages are inserted into RAIN—after the factor of recognition (mindfulness) but before our acceptance of the moment arising—our practice of insight might look more like:

Recognition—Denial—Recognition—Anger—
Recognition—Bargaining — Recognition—
Depression— Recognition—Acceptance (. . . maybe)—
Investigation—Non-identification (. . . maybe)

This sequence feels so much more authentic and realistically human to me. It's never either/or. Life is so much more complex than that. Our experience isn't characterized by just the polar opposites of awakening and not awakening but rather by all of the contours lived in the range in-between. If we can monitor and be aware of the totality of the experience of awakening and not awakening, we can stay connected to both without bypassing either. Reverend Dr. Martin Luther King, Jr., wrote: "We must accept finite disappointment, but we must never lose infinite hope." We need both—the absolute aspiration of unconditioned hope and the relative path, which is filled with constant disappointment. If we have only the aspiration of the enlightened ideal, how do we ever get there? If we only have the path with no guiding North Star, where are we going and what is the point of it all?

The inspiration for our practice often rests on one single moment: the Buddha's awakening beneath the bodhi tree. But that is not the totality of his biography. Tradition tells us it took him thousands of lifetimes to awaken. We have stories about the Buddha's previous lives in the Jataka tales, and in them he was not perfect, not fully awake, even though each illustrates how the perfections (*paramis*) of dharma practice ripened in those lifetimes of the bodhisattva. They show the paramis ripening, *but not yet ripe.* All those moments of non-awakening serve an indispensable purpose in the path to awakening. We must fully live the moments of non-awakening in order for freedom to arise. We can't simply aspire to enlightened states of mind and heart without a realistic, flawed human path.

In the Saccamkira Jataka, a prince in danger of drowning is pulled from the water by a beggar ascetic (the future Buddha). Being an untruthful and ungrateful person, the prince disingenuously tells the future Buddha that he can come any time to his kingdom for support. When the prince becomes king, the ascetic visits his kingdom. Instead of supporting the ascetic, the king has him beaten in the streets and orders his execution. When the ascetic is asked in the streets what the trouble is between him and the king, he tells the story. The populace and guards become so enraged that they kill the king and drag his body through the streets, dumping it in the moat. The ascetic is then anointed the new ruler.

While perhaps indicating a kind of justice, the outcome of the Jataka is not exactly a restorative, compassionate one. As with many of the parables, the Saccamkira concludes with a version of this phrase: *When his (the future Buddha's) days were come to an end, he passed away according to his deeds.* And according to the imperfect deeds of most of his lives, the Buddha did not awaken.

That means, at least metaphorically speaking, before the precious moment of awakening, there were thousands of other times the Buddha-to-be did *not* awaken. If he was practicing mindfulness (and it is said one cannot become a buddha unless there is an initial intention to consciously do so), at some point in each of his unenlightened lives he must have become mindful of the fact that he was not awake. He became aware of his own limitations, his own failures, and his own shortcomings, which, despite his very best efforts, cumulatively were not going to lead to enlightenment in that lifetime. How disillusioning after doing the best he could in service of such goodness. Did the Buddha experience despair? Did he have self-pity over the grief of enlightenment in that particular lifetime? Did the Buddha go through Dr. Elizabeth Kübler-Ross's five stages of grief?

I would have to believe "yes" to all those questions, because he was human. He went through what humans go through when there is significant loss and despair. The future Buddha, in their humanity, needed to experience Denial, Anger, Bargaining, and Depression—before Acceptance is possible.

Yet the Buddha returned to practice—whether he was enlightened or not, whether he was despairing or not. That, to me, is significant. What would you do? What *do* you do? We have all been there, when we have done our best and yet, we may be far from perfect. We try for the best solution we can, and there might be some collateral injury, even serious harm, incurred along the way. We are not enlightened. How do we reconcile the aspiration to be of benefit with the inevitable harm we cause? How do we make all of it our spiritual practice?

When I do *metta* practice, cultivating love and compassion toward all beings in all worlds and in all directions, there is an ancillary blessing that I hold in my mind:

> May I be loving, open, and aware in this moment
> If I cannot be loving, open, and aware in this moment,
>   may I be kind
> If I cannot be kind, may I be nonjudgmental
> If I cannot be nonjudgmental, may I not cause harm
> If I cannot not cause harm, may I cause the least harm
>   possible

Thus, even in my imperfections, even in my failures, I can still incline my heart toward freedom. This is how I see the paths of awakening and non-awakening interweaving. This is freedom in the midst of suffering. This is resilience despite the forces of violence and oppression—both individually and collectively. We can create beautiful lives right where the World is not yet awake.

Each time we practice awareness and kindness, we transform not only our personal world but the World itself. We begin to be able to hold the unholdable, to connect the broken heart and the raging mind. We look for the precious wisdom embedded within that bitter rage, and as soon as we begin to look, we are no longer consumed by the rage itself. We turn toward the direct experience of despair and weave it into care, love, and, dare we say, freedom. This is the magnitude of our collective spiritual practice. It asks us to include all the contradictions and paradoxes of awakening and not awakening and everything in between. It is the in-between—the range from extreme to subtle, the spectrum connecting opposing forces—that constitutes the totality of our lives, our practice, and our freedom.

The Good News
1994

The good news
they do not print.
The good news
we do print.
We have a special edition every moment,
and we need you to read it.
The good news is that you are alive,
that the linden tree is still there,
standing firm in the harsh winter.
The good news is that you have wonderful eyes
to touch the blue sky.
The good news is that your child is there before you,
and your arms are available:
hugging is possible.
They only print what is wrong.
Look at each of our special editions.
We always offer the things that are not wrong.
We want you to benefit from them
and help protect them.
The dandelion is there by the sidewalk,
smiling its wondrous smile,

singing the song of eternity.
Listen. You have ears that can hear it.
Bow your head.
Listen to it.
Leave behind the world of sorrow,
of preoccupation,
and get free.
The latest good news
is that you can do it.

CB

PART III

COMPASSION IN ACTION

Love in Action
1993

T HE ESSENCE OF nonviolence is love. Out of love and the willingness to act selflessly, strategies, tactics, and techniques for a nonviolent struggle arise naturally. Nonviolence is not a dogma; it is a process. Other struggles may be fueled by greed, hatred, fear, or ignorance, but a nonviolent one cannot use such blind sources of energy, for they will destroy those involved and also the struggle itself. Nonviolent action, born of the awareness of suffering and nurtured by love, is the most effective way to confront adversity.

The Buddhist struggle for peace in Vietnam in the 1960s and '70s arose from the great suffering inflicted on our nation by international forces. Blood and fire ravaged the countryside, and people everywhere were uprooted. The Vietnam War was, first and foremost, an ideological struggle. To ensure our people's survival, we had to overcome both communist and anticommunist fanaticism and maintain the strictest neutrality. Buddhists tried their best to speak for all the people and not take sides, but we were condemned as "pro-communist neutralists." Both warring parties claimed to speak for what the people really wanted, but the North Vietnamese spoke for the communist bloc and the South Vietnamese spoke for the capitalist bloc. The Buddhists only wanted to create a vehicle for the people to be heard—and the people only wanted peace, not a "victory" by either side.

During our struggle, many scenes of love arose spontaneously—a monk sitting calmly before an advancing tank; women and children raising their bare hands against barbed wire; students confronting military police who looked like monsters wearing huge masks and holding bayonets; young women running through clouds of tear gas with babies in their arms; hunger strikes held silently and patiently; monks and nuns burning themselves to death to try to be heard above the raging noise of the war. And all of these efforts bore some fruit.

Any nonviolent action requires a thorough understanding of the situation and of the psychology of the people. In Vietnam, we inherited many ideas from the Buddhist tradition and we learned from our mistakes as we went along. In the late nineteenth and early twentieth centuries, Buddhist monks joined the struggle for independence from the French, and they won the support of their countrymen. When the Vietnam War broke out, they still had that support, as well as the knowledge gained earlier to go beyond passive resistance and undertake positive efforts to overcome the war and the oppression. In 1966, when the people of Huê and Da Nang learned that Field Marshall Nguyen Cao Ky was about to bring tanks and troops from Saigon to suppress the movement for peace, the people of those cities brought their family altars—the most sacred objects in their homes—onto the streets, relying on their culture and tradition to oppose the forces of destruction. Some people were critical, saying they used religion for political purposes, but I do not agree. They were using their most potent spiritual force to directly confront the violence. This was not a political act; it was an act of love.

Fasting, the method used most by Mahatma Gandhi to help India in its struggle for independence, was also used in Vietnam. Sometimes, thousands of people fasted, and other times, a single person fasted. We fasted as prayer to purify our hearts, consolidate our will, and arouse awareness and compassion in others. When Thich Tri Quang fasted for 100 days, those who passed the Duy Tan Clinic were jarred into awareness, and compassion was born in them. As a result, they felt compelled to meet, talk, and plan, thereby escalating the struggle. Thich Tri Quang had not planned to fast. He had to fast.

We also used literature and the arts as "weapons" to challenge the oppression. Works by antiwar writers, composers, poets, and artists, although illegal, were widely circulated. Antiwar songs were sung in streets and classrooms, and antiwar literature became the largest category of books sold in Vietnam, even infiltrating army units. *Look Back at Your Homeland, Only Death Allows You to Speak Out,* and *Lotus in a Sea of Fire* sold hundreds of thousands of copies. Our literature was considered dangerous by both sides. One book of poems, *Let Us Pray for the White Dove to Appear,* was submitted to the Ministry of Information, and only two of the sixty poems in it were approved. A group of students published it anyway, and within a week, all copies were sold. In Huê, a policeman saw a copy in a bookstore and warned the owner, "Hide this and only bring it out when someone asks for it." Sister Cao Ngoc Phuong was arrested in Huê for transporting antiwar books, and, before I left the country, I was also arrested and imprisoned for a few days in Bao Loc for "antiwar" activities, although I was charged only with the crime of listening to Hanoi Radio.

Folk poetry was used as means of education. This lullaby was sung throughout the country:

My hand holds a plate of ginger and salt.
Spicy ginger and savory salt: don't go without each
    other!
North and South share the same sorrow.

Loving each other is possible, how can we abandon one
another?

This "Prayer for Peace" was printed by the tens of thousands
and chanted during religious services throughout Vietnam, and
its effects were widely felt:

Homage to all Buddhas in the ten directions.
Please have compassion for our suffering.
Our land has been at war for two decades.
Divided, it is a land of tears,
and blood and bones of young and old.
Mothers weep till their tears are dry,
while their sons on distant fields decay.
Its beauty torn apart,
only blood and tears now flow.
Brother killing brothers
for promises from outsiders.

During the superpower confrontation in Vietnam, while
thousands and thousands of peasants and children lost their lives,
our land was unmercifully ravaged. Yet we were unable to stop the
fighting; we were not able to make ourselves heard or understood.
We had little access to the international news media. People
thought we Buddhists were trying to seize power, but we had no
interest in power. We only wanted to stop the slaughter. The voice
of the Vietnamese people—80 percent Buddhists—was lost in
the melee of shooting and bombs. But we realized that the means
and the end are one, and we never employed any kind of action
that betrayed our commitment to nonviolence.

In 1963, Venerable Thich Quang Duc went to the crossroads

of Phan Dinh Phung, sat in the lotus position, poured gasoline on himself, and transformed himself into a torch. His disciple read his last words to the press. Madame Nhu described it as a "barbecue." By burning himself, Thich Quang Duc awakened the world to the suffering of the war and the persecution of the Buddhists. When someone stands up to violence in such a courageous way, a force for change is released.

Every action for peace requires someone to exhibit the courage to challenge the violence and inspire love. Love and sacrifice always set up a chain reaction of love and sacrifice. Like the crucifixion of Jesus, Thich Quang Duc's act expressed the unconditional willingness to suffer for the awakening of others. Accepting the most extreme kind of pain, he lit a fire in the hearts of people around the world. Self-burning was not a technique or program of action. When anyone wished to burn himself or herself, the Buddhist leaders always tried to prevent it. But many monks, nuns, laymen, and laywomen did sacrifice themselves for peace in this way, including my disciple Nhat Chi Mai, who declared that she wanted to be "a torch in the dark night."

Nhat Chi Mai was one of the first six people ordained into the Tiep Hien Order. In 1966, she placed a statue of Avalokiteshvara, the bodhisattva of compassion, and a statue of the Virgin Mary in front of her, and burned herself alive at the Tu Nghiêm Temple, a nunnery. She left behind letters to the Presidents of North and South Vietnam, imploring them to stop the fighting. She wrote one letter to me: "Thay, don't worry too much. We will have peace soon." Nhat Chi Mai moved the hearts of millions of her countrymen, evoking the force of love.

I know that the self-immolation of monks and nuns was difficult for Westerners to understand. The Western press called it suicide, but it was not really suicide. It was not even a protest. What the monks wrote in the letters they left behind was intended only to move the hearts of the oppressors and call the world's attention to the suffering of our people. To make a statement while enduring such unspeakable pain is to communicate with tremendous determination, courage, and sincerity. During the ordination ceremony in some Buddhist traditions, the ordinee burns one or more very small spots on his body with moxa incense as he takes the 250 vows of a monk, promising to live a life devoted to helping living beings. If he were to say this while sitting comfortably in an armchair, it would not be the same. When uttered while kneeling before the community of elders and experiencing this kind of pain, his words express the full seriousness of his heart and mind.

The Vietnamese monks, nuns, and laypeople who burned themselves were saying with all their strength and determination that they were willing to endure the greatest of suffering in order to protect their people. But why did they have to burn themselves to death? The difference between burning oneself with incense and burning oneself to death is only a matter of degree. What is important is not to die, but to express courage, determination, and sincerity—not to destroy, but to create. Suicide is an act of self-destruction based on the inability to cope with life's difficulties. In Buddhism, self-destruction is one of the most serious transgressions of the precepts. Those who burned themselves had lost neither courage nor hope, nor did they desire nonexistence. They were extremely courageous and aspired for something good in the future. They sacrificed themselves in order to seek help from the people of the world. I believe with all my heart that those who burned themselves did not aim at the death of the oppressors but only at a change in their policy. Their enemies were not other people, but the intolerance, fanaticism, oppression, greed, hatred, and discrimination that lay within the hearts of their fellow men and women.

We did not plan self-immolations or any of the other methods that were used. But confronting the situation and having compassion in our hearts, ways of acting came by themselves. You cannot prefabricate techniques of nonviolent action and put them into a book for people to use. That would be naive. If you are alert and creative, you will know what to do and what not to do. The basic requisite is that you have the essence, the substance of nonviolence and compassion in yourself. Then everything you do will be in the direction of nonviolence.

Besides self-immolation, fasting, and the use of art, literature, and culture, many other tactics were employed in Vietnam. Foreign Minister Vu Van Mau, for example, resigned in 1963 and shaved his head to protest the violent policies of the Diêm regime, and many professors and students followed suit. There were labor strikes at the harbors and markets, and business owners turned in their licenses. University deans, presidents, and professors resigned, and high school and university students boycotted classes and examinations. Draftees refused to fight. All of these acts were met with atrocious reprisals. The government used unbridled brutality—tear gas, suffocation gas, grenades, prisons, and torture—to obstruct and suppress these nonviolent efforts.

Police agents posed as monks and nuns and infiltrated our movement, damaging our prestige and sowing seeds of fear. They excited extremists and fanatics to overturn and destroy the leadership and members of the movement. No one knows exactly how many Buddhist and non-Buddhist leaders of the nonviolent movement were imprisoned or killed, including professors, students, intellectuals, politicians, workers, and farmers. Even social workers trying to help the peasants were terrorized and murdered. From the School of Youth for Social Service, eight people were kidnapped, six killed, and eleven seriously wounded—all because they refused to take sides in the war. In a memorial service organized for those who were killed, the SYSS students openly affirmed their commitment to nonviolence and neutrality: "Now, in the presence of our dear friends whose bodies are lying here, we solemnly proclaim that we cannot consider you who killed them to be our enemies. Our arms are open wide; we are ready to embrace your ideas and advice to help us continue our nonviolent ways of working for the people of Vietnam."

Despite the results—many years of war followed by years of oppression and human rights abuse—I cannot say that our struggle was a failure. The conditions for success in terms of a political victory were not present. But the success of a nonviolent struggle can be measured only in terms of the love and nonviolence attained, not whether a political victory was achieved. In our struggle in Vietnam, we did our best to remain true to our principles. We never lost sight that the essence of our struggle was love itself, and that was a real contribution to humanity.

KENNETH KRAFT

Engaged Buddhism
1988

IN THE MID-1960S, as the war in Vietnam escalated, a group of Vietnamese Buddhist monks and nuns began working in a nonviolent and nonpartisan way to aid their suffering countrymen. One spring day a team of eighteen Buddhists attempted to evacuate about 200 civilians trapped in a combat zone. A participant described what happened:

> The idea was to form two lines of Buddhist monks and nuns in yellow robes and lead the civilians out of the war zone. They asked me to carry a big Buddhist flag so that combatants of both sides would not shoot at us . . . . H. and a nun were quite seriously wounded by stray bullets. The trip lasted terribly long, as we had to stop many times, lying down on the streets and waiting for the shooting to lessen before continuing. We left the district early in the morning, but arrived in Pleiku only after dark. And what a bad time for arrival! It was time for the rockets. Pleiku was shelled. Unfortunately, we were very close to a military camp, and one rocket fell upon us, wounding seven of us. Children and women cried very much. We asked everyone to lie down and tried our best to help those who had been struck by the rocket.

The most wonderful thing that happened that day is
that we went through both Saigon and NFL soldiers but
none of us was shot at. I must say that they were very
thoughtful and kind. Had we not carried the Buddhist
symbol I do not know what would have happened. It
seemed that as soon as they saw and recognized us, they
immediately showed their respect for life.[1]

On that day and on many others, Vietnamese Buddhists
parted the red sea of blood that was flooding their land. They
displayed the equanimity, the courage, and the selflessness of
true peacemakers. Remarkably, the writer of this account even
expressed gratitude toward the soldiers on both sides. Rather
than feeling rage or outrage, he saw the soldiers as thoughtful and
kind, acknowledging them for their ability to respect life even in
the midst of war.

The term "Engaged Buddhism" refers to this kind of active
involvement by Buddhists in society and its problems. Participants
in this nascent movement seek to actualize Buddhism's traditional
ideals of wisdom and compassion in today's world. In times of
war or intense hostility they will place themselves between the
factions, literally or figuratively, like the yellow-robed volunteers
on the road to Pleiku. Roshi Philip Kapleau, an American Zen
teacher, enumerated part of the new agenda:

A major task for Buddhism in the West, it seems to
me, is to ally itself with religious and other concerned
organizations to forestall the potential catastrophes
facing the human race: nuclear holocaust, irreversible

---

1 Letter to Sister Chan Khong, May 1972, quoted in *Zen Bow* (Rochester: The Zen
Center), 5:5, Winter 1973, II.

pollution of the world's environment, and the continuing large-scale destruction of nonrenewable resources. We also need to lend our physical and moral support to those who are fighting hunger, poverty, and oppression everywhere in the world.[2]

Because Buddhism has been seen as passive, otherworldly, or escapist, an "Engaged Buddhism" may initially appear to be a self-contradiction. Isn't one of the distinguishing features of Buddhism its focus on the solitary quest for enlightenment? No enlightenment can be complete as long as others remain trapped in delusion. Genuine wisdom is manifested in compassionate action. When we reexamine Buddhism's 2,500-year-old heritage, we find that the principles and even some of the techniques of an Engaged Buddhism have been latent in the tradition since the time of its founder. Qualities that were inhibited in premodern Asian settings can now be actualized through Buddhism's exposure to the West, where ethical sensitivity, social activism, and egalitarianism are emphasized. We can believe that Buddhism may have unique resources to offer the West and the world, and apply ancient Buddhist insights to actual contemporary problems. Robert Thurman reads the Buddhist philosopher Nagarjuna, active in the second century CE, "as if he were addressing us today."[3]

The touchstone for Engaged Buddhists is a vision of interdependence, in which the universe is experienced as an organic whole, every "part" affecting every other "part." As Joanna Macy writes, "Everything is interdependent and mutually

2 Philip Kapleau, *A Pilgrimage to the Buddhist Temples and Caves of China* (Rochester: The Zen Center, 1983), 26.
3 Robert A. F. Thurman, "Nagarjuna's Guidelines for Buddhist Social Action," 80.

conditioning—each thought, word, and act, and all beings, too, in the web of life."[1] Though classic formulations of this concept push the mind beyond conventional thought, the interconnectedness of things is also evident through ordinary observation. "One sees again and again," says Christopher Titmuss, "the way the mind influences the body, the body influences the mind, the way one influences the world, and the world influences one."[2] On an international level, the interdependence of nations is equally apparent—a Chernobyl meltdown contaminates Polish milk; a Philippine revolution ignites efforts for democratic reform in Korea. In such a world not even the most powerful of nations can solve its problems single-handedly.

For these thinkers, awareness of interconnectedness fosters a sense of universal responsibility. The Dalai Lama states that because the individual and society are interdependent, one's behavior as an individual is inseparable from one's behavior as a participant in society. The darker side of this realization is that each of us contributes in some measure to violence and oppression. The brighter side is that once we recognize our involvement in the conditions we deplore, we become empowered to do something about them. As Thich Nhat Hanh writes:

> We need such a person to inspire us with calm
> confidence, to tell us what to do. Who is that person?
> The Mahayana Buddhist sutras tell us that you are that
> person. If you are yourself, if you are your best, then you

---

1 Joanna Macy, "In Indra's Net: Sarvodaya & Our Mutual Efforts for Peace," in Fred Eppsteiner, ed., *The Path of Compassion: Writings on Socially Engaged Buddhism* (Berkeley: Parallax Press, 1988), 170.

2 Christopher Titmuss, "Interactivity: Sitting for Peace & Standing for Parliament," in Eppsteiner, ibid, 187.

are that person. Only with such a person—calm, lucid, aware—will our situation improve.[3]

Because personal peace is connected with world peace on a fundamental level, we cannot meaningfully "work for peace" as long as we feel upset, angry, or confrontational. "Nonviolence is a day-to-day experience," says Titmuss.[4] The frenzied pace of life in technologically advanced societies exacerbates a tendency to cut oneself off from people and things. That separation is a kind of small-scale violence which breeds violence on a larger scale. Nhat Hanh notes, for example, how rarely we linger over a cup of tea with calm awareness; usually we gulp it down automatically, distracted by conversation, reading, music, or wandering thoughts. We thereby do violence to the tea, to the moment, and to ourselves. This linkage of personal and world peace is one of Buddhism's fresh contributions to politics.

Consistent with Nhat Hanh's gentle way of drinking tea, Engaged Buddhist actions reflect a spirit of tolerance and humility rarely encountered among partisan causes. The fourteen precepts of the Order of Interbeing developed by Thich Nhat Hanh begin with three injunctions: avoid dogmatism, remain open, and do not force your views on others. The first reads, "Do not be idolatrous about or bound to any doctrine, theory, or ideology, even Buddhist ones. Buddhist systems of thought are guiding means; they are not absolute truth."[5] Buddhism is not an infallible system that holds all the answers to the problems we face. In the realm of socioeconomic policy, engaged Buddhist thinkers are willing to take points from a variety of other systems and faiths. Nor is any

---

3 Thich Nhat Hanh, "Please Call Me by My True Names," 109.
4 Titmuss, "Interactivity," *The Path of Compassion,* 186.
5 Fred Eppsteiner, "In the Crucible: The Order of Interbeing," ibid, 150.

conversion to Buddhism required. The ideas and practices offered
are assumed to be effective whether or not a Buddhist label is
attached to them. "As part of our planetary heritage," writes Macy,
"they belong to us all."[1] Thurman's essay in this book shows that
Nagarjuna viewed all belief systems, Buddhist and non-Buddhist
alike, as illnesses to be cured. "It does not matter what symbols or
ideologies provide the umbrella," Thurman explains, "as long as
the function is liberation and enlightenment."

Yet engaged Buddhists refuse to turn away from suffering or
sadness. They believe that no one is really able to avoid feeling
pain for what is happening in the world today, try as one might to
keep such feelings from coming to consciousness. For centuries
Buddhism has focused on suffering as the starting point of the
religious life. Mahayana Buddhism teaches that nirvana is present *within* samsara; that is, awakening or salvation are not separate
from suffering and its causes. Engaged Buddhists are updating
this mysterious alchemy by transmuting despair into empowerment. A rape victim who practices at a midwestern U.S. Zen center reports, even amidst her lingering fear: "I actually was able to
convert this catastrophe into an effective tool for my personal and
spiritual growth."[2]

Buddhism has always emphasized that the spiritual path is
a way that is "walked, not talked." Scattered throughout the literature of Engaged Buddhism are practical insights and specific
techniques that one can apply oneself. If you have a hot temper,
says the Dalai Lama, try timing the duration of your anger, making each bout a minute or two shorter than the last. Macy offers
guided meditations adapted from traditional Buddhist sources on
such themes as death, compassion, empowerment, and mutual

---

1 Macy, "Taking Heart," ibid, 204.
2 Judith Ragir, "Rape," ibid, 191.

trust. For example, the media bombard us continually with evidence of the suffering of fellow beings, but before we can get in touch with our feelings of sadness, empathy, or distress, we are hit with the next alarming image or fact (or distracted by a commercial). Macy suggests that such moments are an opportunity to put down the newspaper, turn down the radio or the TV, and focus on breathing:

> Breathe in that pain like a dark stream ... let it pass
> through your heart ... surrender it for now to the
> healing resources of life's vast web. ... By breathing
> through the bad news, rather than bracing ourselves
> against it, we can let it strengthen our sense of belonging
> in the larger web of being.[3]

Recently, Buddhists have been seen taking action in widely varying contexts around the globe, sometimes nonviolently and sometimes violently. In certain cases their behavior has been deplored by sensitive observers, and troubling issues have surfaced. Some Buddhists might insist that if the collective karma of a nation is to be invaded, even destroyed, then violent resistance would only create further karmic burdens. There is an incident in the Buddhist scriptures in which Shakyamuni Buddha, after failing twice to turn back an invader nonviolently, stands aside and allows his clan to be massacred.[4] There is also a Jataka story in which the Buddha in a former incarnation sacrifices himself for a starving tigress unable to feed her cubs. Are our only options

---

3 Macy, "Taking Heart," ibid, 207.
4 *Ekottaragama;* Hajime Nakamura, "Violence and Nonviolence in Buddhism," in Philip P. Wiener and John Fisher, eds., *Violence and Aggression in the History of Ideas* (New Brunswick, NJ: Rutgers University Press, 1974), 176.

violent self-defense or genocidal self-sacrifice? Gary Snyder, in his essay for this book, offers support for such means as "civil disobedience, outspoken criticism, protest, pacifism, voluntary poverty, and even gentle violence if it comes to a matter of restraining some impetuous crazy."

Because the implications of an engaged Buddhism are only beginning to be explored in a profound and systematic way within the Buddhist tradition, issues like these remain unresolved. To mention some further questions that have arisen: Are ancient Buddhist teachings adulterated or trivialized when linked to specific social goals? What does it mean to present release from suffering in terms of literacy, irrigation, or marketing cooperatives? What are the actual roots of nonviolence in Buddhism? Does "Buddhist nonviolence" differ in any meaningful way from the nonviolence of other traditions? Can Buddhism offer any guidance in our handling of social organization, economics, or technology? Many formerly Buddhist nations are now under the sway of communism; can some form of Buddhism and some form of communism coexist or even support each other? Further inquiry, reflection, and discussion are needed.

"Compassion" is a pleasant-sounding word, newly fashionable in American campaign rhetoric. As a political buzzword, it implies a rejection of attitudes or policies associated with recent constraints on social services. The compassion valued by Buddhists is something different—a deep sense of oneness with all beings, a spontaneous impulse born of suffering. As the yellow-robed Buddhists of Vietnam demonstrated, at times the path of compassion may even be strafed with bullets. Yet it is also as ordinary as a smile of greeting, as close as the hand that offers help. In simple terms, "The philosophy is kindness."[1]

---

1 The Dalai Lama, "Hope for the Future," p. 341.

SULAK SIVARAKSA

Buddhism in a World of Change
1988

WHEN PRINCE SIDDHARTHA saw an old man, a sick man, a dead man, and a wandering monk, he was moved to seek salvation, and eventually he became the Buddha, the Awakened One. The suffering of the present day, such as that brought about at Bhopal and Chernobyl, should move many of us to think together and act together to overcome such death and destruction, to bring about the awakening of humankind.

The origin of Buddhism goes back to the sixth century BCE. The founder was an ordinary man, the prince of a small state in Northern India, now Nepal. He was deeply concerned about the problems of life and death and of suffering, and after much effort, he discovered a solution to these deepest of human problems. His solution was universal and radical. It addressed suffering as such, not just this or that sort of suffering. Neither the cause nor the cure of suffering were matters of revelation. The Buddha simply discovered them, as many others could have done before or since. He appeared as a doctor for the ills of humankind. Buddhist liberation—*nibbana*—is accessible to anyone at any time, indifferent to caste or social standing. It requires neither the mastery of an arcane doctrine nor an elaborate regimen of asceticism. In fact, the Buddha condemned extreme austerity, as well as intellectual learning that does not directly address urgent questions of life and death.

The Buddha's original teaching remains a common fund for all branches of Buddhism, and it is expressed in the Four Noble Truths: Suffering; the Cause of Suffering, namely desire or craving; the Cessation of Suffering; and the Way to do so, namely the Eightfold Path. It is not enough merely to attain an intellectual understanding of these propositions. We have to make them part of our life. Like medicine, they must be taken. It does no good to have aspirins in the bottle; they must be internalized. If we do not regard suffering as something real and threatening, we do not take the message of the Buddha seriously.

The Buddha found that birth is the cause of such suffering as decay and death, and traced the chain back to ignorance. Then he contemplated the way in which ignorance gives rise to karmic formation, which in turn produces consciousness and so on through the twelve-link chain of causation (*paticcasamuppada*), until he came to birth as the cause of decay and death. Working backward, he saw that cessation of birth is the cause of the cessation of suffering, and finally, he discovered that the cessation of ignorance is the ultimate cause of cessation of the whole chain. He is said to have become the Buddha by means of this contemplation up and down the chain of causation. In other words, he contemplated the way to deliverance from suffering and found that the cause of suffering is ignorance and that by extinguishing ignorance, suffering is extinguished.

The Buddha, having attained the peaceful state of nibbana, is full of compassion. This attitude of compassion or benevolence should be taken as the fundamental principle in our social life. Compassion or love toward one's neighbors is highly esteemed in Buddhism. Compassion is expressed in the Pali word *metta,* which is derived from *mitta* (friend). Compassion therefore means "true friendliness."

Buddhism enters the life of society through the presence of individuals who practice and bear witness to the Way, through their thought, speech, and actions. Anyone who looks at this world and society and sees its tremendous suffering, injustice, and danger, will agree on the necessity to do something, to act in order to change, in order to liberate people. The presence of Buddhist sages—or indeed of any humanist leaders who have attained the Way—means the presence of wisdom, love, and peace. In most societies, the so-called leaders are themselves confused, engrossed in hatred, greed, or delusion, so they become the blind who lead the blind. When they do not have peace of mind, how can they lead others without love or compassion? In Buddhism, we believe that the presence of one such person is very important, and can have an important influence on society. In Buddhist terminology, we use the term "emptiness of action," or "non-action." To act in a way that arises from non-action is to act in a way that truly influences the situation in a nonviolent way. Naturally, humanists and masters of the Way contribute to the ends to save life, but their most valued contribution is their presence, not their actions. When they act, their actions are filled with the spirit of love, wisdom, and peace. Their actions are their presence, their mindfulness, their own personalities. This non-action, this awakened presence, is their most fundamental contribution.

Since the time of the Buddha there have been many meditation masters. They may appear not to be involved with society, but they contribute greatly. For me, they are the spring of fresh water, living proof that saints are still possible in this world. Without them, religion would be poorer, more shallow. These meditation masters, monks who spend their lives in the forests, are very very important for us and for society. Even those of us who are in society must return to these masters from time to time and look within. We must practice our meditation, our prayer, at least every morning or evening. In the crises of the present day, those of us who work in society, who confront power and injustice daily, often get beaten down and we become tired. At least once a year, we need to go to a retreat center to regain our spiritual strength, so we can return to confront society. Spiritual masters are like springs of fresh water. We who work in society need to carry that pure water to flood the banks, to fertilize the land and the trees, to be of use to the plants and animals, so that they can taste something fresh, and be revitalized. If we do not go back to the spring, our minds get polluted, just as water becomes polluted, and we are not of much use to the plants, the trees, or the earth.

Most of us who are in society must be careful, because we can become polluted very easily, particularly when confronted with so many problems. Sometimes we feel hatred, sometimes greed, sometimes we wish for more power, sometimes for wealth. We must be clear with ourselves that we do not need much wealth or power. It is easy, particularly as we get older, to want softer lives, to want recognition, to want to be on equal terms with those in power. But this is a great danger. Religion means deep commitment, and personal transformation. To be of help we must become more selfless and less selfish. To do this, we have to take more and more moral responsibility in society. This is the essence of religion, from ancient times right up to the present.

Many people, particularly in the West, think that Buddhism is only for deep meditation and personal transformation, that it has nothing to do with society. This is not true. Particularly in South and Southeast Asia, for many centuries Buddhism has been a great strength for society. Until recently, Buddhist values permeated Burma, Siam,[1] Laos, Cambodia, Sri Lanka, and other Buddhist countries. But things have changed, due mainly to colonialism, materialism, and Western education. Many of us who were educated abroad look down on our own cultures, on our own religious values.

Society has become much more complex. Whether we like them or not, industrialization and urbanization have come in, and traditional Buddhism does not know how to cope with them. It did very well in rural, agrarian societies, but in urbanized societies, with the complexities of modern life, Buddhism does not know what to do. The Buddhist university in Siam, for example, is a place where monks read only the scriptures, study only the life of the Buddha in the traditional way. Meanwhile, Bangkok has become like New York or Chicago, but the monks are not aware. They think it is just a big Siamese village, as it was when I was born. They do not realize how complex Bangkok has become. Indeed, the monks still have food offered to them in the traditional way, so why should they think things have changed?

They still feel that because we have a king, the government must be just, since the government supports the Sangha. This is the *Dhammaraja,* or "Wheel-Turning King" theory. But in reality the governments have been corrupt in Siam for at least thirty or forty years. Most came to power through coups d'état, often

---

1 My country has become very Westernized, perhaps more than anywhere else in Southeast Asia. We even changed our name from Siam to Thailand. This kingdom was known as Siam until 1939 when it was changed to Thailand, and it remains so officially. It has been ruled by one dictator after another, and Bangkok has become a kind of second- or third-rate Western capital. There is not a single Buddhist value left in Bangkok, except as decoration for the tourists, or for mere religious ceremony, and Western urbanization is really beyond our grasp. To me, the name "Thailand" signifies the crisis of traditional Siamese values. Removing from the nation the name it had carried all its life is the first step in the psychic dehumanization of its citizens, especially when its original name was replaced by a hybrid, Anglicized word. This new name also implies chauvinism and irredentism, and I refuse to use it. I prefer to use the name Siam.

violent. In the last coup d'état, several hundred people, mostly students, were killed, and several thousand were put in jail. Still, many of the monks feel that the governments are just, so it is the duty of those of us who have a certain spiritual strength and who can see what is going on to tell them that it is otherwise. This is the duty of any religious person. We have to build up political awareness. Politics must be related to religion.

We must also build up economic awareness. Economics also relates to religion. We need what E. F. Schumacher called Buddhist economics—not just Western capitalistic economics, which is unethical and unjust, which only makes the rich richer and the poor poorer. Yes, we also need some socialist economics, but socialist economics makes the state too powerful. We really need Buddhist economics. If we are to be poor, we must be poor together, poor but generous, share our labor, share our thought, share our generosity. We need to build on that. So it is our duty to make economists aware of Buddhist economics.

In *Small Is Beautiful,* Schumacher reminds us that Western economists seek maximization of material gain as if they hardly care for people. He says that in the Buddhist concept of economic development, we should avoid gigantism, especially of machines, which tend to control rather than to serve human beings. With gigantism, we are driven by an excessive greed in violating and raping nature. If bigness and greed can be avoided, the Middle Path of Buddhist development can be achieved, i.e., both the world of industry and agriculture can be converted into a meaningful habitat.[1] I agree with Schumacher that small is beautiful in the Buddhist concept of development, but what he did not stress is that cultivation must first come from within. In the Sinhalese experience, the

---

1   E. F. Schumacher, *Small Is Beautiful* (London: Blond & Briggs, 1973).

Sarvodaya Shramadana movement applies Buddhism to the individual first. Through cultivated individuals a village is developed, then several villages, leading to the nation and the world.

Political awareness and economic awareness are related to ourselves and our society, and very much related to our own culture. To drink Coca Cola, to drink Pepsi Cola, for example, is a great mistake. It is not only junk food, it is exploiting our country economically. Both the Coca Cola Thailand Company and the Pepsi Cola Thailand Company have an ex-prime minister as president. This already makes us suspect something exploitative politically and economically. Culturally, the exploitation is insidious. Pepsi Cola and Coca Cola make the villagers feel ashamed to offer us rainwater to drink. They feel they must offer us something in a bottle. And each bottle costs them one day of their earnings.

For another example, a multinational pineapple company recently expanded its empire into my country. They bought a lot of land from our farmers, who were very proud—poor but proud to be farmers. Now they have become landless. They do not grow rice any more, they just grow pineapples for that company. At first, the company bought at a very good price; later on, they lowered the price; still later on, the farmers just became their employees. In a country without labor unions, without the right to strike, the farmers are at the mercy of the pineapple company (which was started by a missionary).

Some Westerners want to become Buddhist monks only to escape from the world of turmoil, to benefit only themselves. My own experience over the past thirty years clearly indicates that Buddhism in the West has been practiced by many who did not want to get involved with society. However a new generation of Buddhists in England and America have displayed a robust feeling and an inclination to become involved in the spirit of Buddhism.

Phrakru Sakorn is a good example of what I mean by the spirit of Buddhism. He is a Thai monk in his fifties, the abbot of Wat Yokrabat in Samut Sakorn province, a provincial monk who only completed elementary education. Samut Sakorn is only one province away from Bangkok. The people there are mostly impoverished, illiterate farmers. The province is usually flooded with seawater, which perennially destroys the paddies, leaving the people with little or no other means of subsistence.

Most of the people had been driven to gambling, drinking, or playing the lottery. Being fully aware of the people's situation, Phrakru Sakorn decided to try to help the people before attempting to make any improvements in his own temple or spending a lot of time preaching Buddhist morals. Phrakru organized the people to work together to build dikes, canals, and to some extent, roads. He realized that poverty could not be eradicated unless new crops were introduced, since saltwater was ruining the rice fields. He suggested coconut as a substitute, based on the example of a nearby province.

Once the people of Samut Sakorn started growing coconuts, Phrakru advised them not to sell them because middlemen kept the price of coconuts very low. He encouraged them to make coconut sugar, using traditional techniques to do so. With the help of three nearby universities that were interested in the development and promotion of community projects, Phrakru received assistance, and the people of Samut Sakorn began selling their coconut sugar all over the country. He has since encouraged the growing of palm trees for building material, and the planting of herbs to be used as traditional medicine.

Before the end of the Vietnam War, I asked Ven. Thich Nhat Hanh whether he would rather have peace under the communist regime which would mean the end of Buddhism or rather the victory of the democratic Vietnam with the possibility of Buddhist revival, and his answer was to have peace at any price. He argued that Buddhism does not mean that we should sacrifice people's lives in order to preserve the Buddhist hierarchy, the pagodas, the monasteries, the scriptures, the rituals, and the tradition. When human lives are preserved and when human dignity and freedom are cultivated toward peace and loving-kindness, Buddhism can again be reborn in the hearts of men and women.

The presence of Buddhism in society does not mean having a lot of schools, hospitals, cultural institutions, or political parties run by Buddhists. It means that the schools, hospitals, cultural institutions, and political parties are permeated with and administered with humanism, love, tolerance, and enlightenment, characteristics which Buddhism attributes to an opening up, development, and formation of human nature. This is the true spirit of nonviolence.

Having grasped the spirit of Buddhism, we must face the world in full awareness of its condition. In Buddhist terminology, the world is full of *dukkha,* i.e., the dangers of impending world destruction through nuclear weapons, atomic fallout, air, land, and sea pollution, population explosion, exploitation of fellow human beings, denial of basic human rights, and devastating famine. We must realize that if we wish to avoid these catastrophes, humanity must immediately stop all partisan brawls and concentrate all its abilities and energy in the urgent effort to save ourselves.

The struggles of the peoples in developing nations might go on for many more dozens of years. Because of wars, resources are wasted and economies cannot be built up. Governments in developing nations want to spend more and more money to buy weapons from rich countries to fight civil wars, and they fall farther and farther behind on the path of development. The situation grows more and more complex. The fate of humanity is too great a burden. What can we do?

World dukkha is too immense for any country, people, or religion to solve. We can only save ourselves when all humanity recognizes that every problem on earth is our own personal problem and our own personal responsibility. This realization can only occur when the divisions and strife between religions, peoples, and nations cease. We can only save ourselves when, for example, the rich feel that they should contribute towards alleviating the famine of the world. Unless the rich change their lifestyle considerably, there is no hope of solving this problem. Those in the northern hemisphere must see the difficulties in developing countries as their own problem. They must see the denial of basic human rights in Siam and Chile as their own problem, and the famine in Calcutta as their own agony.

The thoughts and spirit of Buddhism are well suited to the needs of a united world and to the removal of dividing, painful boundaries. The wisdom of Buddhism can provide a shining and illuminating outlook. The language of Buddhism must offer answers which fit our situation. Only then will Buddhism survive, today and tomorrow, as it has in the past, influencing humankind positively and generating love, peace, and nonviolence. The Buddha himself declared:

> All actions, by which one acquires merits are not worth
> the sixteenth part of friendliness (metta) which is
> the emancipation of mind; for friendliness radiates,
> shines and illumines, surpassing those actions as the
> emancipation of mind, just as all the lights of the stars
> are not worth the sixteenth part of the moonlight, for

the moonlight, surpassing them all, radiates, shines, and illumines.[1]

In the whole of Buddhist history, there has never been a holy war. Surely Buddhist kings waged war against one another, and they might even have claimed to do so for the benefit of mankind or for the Buddhist religion, but they simply could not quote any saying of the Buddha to support them however just their war might have been. The Buddha said,

> Victory creates hatred. Defeat creates suffering. The wise ones desire neither victory nor defeat.... Anger creates anger.... He who kills will be killed. He who wins will be defeated ... Revenge can only be overcome by abandoning revenge.... The wise ones desire neither victory nor defeat.

There is much to be learned from the wisdom and compassion of the Buddha in this pluralistic world.

---

1 Anguttara-nikaya.

ROBERT A. F. THURMAN

Nagarjuna's Guidelines for Buddhist Social Action 1988

[O King!] Just as you love to consider
What to do to help yourself,
So should you love to consider
What to do to help others![1]

Nagarjuna thus expresses the basic principle of Buddhist social action: the universal altruism of "great love" (*mahamaitri*) and "great compassion," or "great empathy" (*mahakaruna*). The primary Buddhist position on social action is one of total activism, an unswerving commitment to complete self-transformation and complete world transformation. This activism becomes fully explicit in the Universal Vehicle (Mahayana), with its magnificent

---

1 All Nagarjuna references are from Nagarjuna, *The Precious Garland,* translated by Jeffrey Hopkins (London: Allen & Unwin, 1975). I have, however, used the Sanskrit original (Vaidya, 1960) in certain places, and on that basis altered the terminology to suit my own preference, thus to maintain coherence between quotes and commentary. [Ed. note: For the verse number of each quote from Nagarjuna, see Professor Thurman's article from which this essay is excerpted, published in *The Eastern Buddhist,* Vol. XVI, No. I, Spring 1983.]

literature on the Bodhisattva career.[1] But it is also compellingly implicit in the Individual Vehicle (Hinayana) in both the Buddha's actions and his teachings: granted, his attention in the latter was on self-transformation, the prerequisite of social transformation. Thus, it is squarely in the center of all Buddhist traditions to bring basic principles to bear on actual contemporary problems to develop ethical, even political, guidelines for action.

This is just what Nagarjuna did during the second century CE, when he wrote his *Jewel Garland of Royal Counsels* to his friend and disciple, King Udayi of the powerful Satavahana dynasty of south central India. It should thus prove instructive to examine his counsels in some detail. In this essay, I will extrapolate from his specific prescriptions a set of modern "counsels" for today's "kings," in hopes that it will help the buddhistic intellectual clarify his or her own thinking about the emergencies that beset us. I will use these prescriptions as a framework on which to outline guidelines for Buddhist social action in our modern times. The fact that it is counsel to a "king" does not invalidate this approach in the least, for, as R. B. Fuller says, the average citizen of any modern, industrial, or postindustrial society lives better in many ways than most kings of bygone eras; indeed is more king of his own fate than they were in many ways.[2] Therefore, everyone can apply these counsels in their own sphere of activity. Political parties

---

1 I use "Universal" and "Individual" to translate *Maha-* and *Hina-*, based on the fact that the Mahayana is a vehicle designed for riders who wish all other beings to share the ride, and the Hinayana is a vehicle designed for riders who also hope others will get aboard, but who are primarily concerned with hanging on themselves at least. The former thus emphasizes "Universal" liberation, the latter "Individual" liberation. Finally, since universal liberation certainly cannot take place unless it is "universal individual" liberations in totality, these translations also capture the relationship between the two vehicles.

2 R. B. Fuller is fond of making this point in his essays in *Utopia or Oblivion* (Overlook Press, out of print, 1973).

could be formed with such principles in their platforms (indeed many parties do have such planks), and Buddhist communities and individuals in particular could work to spread such principles and attitudes. So, let us now read Nagarjuna as if he were addressing us today.

There are forty-five verses (#301–345), which contain the whole quintessence of the matter. This section begins with some acknowledgment that good advice is often unpleasant at first hearing, especially to a rich and powerful king who is used to being flattered and having his own way. The king is urged to be tolerant of the "useful but unpleasant" words, and to consider them as true words spoken without anger and from compassion, hence fit to be heard, like water fit for bathing. "Realize that I am telling you what is useful here and later. Act on it so as to help yourself and others."

People in power are still the same. In fact, the entire populations of the "developed" countries are in a way full of people of royal powers, used to consuming what they want, being flattered and waited upon by people from "underdeveloped" lands, used to having unpleasantly realistic things such as corpses, sicknesses, madnesses, the deformities of poverty, kept out of their sight. They do not want to hear that all is impermanent, that life is essentially painful and fundamentally impure. They do not want to acknowledge that all beings are equal to them and their dear ones, equally lovable and deserving. They do not want to hear that there is no real self and no absolute property and no absolute right. But that they do hear it, and hear it well, is quite the most crucial necessity of our times. The hundreds of millions of "kings" and "queens" living in the developed world must face their obligations to other peoples, to other species, and to nature itself. This is the crisis of our times, the real one, not the supposedly important competitions among the developed powers.

Nagarjuna's first real statement is straight to this most crucial point. "If you do not make contributions of the wealth obtained from former giving, through such ingratitude and attachment you will not gain wealth in the future." There are two beliefs behind this simple yet far-reaching injunction to generosity, an injunction essential today. First, wealth accrues to an individual as the evolutionary effect of generosity in former lives or previously in this life. Second, wealth in this life accrues to one by the generosity of others who give to one, for whatever reason, and therefore one must be grateful to them. Bracketing the question of former lives, which is difficult for modern people, it is a fact that people who are wealthy today usually are so because previous generations worked hard and gave of themselves to the future. Capitalism itself is, in its essence, not a matter of hoarding and attachment, but a matter of ascetic self-restraint, the "investment" of wealth or the giving it up to a larger causality. The more given up from present consumption to productive investment, the more is produced for future consumption. Those who lose sight of the essence of this process and simply consume and hoard, soon lose their wealth, just as Nagarjuna states. It is a fact of economics that the basis of wealth is generosity.

Petty-mindedness, scarcity psychology, short-term profit seeking, destructive rapacity—these are the real enemies. Their opposite is magnanimity, which makes all people friends. In sum, transcendence is the root of generosity. Generosity is the root of evolutionary survival. Evolutionary survival eventually brings forth freedom for the bliss of transcendence. This is a golden three-strand cord more powerful than the usual heap-habit, ego-habit, addiction cycle. The former is a living Nirvana. The latter is the samsara of continual dying.

The foremost type of giving is, interestingly, not just giving of material needs, although that is a natural part of generosity. That of

greatest value to beings is freedom and transcendence and enlightenment. These are obtained only through the door of Dharma,
Transcendent Truth of Selflessness, Voidness, Openness, and so
forth. Therefore, the educational system of a society is not there
to "service" the society, to produce its drone-"professionals," its
workers, its servants. The educational system is the individual's
doorway to liberation, to enlightenment. It is therefore the brain
of the body politic. Society has no other purpose than to foster it.
It is society's door of liberation. By giving others the gift of education, they gain freedom, self-reliance, understanding, choice, all
that is still summed up in the word "enlightenment." Life is for the
purpose of enlightenment, not enlightenment for life. The wondrous paradox is, of course, that enlightenment makes life worthwhile: because it makes it less important, it makes it easier to give
it away, whereby at last it becomes enjoyable. Therefore, human
evolution is consummated in transformative education. Society
becomes meaningful when it fosters education. Life is worth living when it values education supremely. And so our "royal" giving
should first of all go to support universal, total, unlimited education of all individuals. Nagarjuna is very specific: "Create centers
of Teaching, institutions of the Three Jewels, whose name and
glory are inconceivable to lesser kings, for fear of their ill-repute
after death (if they rule unwisely and selfishly)."

Nagarjuna is not talking about merely creating "religious centers." He is not even talking about creating "Buddhist centers,"
"Buddhism" understood in its usual sense as one of a number of
world religions. It does not matter what symbols or ideologies
provide the umbrella, as long as the function is liberation and
enlightenment. Clearly Nagarjuna, who proclaims repeatedly
that "belief-systems," "dogmatic views," "closed convictions,"
"fanatic ideologies," and so forth, are sicknesses to be cured by
the medicine of emptiness, is not a missionary for any particular

"belief-system," even if it is labeled "Buddhism." Rather, he wants the social space filled with doorways to Nirvana, shrines of liberating Truth, facilities for Teaching and Practice, where "things," "duties," "laws," "religions," and "doctrines" can be examined, criticized, refined, used, transcended, and so forth. As already mentioned, these centers are not primarily even for the service of society, although in fact they are essential facilities for the evolutionary betterment of the people. They are the highest product of the society. As society itself has the main function of service to the individual, its highest gift to its individuals is to expose them to the transcendent potential developed by education.

Now these are institutions of the Three Jewels: the Buddha, the Dharma, and the Sangha. And, under the above, critically "de-religionized" interpretation, fully in keeping with Nagarjuna's own centrist (Madhyamika) critical style, these Three Jewels can demonstrate their value without any sectarian context. In universal social terms, the Buddha is the ideal of the educated person, the full flowering of human potential, the perfectly self-fulfilled and other-fulfilling being. He/she[1] is not a god, not an object of worship, but an object of emulation, a source of enlightenment teaching. He/she is the standard of achievement. The Dharma is his/her Teaching, the Truth and Nirvana he/she realized, which all people can educate themselves to realize, as already explained. The Sangha is the Community of those dedicated to teaching and practicing this Dharma with a view of becoming and helping all become such Buddhas. Very often they are so concentrated on

---

1 When speaking of Buddha in the context of ideal archetypes, it is important to use the double pronoun, as a modern Buddhist, for males not to monopolize access to religious virtuosity and spiritual perfection. In fact, the 112 superhuman signs of a Buddha contain definite symbols of androgyny, subliminally resonating with the famous pronouncement that "ultimate reality is beyond male and female," found in many Universal Vehicle Scriptures.

these tasks, they have no time for ordinary social activities, business, professions, family, and so forth, but are specialists in practice and teaching. These become mendicants, identityless, propertyless, selfless monastics, and often in Buddhist history they served as the core staff of Teaching centers. Sometimes, however, part of their Teaching and practice involved, as in the case of Vimalakirti and later the Great Adepts (*mahasiddhas*), participation in ordinary living patterns, so it is not necessary at all times and places and at all stages of development that they observe the monastic lifestyle.

These institutions will gain fame, as the people come to know that they are verily the gateways to a higher order of living, a higher awareness, a fuller sensibility, a more valid knowledge. They radiate glory as the persons who have developed themselves and have transcended their previous addictive habits naturally and compassionately give invaluable assistance toward the betterment of others according to their capacities and inclinations.

In the second verse, Nagarjuna puts in an important criterion of a genuine institution of Enlightenment Teaching: it must not become a servile establishment in service of the elites of existing societies, there to provide professional training and ideological indoctrination. Its teachers and students must live transcendently, that is, valuing Truth above all personal considerations. They must thus be intensely critical of all falsehood, pretense, delusion, sham. Therefore, their sayings and writings must be so ruthlessly clear and straightforward that inferior persons, elite members as well as kings, must be terrified of being exposed in their pretenses and faults, hence inspired themselves to live and act transcendently. If the institutions are not truly liberal, i.e., liberating in this manner, they had better not be established at all.

To take Nagarjuna's counsel to heart in modern times, this means a drastic revision of our practice nowadays. Liberal education should no longer be seen as an institution necessary for the preservation and enrichment of a free society. Rather liberal education as an institution should represent the fulfillment of the very founding purpose of a free society. Kant's call for enlightenment as the "emergence from the tutelage of others" and Jefferson's call for "universal enlightenment throughout the land" should be seen as expressing the prime priority of the whole nation. Thus, it is quite proper that the major expenditure in the national budget should be for education; and it should be offered free to all, regardless of class affiliation, regardless of utilitarian calculations. "If it takes all your wealth, you should disabuse the magnificent elite of their arrogance, inspire the middle classes, and refine the coarse tastes of the lowly."

Nagarjuna seems to have been aware of the economic costliness of his insistence on the priority of education, for he devotes the next five verses to persuading the king that wealth should not be hoarded for lesser necessities, and that he should go the whole way in support of higher education. He harps on the king's death, how such contributions are an investment in his future evolution, how his successor will probably waste it, how happiness comes from the generous use of wealth, not from hoarding and eventual wasting, and how, finally, if he does not do it now while he is young and in control of his ministers, they will not respect his wishes when he sees clearly on his deathbed. In his own words:

> Having let go of all possessions (at death)
> Powerless you must go elsewhere;
> But all that has been used for Dharma
> Precedes you (as positive evolutionary force).
> All the possessions of a previous King come under the
>   control of his successor.

Of what use are they then to the previous King,
Either for his practice, happiness, or fame?
Through using wealth there is happiness in the here
    and now.
Through giving there is happiness in the future.
From wasting it without using it or giving it away there
    is only misery.
How could there be happiness?
Because of impotence while dying,
You will be unable to make gifts through your ministers.
Shamelessly they will lose affection for you,
And will only seek to please the new King.
Therefore, now while in good health,
Create Centers of Learning with all your wealth,
For you are living amid the causes of death
Like a lamp standing in the breeze.
Also other Teaching Centers established by the
    previous kings,
All temples and so forth should be sustained as before.

From the universalism underlying the educational emphasis of Buddhist activism, Nagarjuna moves to the principle of pacifism, in specific application to the appointment of ministers, generals, officials, administration of justice, and vigilance over the actual conditions in the nation.

The choice of ministers, generals, and officials is mainly determined by whether or not they practice the Teachings, and manifest this personally by honesty, generosity, kindliness, and intelligent discrimination. Even with such people, the ruler should be in constant contact with them, and constantly admonish them to remember the overall aim and purpose of the nation: namely the Teaching, realization, and practice of the liberating Truth. "If your kingdom exists for the Truth, and not for fame, wealth, or consumption, then it will be extremely fruitful; otherwise all will finally be in vain." In modern terms, this counsel accords well with the experience of successful corporations and government administrations and agencies. They always choose their leaders from among liberally educated persons, rather than from narrow professional circles, as it takes the special "enlightened" ability of clear critical insight to manage large complex affairs successfully.

In regard to justice, Nagarjuna tells the king to appoint elder judges, responsible, well-educated, virtuous, and pleasant persons, and even so he should intervene as much as possible to exercise compassion for criminals. "Even if they (the judges) have rightfully fined, bound, or punished people, You, being softened with compassion, should still take care (of the offenders). O King, through compassion you should always generate an attitude of help, even for all beings who have committed the most appalling sins. Especially generate compassion for those murderers, whose sins are horrible; those of fallen nature are receptacles of compassion from those whose nature is great." Nagarjuna goes to the central issue concerning violence and nonviolence in a society, the issue of murder and its retribution. Taking of life is the worst violence, especially in enlightenment-valuing nations, where the precious human life, hard-won by struggle up from the tormented lower forms of evolution, is the inestimably valuable stage from which most effectively to attain freedom and enlightenment. But to take a second life to avenge the first is to add violence to violence, and hence capital punishment is abolished by Nagarjuna. Punishment must be rehabilitative, and Nagarjuna's formulation of this principle may be the earliest on historical record. "As long as the prisoners are not freed (which, he says, they should be as soon as possible) they should be made comfortable with barbers, baths, food, drink, medicine, and clothing. Just as unworthy sons are punished out of a wish to make them worthy, so punishment should be enforced with compassion and not from hatred or concern for wealth. Once you have examined the fierce murderers and judged them correctly, you should banish them without killing or torturing them." The nonviolent treatment of criminals, even capital offenders, accords with every principle of Buddhist teaching: 1) compassion, of course, in that love must be extended most of all to the undeserving, the difficult to love; further, for society to kill, sanctions killing indirectly, setting a bad example; 2) impermanence, in that the minds of beings are changeable, and commission of evil once does not necessarily imply a permanent habit of doing evil; 3) selflessness implies the conditionality of each act, and the reformability of any personality; 4) the preciousness and value of life, especially human life.

In modern times, it is to the great credit of those modern societies founded on enlightenment principles that they finally have abolished capital punishment. By the same token, it is sad that there are strong political pressures to reinstate it. In such a context, it is even more astounding that Nagarjuna should have set forth this clear-cut principle almost two thousand years ago, in such specific, practical terms.

Nagarjuna gives specific advice regarding socialistic universal welfare policy: "Cause the blind, the sick, the humble, the unprotected, the destitute, and the crippled, all equally to attain food and drink without omission." He does not elaborate upon this in specific policy terms. It is perfectly clear that he considers it obvious that the king is obligated to care for everyone in the whole nation as if they were his children. In modern terms, the welfare system created by Roosevelt in the United States, and the welfare socialism the socialist states have implemented, fit extremely well with this policy. But recently, we can observe a trend of assumption that, while any reasonable person would like to give everything to everyone, it is bad for people to get goods for nothing, and it is impossible to support everyone; there is not enough wealth for that purpose. The assumptions underlying this anti-welfare reaction we see around the world are that 1) people are inherently lazy, and 2) wealth is inherently insufficient. Indeed, there were certainly such attitudes in Nagarjuna's day and earlier. The central Buddhist story of Prince Vessantara turns on the paradox of generosity and wealth. Everyone loves him because he gives everyone everything they ask for. Yet the nation comes to fear him when it seems he will give away even the very sources of their wealth. So they shrink back in fright, clutch what they have to themselves, and banish their real source of joy, the generous Prince.

Since the welfare system was installed in the United States, that nation has produced the greatest wealth ever produced by any nation in history, including inventions, in principle, capable of infinite productivity; and this in the midst of a series of disastrous wars, with their aftermaths wherein the nation gave enormous treasure to rebuild the nations it had defeated. Now, the rulers of America confusedly think that their gifts to the people, the real source of their optimism, the energy of real productivity, are exhausting them, and so they want to take it all away. In this confused effort to clutch onto what they see as scarce and shrinking wealth, they will destroy the source of that wealth, the love and optimistic confidence and creativity of the people. Fortunately, this will result in a rapid disaster for all, so the error will soon come to light, and Prince Vessantara will return in triumph from his banishment. Hoarding creates poverty. Giving away creates wealth. Imagination of scarcity is thus the cause of loss. Imagination of abundance creates endless wealth. It is terrible or wonderful, depending on one's tolerance, that life must always be so subtle, so paradoxical, and complex.

Nagarjuna seems to be aware of the charge of "impractical idealism" that tends to be levelled against his *Counsels,* and so his verses closing this passage address the practicality question. "In order to maintain control, oversee your country through the eyes of agents; attentive and mindful, always act in accordance with the principles." An effective intelligence system seems to be necessary! The king must know what is happening throughout his realm to prevent abuses and forestall disasters. In modern terms, Nagarjuna allows for the vital role of "intelligence," the gathering of insightful information about the state of the people. The very mention of an "Intelligence Agency" is so sensitive nowadays, it is hard to remember that it is not the "intelligence" but the stupidity and violence in the paramilitary activities of the CIA, KGB, and their colleagues in other nations that have caused their aura of horror. Theoretically, if the responsible leaders of all nations really had all the information about all consequences of their actions, they surely would desist from the foolish and self-destructive policies they currently espouse.

Nagarjuna sums up his practical counsels with a pleasant metaphor: "The birds of the populace will alight upon the royal tree that gives the cool shade of tolerance, that flourishes with the flowers of honors, and that provides the bounteous fruit of great rewards." That is, an idealistic social policy is realistic. Tolerance, justice, and generosity are not merely lofty ideals, "ultra-obligations" for a few saints and heroes to aspire to embody, but are the essential components of any viable social policy. The ruler or government must manifest them first, and each citizen must strive to cultivate them. Since animals' habits do not automatically tend away from anger, delusion, and greed toward tolerance, justice, and giving, these virtues must gradually be cultivated. As each must do this for himself or herself, individualistic transcendentalism is the foundation of any viable activism. From this basis, pacifism is the social expression of tolerance; educational universalism is the social expression of wise justice; and socialistic sharing of wealth is the social expression of generosity.

These four principles seem to encompass mainstream Buddhist social practice, as counseled by Nagarjuna. These four guidelines should be reliable in choosing a line of action in particular situations. It is always essential to remember, however, the fundamental inconceivability of all things, for which great love seems finally the only adequate response. Nagarjuna insists that "the profound, enlightenment in practice, is emptiness creative as compassion." Jesus Christ's "Love God with all thy heart, and thy neighbor as thyself," and Augustine's "Love God and do what you will"—these two great "pivotal phrases" are very much in the same vein, using of course the theistic term for emptiness. In a culture more used to those great statements, we might express Nagarjuna as follows: "Open thy heart to absolute emptiness, and love all thy neighbors as thyself!" It is such love that is the whole "Law," and is the very body of all Buddhas. Vimalakirti describes it to Manjusri:

> The love that is firm, its high resolve unbreakable like a diamond; . . . the love that is never exhausted because it acknowledges voidness and selflessness; the love that is generosity because it bestows the gift of Truth without the tight fist of bad teachers; the love that is justice because it benefits immoral beings; the love that is tolerance because it protects both self and others; the

love that is enterprise because it takes responsibility
for all living things; the love that is meditation because
it refrains from indulgence in tastes; the love that is
wisdom because it causes attainment at the proper time;
the love that is liberative technique because it shows
the way everywhere; the love that is without formality
because it is pure in motivation; the love that is without
deviation because it acts decisively; the love that is high
resolve because it is free of passions; the love that is
without deceit because it is not artificial; the love that
is happiness because it introduces living beings to the
happiness of a Buddha. Such, Manjusri, is the great love
of a bodhisattva.[1]

---

1 Thurman, *The Holy Teaching of Vimalakirti* (University Park, Pennsylvania: Penn
State University Press, 1976), 57.

THICH NHAT HANH

Please Call Me by My True Names
1988

I HAVE A poem for you. This poem is about three of us. The first is a twelve-year-old girl, one of the boat people crossing the Gulf of Siam. She was raped by a sea pirate, and after that she threw herself into the sea. The second person is the sea pirate, who was born in a remote village in Thailand. And the third person is me. I was very angry, of course. But I could not take sides against the sea pirate. If I could have, it would have been easier, but I couldn't. I realized that if I had been born in his village and had lived a similar life—economic, educational, and so on—it is likely that I would now be that sea pirate. So it is not easy to take sides. Out of suffering, I wrote this poem. It is called "Please Call Me by My True Names," because I have many names, and when you call me by any of them, I have to say, "Yes."

Don't say that I will depart tomorrow—
even today I am still arriving.

Look deeply: every second I am arriving
to be a bud on a Spring branch,
to be a tiny bird, with still-fragile wings,
learning to sing in my new nest,

to be a caterpillar in the heart of a flower,
to be a jewel hiding itself in a stone.

I still arrive, in order to laugh and to cry,
to fear and to hope.

The rhythm of my heart is the birth and death
of all that is alive.

I am the mayfly metamorphosing
on the surface of the river.
And I am the bird
that swoops down to swallow the mayfly.

I am the frog swimming happily
in the clear water of a pond.
And I am the grass-snake
that silently feeds itself on the frog.

I am the child in Uganda, all skin and bones,
my legs as thin as bamboo sticks.
And I am the arms merchant,
selling deadly weapons to Uganda.

I am the twelve-year-old girl,
refugee on a small boat,
who throws herself into the ocean
after being raped by a sea pirate.
And I am the pirate,
my heart not yet capable
of seeing and loving.

I am a member of the politburo,
with plenty of power in my hands.
And I am the man who has to pay
his "debt of blood" to my people,
dying slowly in a forced-labor camp.

My joy is like Spring, so warm
it makes flowers bloom all over the Earth.
My pain is like a river of tears,
so vast it fills the four oceans.

Please call me by my true names,
so I can hear all my cries and my laughter at once,
so I can see that my joy and pain are one.

Please call me by my true names,
so I can wake up,
and so the door of my heart
can be left open,
the door of compassion.

I still have the theme of this poem in my mind. "Where is our enemy?" I ask myself this all the time. Our Earth, our green, beautiful Earth, is in danger and all of us know it. We are not facing a pirate, but we are facing the destruction of the earth where our small boat has been. It will sink if we are not careful. We think that the enemy is the other, and that is why we can never see him. Everyone needs an enemy in order to survive. Russia needs an enemy. The United States needs an enemy. China needs an enemy. Vietnam needs an enemy. Everyone needs an enemy. Without an enemy we cannot survive. In order to rally people, governments need enemies. They want us to be afraid, to hate, so we will rally behind them. And if they do not have a real enemy, they will invent one in order to mobilize us. Yet many people in the United States have gone to Russia and discovered that the Russian people are very nice, and there are Russian citizens who visit the U.S., and when they return home, report that the American people are fine. This after so many decades of both sides telling their own people how evil the other country's people are.

One friend in the peace movement told me, "Every time I see the President on television, I cannot bear it. I have to turn the TV off, or I become livid." He believes that the situation of the world is in the hands of the government, and if only the President would change his policies, we would have peace. I told him that that is not entirely correct. The "President" is in each of us. We always deserve our government. In Buddhism, we speak of interdependent origination. "This is, because that is. This is not, because that is not." Do our daily lives have nothing to do with our government? Please meditate on this question. We seem to believe that our daily lives have nothing to do with the situation of the world. But if we do not change our daily lives, we cannot change the world.

In Japan, in the past, people took three hours to drink one cup of tea. You might think this is a waste of time, because time is money. But two people spending three hours drinking tea, being with each other, has to do with peace. The two men or two women did not speak a lot. They exchanged only a word or two, but they were really there, enjoying the time and the tea. They really knew the tea and the presence of each other.

Nowadays, we allow only a few minutes for tea, or coffee. We go into a cafe and order a cup of tea or coffee and listen to music and other loud noises, thinking about the business we will transact afterwards. In that situation, the tea does not exist. We are violent to the tea. We do not recognize it as living reality, and that it is related to why our situation is as it is. When we pick up a Sunday newspaper, we should know that in order to print all the copies of that edition, which sometimes weighs 10 or 12 pounds, they had to cut down a whole forest. We are destroying our Earth without knowing it.

Drinking a cup of tea, picking up a newspaper, using toilet paper, all of these things have to do with peace. Nonviolence can be called "awareness." We must be aware of what we are, of who we are, and of what we are doing. When I became a novice in a Buddhist monastery, I was taught to be aware of every act during the day. Since then, I have been practicing mindfulness and awareness. I used to think that practicing like that was only important for beginners, that advanced people did other important things, but now I know that practicing awareness is for everyone, including the abbot. The purpose of Buddhist meditation is to see into your own nature and to become a Buddha. That can be done only through awareness. If you are not aware of what is going on in yourself and in the world, how can you see into your own nature and become a Buddha?

The word "Buddha" comes from the root, *buddh*, which means "awake." A Buddha is one who is awake. Are we really awake in our daily lives? That is a question I invite you to think about. Are we awake when we drink tea? Are we awake when we pick up the newspaper? Are we awake when we eat ice cream?

Society makes it difficult to be awake. We know that 10,000 children die every day of hunger, but we keep forgetting. The kind of society we live in makes us forgetful. That is why we need exercises for mindfulness.

One day I asked a Vietnamese refugee boy, who was eating a bowl of rice, whether children in his country eat such high-quality rice. He said, "No," because he knows the situation. He experienced hunger in Vietnam—he only ate dry potatoes and he longed for a bowl of rice. In France, he has been eating rice for a year, and sometimes he begins to forget. But when I ask him, he remembers. I cannot ask the same question of a French or American child, because they have not had that kind of experience. They cannot understand. I realize how difficult it is for the people who live in Western countries to know what the situation in the developing countries really is. It seems to have nothing to do with the situation here. I told the Vietnamese boy that his rice comes from Thailand, and that most Thai children do not have this rice to eat. They eat rice of a poor quality, because the best rice is for export. Their government needs foreign currency, and they reserve the best rice for Westerners and not them.

In Vietnam we have a delicious banana called *due duja,* but now children and adults in Vietnam do not have the right to eat these bananas because they are all for export. And what do we get in return? Guns. Some of us practice this exercise of mindfulness: We sponsor a child in a developing country in order to get news from him or her, thus keeping in touch with the reality outside. We try many ways to be awake, but society keeps us forgetful. It is so difficult to practice awareness in this society.

It is said that if we reduce consumption of meat and alcohol by 50 percent, that would be enough to relieve poverty and protect the planet from the destructive effects of industrial farming. But how can we do it when we do not remember to be aware? We are intelligent people, but we keep forgetting. Meditation is to help us remember.

There are means for us to nourish awareness, to enjoy silence, to enjoy the world. There was a thirteen-year-old boy from Holland who came to our Center and ate lunch with us in silence. It was the first time he had eaten a silent meal, and he was embarrassed. The silence was quite heavy. After the meal, I asked whether he felt uneasy, and he said, "Yes." So I explained that the reason we eat in silence is in order to enjoy the food and the presence of each other. If we talk a lot we cannot enjoy these things. I asked him if there was some time when he turned off the TV in order to better enjoy his dinner or the conversation with friends, and he said, "Yes." I invited him to join us for another meal, and he ate with us in silence and enjoyed it very much.

We have lost our taste for silence. Every time we have a few minutes, we pick up a book to read, or make a phone call, or turn on the TV. We do not know how to be ourselves without something else to accompany us. We have lost our taste for being alone. Society takes many things from us and destroys us with noises, smells, and so many distractions. The first thing for us to do is to return to ourselves in order to recover ourselves, to be our best. This is very important. We need to reorganize our daily lives so that we do not allow society to colonize us. We have to reclaim our independence. We have to be real persons and not just the victim of society and other people.

The boat people said that every time their small boats were caught in storms, they knew their lives were in danger. But if one person on the boat could keep calm and not panic, that was a great help for everyone. People would listen to him or her and keep serene, and there was a chance for the boat to survive the danger. Our Earth is like a small boat. Compared with the rest of the cosmos, it is a very small boat, and it is in danger of sinking. We need such a person to inspire us with calm confidence, to tell us what to do. Who is that person? The Mahayana Buddhist sutras tell us that you are that person. If you are yourself, if you are your best, then you are that person. Only with such a person—calm, lucid, aware—will our situation improve. I wish you good luck. Please be yourself, please be that person.

I would like to suggest that in each home we have a small room for breathing. We have rooms for sleeping, eating, and cooking, why not have one room for breathing? Breathing is very important. I suggest that that room be decorated simply, and not be too bright. You may want to have a small bell, with a beautiful sound, a few cushions or chairs, and perhaps a vase of flowers to remind us of our true nature. Children can arrange flowers in mindfulness, smiling. If your household has five members, you can have five cushions or chairs, plus a few for guests. From time to time, you might like to invite a guest to come and sit and breathe with you for a few minutes.

I know of families where children go into a room like that after breakfast, sit down and breathe ten times, in-out-one, in-out-two, in-out-three, and so on, before they go to school. This is a beautiful practice. Beginning the day with being a Buddha is a very nice way to start the day. If we are a Buddha in the morning and we try to nourish the Buddha throughout the day, we may be able to come home at the end of a day with a smile—the Buddha is still there. It is really beautiful to begin the day by being a Buddha. Each time we feel ourselves about to leave our Buddha, we can sit and breathe until we return to our true self. Doing these kinds of things can change our civilization.

CHARLES JOHNSON

Be Peace Embodied
2004

D URING THIS PRESIDENTIAL election year, which many political commentators tell us may prove to be one of the most polarizing, divisive, and rancorous in American history, followers of Buddhist dharma will, like all citizens, be faced with what philosopher Jean-Paul Sartre once called "the agony of choice." To my eye, this is the most glorious of civilization's regular trials, one that defines the nature of a democratic republic. For when the framers of the Constitution declared that the nation's president "shall hold his office during the term of four years," they ingeniously guaranteed that a healthy degree of quadrennial change, suspense, tumult, renewal, and spirited debate would be inscribed into our political and social lives. Put another way, American voters, if they take their civic duty seriously, can never rest. Every four years they must decide on the direction of their collective destiny. Twenty-five times in each century they must define for themselves their understanding of the "good life," and vote for candidates and proposals that embody their vision of what this country and its influence on the world should be.

Yet for all its virtues, this necessary process, which the media frequently presents as a highly competitive "battle" or "war," can fuel the most ugly partisan passions, fears, frustrations, incivility, and forms of dualism we are likely to find in the realm of *samsara*.

If perceived through the distorting lens of conflict-laden language and concepts that deliberately pit one citizen against another ("Speech has something in it like a spider's web," Thomas Hobbes once remarked), politics divides people on election night into "winners" and "losers," and creates bitterness and attachment that can cloud consciousness and cripple spiritual development, though one of our greatest American leaders, Dr. Martin Luther King, Jr., proved time and again that this need not be so.

On December 20, 1956, the day the Montgomery bus boycott ended, King—whose model for nonviolent civil disobedience in Alabama drew inspiration from Gandhi's struggle with the British—said, "We must seek an integration based on mutual respect. As we go back to the buses, let us be loving enough to turn an enemy into a friend." Though his home was bombed and his wife and baby endangered during the campaign to end segregation in the "Cradle of the Confederacy," the twenty-six-year-old King never forgot that "all life is interrelated," nor that we are all "caught in an inescapable network of mutuality, tied in a single garment of destiny. Whatever affects one directly, affects all indirectly." He called this the "beloved community," which in my view is simply sangha by another name.

If we can, through the kind of mindfulness exhibited by Dr. King during one of the most revolutionary moments in American history, remember that politics is merely the skin of social life beneath which we find a more profound experience of ourselves and others, then our Constitution-mandated sea change every four years can potentially be an uplifting experience rather than a spiritually debilitating one. For as the Buddhist nun Jingnuo wrote four centuries ago, "If you bring to everything an illumined mind, you won't get lost."

The buddhadharma captures such course-correcting illumination in the terse Pali description of existence known as "the three marks": *anicca, dukkha, anatta,* often translated as, "Life is transient, sorrowful, and selfless." In this eidetic formulation about the marks that stain all phenomena, *anatta* reminds us that the belief in a substantive, enduring self is an illusion, while *dukkha* emphasizes the First Noble Truth of universal suffering based on selfish desire and clinging to the things of this world (including our thoughts and feelings about those things). Both the latter terms are experientially and logically grounded in the first mark, *anicca,* which means "impermanent," and speaks to Shakyamuni Buddha's insight that, "whatever is subject to arising must also be subject to ceasing."

With that general statement, the Buddha is referring to everything in our experience—all material and immaterial objects, men and women, societies and states of mind, legislation and governments. Any physicist would add that even the thirteen-billion-year-old universe itself will one day be reduced to black holes that will eventually disintegrate into stray particles, and these, too, will decay. From the moment of our so-called "birth" we have been dying, "changing all the time," says Thich Nhat Hanh, "Not a single element remains the same for two consecutive moments." In essence, we are verbs, not nouns; processes, not products. Therefore, the *Diamond Sutra* ends with this memorable verse:

Thus shall ye think of all this fleeting world:
A star at dawn, a bubble in a stream;
A flash of lightning in a summer cloud,
A flickering lamp, a phantom, and a dream.

We can all understand this. There is nothing particularly mystical about the fundamental nature of reality being change, process, and transformation. Nor is there anything esoteric in the wisdom that we err if we desire or try to cling to evanescent phenomena that change faster than we can chase them. In the buddhadharma, the true nature of things is *shunyata*, Sanskrit for "emptiness." But we would be wrong if we interpreted this emptiness as a lack, or as vacuous. In his outstanding book *Nonduality*, scholar David Loy provides a concise account of shunyata: "It comes from the root *shunya*, which means 'to swell' in two senses: hollow or empty, and also like the womb of a pregnant woman. Both are implied in the Mahayana usage: the first denies any fixed self-nature to anything; the second implies that this is also fullness and limitless possibility, for lack of any fixed characteristics allows the infinite diversity of impermanent phenomena." Those who experience shunyata know that all things have eternally been in a perfect state of tranquility, and that as Buddhaghosa says in the *Visuddhimagga*:

> Suffering alone exists, none who suffers
> The deed there is, but no doer thereof;
> Nirvana is, but no one seeking it;
> The Path there is, but none who travel it.

In *The Buddhist Vision*, Alex Kennedy points out that the recognition of impermanence or emptiness necessarily leads to the nonconceptual intuition that all perceived conditioned and transitory things are interdependent. Thich Nhat Hanh's word for this is "interbeing," a neologism he coined to express the traditional Buddhist understanding of the concatenated links in dependent origination. Kennedy says, "When we analyze any object, we can never come to a substance beyond which our analysis cannot penetrate. We can never find anything conditioned which has an underlying substantial reality. . . . All things, whether subject or object, are processes linked together in an intricate network of mutual conditions. . . . The ordinary man is distracted by the bright surface of the world and mistakes this for reality."

All things are empty in themselves, only existing—as Dr. King said—in a delicate "network of mutuality" where, as we are told in the *Visuddhimagga*, "it is not easy to find a being who has not formerly been your mother, your father, your brother, your sister, your son, your daughter." After awakening, or the experience of nirvana, which in Sanskrit literally means to "blow out" selfish desire and the illusory belief in a separate sense of one's life, the student of the Way experiences ultimate reality as a "we-relation." "Perfect peace," said Shakyamuni, "can dwell only where all vanity has disappeared."

However, in Buddhism we must acknowledge two levels of truth. First, there is ultimate, ontological truth. In *The Long Discourses of the Buddha*, Maurice Walshe explains that on this level, existence is experienced as "a mere process or physical and mental phenomena within which, or beyond which, no real ego-entity nor any abiding substance can be found." Secondly, there is conventional or relative truth, described by Walshe as the samsaric world "according to which people and things exist just as they appear to the naïve understanding." For myself, I enjoy thinking of these two truths in terms of our knowing the subatomic realm of electrons and positrons exists, but in our everyday lives we necessarily conduct ourselves in terms of Newtonian physics, because if we step out a tenth-floor window or in front of a fast-moving truck, we will go *splat*.

The great dialectician Nagarjuna, founder of the Madhyamaka school, demonstrated that these two truths are not in conflict, because samsara is nirvana. The sacred is the profane. The everyday is the holy. The dream world of samsara, which is the world of so much suffering and the world of relative truth, is the projection of our delusions and selfish desires onto nirvana. Yet samsara is logically prior to and necessary for the awakening to nirvana. The important point here, says John Blofeld in *The Zen Teachings of Huang Po*, is that "the enlightened man is capable of perceiving both unity and multiplicity without the least contradiction between them." His words echo in the lambent verse of Jingnuo, which appears in the wonderful book edited by Beata Grant, *Daughters of Emptiness: Poems by Buddhist Nuns of China*: "Everything is in the ordinary affairs of the everyday world." That is, if one is guided by mindfulness, the transcendent is found no less in quotidian tasks, such as serving tea, motorcycle maintenance, or the arranging of rock gardens, than in the recitation of mantras; no less in washing the dishes, writing this article, or actively participating in mercurial political affairs, than in the oldest monastic rituals.

Insofar as Buddhist practitioners grasp reality as a we-relation, they are unshakeable in the experience of the Other as themselves. Thus, in the social and political world of samsara, there can be but a single proper response to all sentient beings, regardless of their political affiliations or views: compassion and lovingkindness. That ethical posture is codified in the bodhisattva vows and Shantideva's Guide to the Bodhisattva's Way of Life:

> First of all I should make an effort
> To meditate upon the equality between self and others:
> I should protect all beings as I do myself
> Because we are all equal in (wanting) pleasure and
>   (not wanting) pain.

> Hence I should dispel the misery of others
> Because it is suffering, just like my own,

And I should benefit others
Because they are sentient beings, just like myself.

When both myself and others
Are similar in that we wish to be happy,
What is so special about me?
Why do I strive for my happiness alone?

For those following the Way, individual salvation is never enough; they work tirelessly for the liberation, not just of men and women, but of all sentient beings. Politics, therefore, offers the opportunity to use samsaric means for nirvanic ends—or what Shakyamuni might call "skillful means" that adapt the dharma to those imperfect tools we are obliged to work with in the relative-phenomenal world. The step on the Eightfold Path called "right conduct" demands such conscientious involvement in the relative-phenomenal realm, for we ourselves are inseparable from that world and can live here and now, nowhere else. But it is how the dharma student works in the world that is of all importance. He or she will, I believe, bring one dimension of "right view" to the political arena—that is, the understanding that our perspectives and views on a particular issue are not the only veridical or possible ones. The follower of the Way will practice civility and "right speech," which the *Mahasatipatthana Sutta* says involves "refraining from lying, refraining from slander, refraining from harsh speech, refraining from frivolous speech." He or she will listen with full empathy to the political Other, listening as carefully as they do when following their own breaths and thoughts in meditation, for egoless listening is one of the attributes of love.

They will dispassionately examine evidence, tame their minds, know where their thoughts have come from, and be able to distinguish what in the mind is the product of past conditioning and received opinion (political ads, propaganda), what thoughts are genuinely their own, and what their desires may be projecting on reality. (We all learned the hard way the importance of this kind of epistemological humility when members of the current administration, driven by their desire for change in the Middle East, rushed into a war with Iraq based on less than reliable "intelligence.")

And if peace is their goal, they will in the field of politics be themselves peace embodied. They will work indefatigably in the present moment, but without the beggarly attachment to reward, recognition, or future results. And when disappointment comes, as it must—as it did so often to those unsung heroes of the Civil Rights movement—Buddhists doing political work would do well not to despair, thinking, "I have lost, they have won," but remember that no victory won for the sangha or "beloved community" can last forever (nor any defeat), because every worldly thing is stained by anicca. In "defeat," if it comes, they might find solace in a judicious distinction that my friend, mystery writer Candace Robb, a Tibetan Buddhist practitioner in Seattle, makes when she says, "Pain is something that comes in life, but suffering is voluntary or optional." (Or on their refrigerator door they might tape this quote from seventy-five-year-old Chan master Sheng Yen: "I follow four dictates: face it, accept it, deal with it, then let it go.")

Finally, they will take as a reliable guide for spiritually informed political action the statement Dr. King made in his stirring Nobel Prize acceptance speech exactly forty years ago:

> Civilization and violence are antithetical concepts.
> Nonviolence is the answer to the crucial and moral
> question of our time. . . . The foundation of such a

method is love. . . . I have the audacity to believe that
peoples everywhere can have three meals a day for
their bodies, education and culture for their minds, and
dignity, equality, and freedom for their spirits.

Dr. King's political objectives in 1964 were, at bottom, of a
piece with bodhisattva goals, and they complement nicely the
ones Buddhists in the countries of the Far East have traditionally
worked to achieve. In *Inner Revolution*, Robert Thurman informs
us that Nagarjuna was the mentor of a great king of a dynasty in
southern India, King Udayi Satavahana, sometime between the
first century BCE and the second century CE. Nagarjuna first
instructed the king on what he needed to know for the king's own
liberation, then he advised him on how a ruler should oversee an
enlightened society. He said, "O King! Just as you love to consider
what to do to help yourself, so should you love to consider what
to do to help others!" According to Thurman, Nagarjuna "taught
his friend the king how to care for every being in the kingdom:
by building schools everywhere and endowing honest, kind, and
brilliant teachers; by providing for all his subjects' needs, opening
free restaurants and inns for travelers; by tempering justice with
mercy, sending barbers, doctors, and teachers to the prisons to
serve the inmates; by thinking of each prisoner as his own way-
ward child, to be corrected in order to return to free society and
use his or her precious human life to attain enlightenment."

Thurman says, "This activism is implicit in the earlier teachings of the Buddha, and in his actions, though his focus at that
time was on individual transformation, the prerequisite of social
transformation." In our brief passage through this life, we must
have both inner and outer revolutions, since the former is essential for deepening the latter. When we no longer divide the great

emptiness, shunyata, into "this" and "that," we are empowered to reduce without discrimination the suffering of all sentient beings in the six realms of existence, as Thich Nhat Hanh and his monks demonstrated so beautifully during the Vietnam War, coming to the aid of orphans, widows, and the wounded on both sides of the civil war that devastated their country.

Naturally, lay Buddhists will need the support of their sangha as they engage in political action. No one understands better the importance of taking refuge in the community of dharma followers than Buddhist monk and mendicant Claude AnShin Thomas. Last year he completed the building of a meditation center in Florida as a place where activists can momentarily retire to refresh and renew themselves.

Thomas understands suffering as a teacher and "sangha as the entire spectrum of the universe." In his upcoming memoir, *At Hell's Gate: A Soldier's Journey from War to Peace*, he says, "As a Buddhist, I cannot think myself into a new way of living, I have to live myself into a new way of thinking." That wisdom is captured concisely in his reflections on how dharma followers approach the goal of peace:

> Peace is not an idea. Peace is not a political movement, not a theory or a dogma. Peace is a way of life: living mindfully in the present moment. . . . It is not a question of politics, but of actions. It is not a matter of improving a political system or even taking care of homeless people alone. These are valuable but will not alone end war and suffering. We must simply stop the endless wars that rage within. . . . Imagine, if everyone stopped the war in themselves—there would be no seeds from which war could grow.

Days and Months
1993

I T SEEMS LIKE only yesterday that I stopped by to see my dear friend, Nhat Chi Mai. Mai was a sister in the Dharma, my closest fellow traveler along the Buddha's path of understanding and love. Whenever she spoke, her voice was filled with affection and a unique blend of innocence and wisdom that my friends and I began to call "the special accent of Mai."

"Where have you been? You're all covered with sweat," she said to me, with her eyebrows knit and her lips pursed, like a mother worrying about her only child.

"Do I look as if I've been working in the rice fields? I've just come from Tan Dinh Market collecting pledge money from our school's supporters." Mai laughed and served me a large glass of cool water—exactly what I needed that hot July day.

Her dress was as simple as a nun's robe, and it made her look especially beautiful. After a moment, I became serious and asked Mai what she thought about Thay's appeal for peace. She sat silently, and then, stroking my hair, she said, "You know I love and respect Thay, especially his vision of social service, but his political activities worry me."

I understood. Thay's appeal for a cease-fire and the withdrawal of American troops was still very early. A "nationalist" wouldn't dare demand such a thing, and our government and newspapers condemned him. As the youngest in her family, protected by her parents, Mai had never even seen a bombed village, so how could she not worry when the radio, newspapers, and even the President himself accused Thay of being a communist?

Anxiously, on the verge of tears, I said, "Please consider this, dear sister. The Buddha taught us not to take life, so how can we sit by while our people kill one another? For 4,000 years, our country has defeated every single invader. Why do we need the help of foreign troops now? Mai, do you know that when Thay's 'Prayer for Peace' was printed in the *Buddhist Weekly*, I asked the Executive Council of the Buddhist Church to support eight of us in a fast until death as a prayer for peace? But the Council did not approve, and, without their backing, we knew that our act would be useless."

"Of course they wouldn't approve!" she interrupted. "Who would care for your aged mother?"

"I know that I would commit the sin of impiety towards my mother by killing myself, but if my death could help shorten the war and save lives, I would be willing to pay for the sin of impiety in another life."

Mai sat still for a long moment, then she took my hands, looked deeply into my eyes, and said, in a determined voice, "Dear younger sister, you are right. If there is ever another opportunity to fast for peace, count on me to join you." The sincerity of her words moved me so, and I wept.

Three months later, Mai joined our work for peace at Van Hanh University. As the daughter of a well-off family, this kind of "underground" work was new to her, but with copies of Thay Nhat Hanh's book *Lotus in a Sea of Fire*, hidden in her white Volkswagen, she delivered ten to this school, twenty to that, and through her efforts, Thay's book made its way into the hands of almost every teacher and student organization in Saigon.

One Saturday, during our weekly Day of Mindfulness, Mai invited me into her room, took my hand in hers and said, "Younger sister, I have an idea. Remember how the eight of you wanted to fast for peace? What if I and one other person joined you, and ten of us left a statement for peace and then disemboweled ourselves? Our act could reach many people, and it might move them to end this dreadful war! Fasting and even self-immolation no longer wake people up. We have to be imaginative!" I was shocked, but I promised Mai I would consider her proposal.

I stayed in my room for four days, weighing the pros and cons, and finally I told her that I thought we shouldn't do it. The eight of us had been single when we proposed the fast for peace. Now all the others were married, and some lived far away. I suspected there would be only Mai and me.

"The peace movement is still quite weak," I said. "If we sacrifice ourselves, the only thing we can be sure of is that our brothers and sisters in the peace movement will be without us. And we promised Thay Nhat Hanh that we would help Thay Thanh Van manage the School of Youth for Social Service, at least until the first students complete their training." Mai knew that the financial crisis of the SYSS was critical after Thay Nhat Hanh's departure. If we two, the main fundraisers for the school, died, who would care for the students? I spoke with all my heart, and she agreed to abandon the idea, although she wanted to wait for the final word from Thay Nhat Hanh. She had sent him a letter but hadn't received a response yet. A week later, she cheerfully told me that Thay had written back forbidding the sacrifice.

Feeling a great sense of responsibility for the School of Youth for Social Service, Mai said to me, "We need to work as much as we can. You must make me work harder. You are so good in your work in the slums, the peace movement, and the school. I wish I could be more like you." I held her shoulder tenderly and said, "Dear elder sister Mai, each person is unique, and you are a beautiful flower. There is no need to be like anyone else, especially me!" At the beginning of the second year of the SYSS, we were having a severe financial crisis. When Nga and I collected more sacks of rice than Uyen or Mai, Mai reproached herself, but her disappointment caused her to be even more diligent in starting self-support projects for the school. Each week, she presented a new list of proposals.

Thay Nhat Hanh was far away, and no one had taught us Avalokiteshvara's great art of listening or the Buddha's art of Sangha building—living in harmony with those around you. So, instead of sitting with Mai, listening deeply, and kindly showing her the strong and weak points of each proposal, we became impatient and ignored her. Many people would have felt frustrated and accumulated internal wounds that might explode at some time, but Mai seemed able to look deeply into herself and heal and transform each wound with ease.

Every week, she would propose something new. In a soft voice, she said to me, "Phuong, if you are free Monday, please come with me to the rice market. We can buy large quantities of rice and then sell it in smaller amounts to raise money." The next week she would suggest, "Phuong, perhaps we can sell soap to the families that support the school." And the following week, she would have yet another plan, and the next week another. Her proposals were not particularly wise, but I did not want to hurt her, so I didn't say anything. Then one day, when too many silent disagreements had accumulated in my mind's "store consciousness," I answered in a very irritated way: "Just go ahead and do it, Mai! But don't force me to do everything with you. I have my own work."

As soon as the words left my mouth, I regretted them, but I could not take them back. At dinnertime, I walked up behind

Mai, hugged her, and said, "Where would you like me to go Monday?" She smiled sweetly, and I knew she bore no grudge. The next Monday we went to the soap market together, and on Tuesday we went to the home of a sponsor to sell our soap. On Wednesday we picked up rice, and it was only on Thursday that I got around to my own work. Mai could have done those errands by herself, but she always insisted how much fun it would be to do things together.

To satisfy Mai, Uyen and I would have had to spend two or three days each week just accompanying her. Looking back, I wish we had done so. But at the time, we grumbled to each other, "We spent 1,000 *piasters* on rice, carried it across the city in traffic, and arrived at the home of a sponsor to sell it for a profit of fifteen piasters, while it cost us eight piasters for gas, and took the whole morning! I could earn 300 piasters an hour teaching math." Uyen and I had not yet learned the joy of just being together with a friend, the work, the rice sellers, and the sponsors. Uyen and I did not know how to practice peace with every step, but it seems that Mai did. With or without us, she embarked on many projects just to earn small amounts of money for the school. Then one day, she touched the heart of a wealthy man with her gentle way of being, and he gave the school 20,000 *dong* that we used to start many self-supporting projects. Little by little, we repaid the construction loans, and the sponsors' pledges were again used to buy food.

One evening after we had recited the Tiep Hien precepts, I suggested that we build a bungalow with six tiny meditation rooms for each Tiep Hien brother and sister to use for a half-day solitary retreat every week. I knew that would be a real treasure. Uyen and the other brothers and sisters were overjoyed by the idea, but Mai opposed it, saying that sharing a room with others was practicing the way also, that it would be too much of a luxury to have our own rooms. I did not want a fancy building, just a palm-leaf and bamboo hut, a place to be alone to calm our emotions after six days of strenuous work.

Mai sat silently and then reminded us that we did not have the money and that if we did, we should use it for the school, not to build a house for ourselves. I was afraid that if we did not build this bungalow, we might lose ourselves and be unable to serve anyone. Seeing my determination, Mai finally agreed. At times, I felt she did not understand my suffering. I suppose that was because she lived on a different level from most of us. She always seemed refreshed and in touch with her deepest self.

To raise the money, I began by asking my older sister, "Nam, if I get married, how much will you give me as a wedding gift?" My family had been concerned about me not getting married, so when Nam heard this, she answered right away, "Three thousand piasters!" "That's all?" I responded, "How about 5,000?" She said, "Okay, 5,000." I put out my hand and said, "For people who want a family, a wedding is important. But for someone who wants to be a resource for many people, having a special room to quiet her mind is equally important, don't you agree? How about giving it to me right now so we can build a bungalow for a solitary retreat?" Nam laughed and gave me 3,000 piasters.

Mai donated 5,000 piasters of her own money, and with a few other donations, we were able to build a small house. Uyen and I always had a simple arrangement of bamboo or wildflowers in our rooms, while the flowers in Mai's room were always arranged in the formal, traditional way. Every time I entered it, I was struck by the resplendent Buddha on gold paper hanging on her wall—the Buddha sat in a full lotus, surrounded by clouds, flowers, and a halo—and a set of eight pictures of Thay Quang Duc. Mai also had a hanging pot with a branch of golden plum flowers and one bright red, plastic rose. It was exactly like entering an old-style nun's room, except that her bed always had many covers and a pink satin pillowcase—appropriate for the favorite daughter of a well-to-do family!

One day Mai entered my room and exclaimed, "Your room is so sad. There are no pictures at all here." When she looked more closely, she noticed a tiny photo of a lake and a forest just above the floor, and near my bed, at eye level, sketches of crying children.

Surprised, she asked, "Why are the pictures so close to the ground where no one can see them?" I answered, "I did not arrange the room for others. I placed the pictures low so I can see them when I lie down." Mai shook her head and said, "How selfish!" When she accused me of being selfish, I felt angry, but my irritation dissipated quickly when I remembered how different her nature was from mine. We laughed, and everything was fine.

One Saturday in April, when it was Mai's turn to read the Precepts of the Order of Interbeing, her voice faltered as she said, "Do not kill. Do not let others kill. Find whatever means possible to protect life and build peace." From that moment on, she spoke so softly it was nearly impossible to hear her. As we were putting the precept books back on the shelves, Uyen asked, "What happened, Mai?" And I added, "You seemed to lose your concentration during the recitation. Are you all right?" Mai just smiled and returned to her room early that evening. The following two Saturdays she did not come to our Days of Mindfulness. Because the situation in Saigon was so dangerous—four friends from the school had been murdered—I assumed that her parents had forbidden her from spending the night with us. But when she didn't show up for a third Saturday, I thought that even if her parents wanted her home at night, they would certainly let her recite the precepts with us in the afternoon.

I wondered if something could be wrong, yet, at the same time, I was upset with Mai for not taking our Days of Mindfulness more seriously. At least she could have told us why she had missed the SYSS staff meetings, the Days of Mindfulness, and her work at the university.

Then, on Sunday, May 14, 1967, she came to her last Morning of Mindfulness. I was in my room, looking out the window onto a field of green bamboo, and I didn't hear her car pull up. Uyen knocked gently at my door and said, "Sister Mai is here, wearing a beautiful violet *ao dai* with gold embroidery!" I stood up and walked slowly from my room, intending to reproach her. But as I entered the hallway, I saw Mai surrounded by friends, all trying to tell her something, and then, like baby chicks with their mother, we all followed her into the dining room.

Mai's hair was arranged beautifully, and her new dress made her look as if she were about to attend a ceremony. Right away, she began slicing the banana cake she had baked especially for us. I smiled and said, teasingly, "First you abandon us for three weeks, and now you dress so beautifully and bring a delicious cake! Are you going to get married?" Others joined in, "Very possible! Mai looks so pretty today!" We all laughed, but Mai just smiled silently.

I felt disappointed that, once again, our dream for peaceful social change was being pushed aside. So many young friends shared our aspiration, but then they married and had children, and always had excuses for not helping with the work. Now Mai was going too. At that moment, her voice pierced my thoughts, "Sister Chan Khong, please come to Tu Nghiêm Pagoda early on Tuesday morning. It is Wesak, the Buddha's nativity, and something interesting will happen." Mai was always kind to the old nuns at the pagoda, so I thought she was asking me to help decorate their temple for Wesak. "I respect your wish," I said, somewhat irritably, "but is it really necessary for me to be at the temple so early?" Nhat Chi Mai looked directly at me and said, "If you don't want to come, it's okay, but please don't speak so strongly about it!" When she left, I felt ashamed, and I resolved to go to the pagoda early on Tuesday, just to please her.

On Tuesday morning, Ngoc ran frantically into my family's house and told me that Sister Mai had set herself on fire, right outside the Tu Nghiêm Pagoda! I couldn't believe my ears! I sat perfectly still for a long while, and then I said, "Sister Mai has sacrificed herself for peace." My mother, sitting next to me, burst into tears. "Your friend's act," she said, "will lead her parents to the grave!" She looked at me with each word, preparing herself for the day I might do the same.

Without a word, Ngoc and I went out, knowing that much needed to be done. I went straight to Mai's parents' home, and when I entered the house, they embraced me, sobbing. As we sat together, her mother actually passed out several times. Then I drove them to the pagoda, and they went inside. I don't know why, but I was unable to enter the pagoda and see Mai in death. Instead I ran to the Cau Muoi Market and told our vendor friends of Mai's sacrifice. As I was sharing the news with dear old Aunt Ba, I started to cry and she began to weep with me. Soon everyone in the market was in tears. Aunt Ba walked over to the taxi and pedicab drivers, spoke a few words to each, and immediately the drivers began to carry all the vendors from the market to the pagoda to see Mai for the last time.

The well-known writer Bae Thieu Son also came to the pagoda, joined by several other intellectuals. His face was drawn, and when he saw me, he could only manage to say, "Phuong!" and tears rolled down his cheeks. The printer who had refused to print our peace books was also there. He came up to me, sobbing, and said that in the future he would help us in any way we needed. Even government officials and military men came and offered to help our work for peace. It was only then that I realized that my words of advice to Mai against sacrificing ourselves—"We are too few. If we are gone, there will not be enough people to do the work"—were wrong. Her sacrifice had indeed moved the hearts of many people and caused the peace movement to swell like waves in a storm. Even friends who had become guerrillas in the jungle sent back news and asked, "How can we help realize Mai's wish for peace and reconciliation?"

Before she died, Nhat Chi Mai placed two statues in front of her, the Virgin Mary and Avalokiteshvara Bodhisattva. In her poems and letters, she asked Catholics and Buddhists to work together for peace so that people might realize the love of Jesus and the compassion of the Buddha.

I never saw Thay Tri Quang more moved. At one o'clock in the morning, he sent a message to Tu Nghiêm Pagoda to ask the nuns to provide a car for me to come to An Quang Pagoda. (He was afraid I would be arrested or kidnapped if I came by myself.) When I arrived at his pagoda, the gate was locked, and I had to climb over it. As I entered his room, he was trying to repair an old tape recorder, and he told me, "This machine hardly works, but I want to have a tape of someone reading the poems and letters of the young woman who sacrificed herself so I can come to know her better. Will you read them? You are also a young woman from the South, so your voice must be close to hers."

The next day, at four o'clock in the morning, Thay Tri Quang disguised himself as a novice and had someone take him to Tu Nghiêm Pagoda. He had been under house arrest for some time, so he could not travel openly. In front of Mai's coffin, he chanted sutras for her. When he finished, he called me into a room of the pagoda and said, "You must find a way to print Mai's letters and distribute them widely. I will pay for the paper and the printing. Ask some of the Buddhist elders to lend you the money, and my younger sister will pay them back."

The following day, Thay Tri Quang called me again, "Mai's prayer was for all religions to work together for peace. I've heard that Father Nguyen Ngoc Lan is a progressive Catholic and close to us. Please ask him to write a preface to Mai's letters." I was very moved. In the past, Thay Tri Quang had been skeptical about working with Catholics. In fact, Father Lan had already offered to print Mai's letters and write a foreword to them. He even agreed to circulate them, a very dangerous thing to do. With each heartfelt act, I thought of Mai's smiling face, and I could hear her saying, "Isn't that wonderful?" Just as she had prayed, the elders of the Buddhist Church tried every day to find opportunities to work with the Catholics, and the Catholics also began to have more sympathy for the Buddhists. It all began with everyone's appreciation of Sister Mai.

During the three days her body lay in Tu Nghiêm Pagoda, I tried to keep busy. I went to meet students both inside and outside our movement. I went to all the markets. I visited many organizations and friends. When I saw Hiep and other friends sitting by her body, weeping and clutching the yellow cloth that covered her, I didn't have the courage to come near. I could only think that my body should be there too, or in a pagoda in Hue, Ben Tre, or Can Tho. Hadn't that been Mai's wish? But I was alive, able to stand, walk, eat, drink, and sleep.

Day after day, I met with friends to inform them of Mai's sacrifice for peace. And night after night, I stayed up translating her poems into English and French for newspapers and peace groups around the world. But it was not until Ngoc brought me Mai's final letters and poems that I understood how she had spent her last three weeks: she had stayed with her parents in order to give them those last precious hours of her life. She was "sweet bananas, fragrant rice, and precious honey," a loving child for them, all the while preparing for her sacrifice.

Students came to the pagoda to prevent the police from taking Mai's body away. The police, afraid that the news of her sacrifice would travel to other provinces and inspire others to work for peace, tried to persuade her parents to bury her right away. Mai's father resisted, but his wife's grief was so great that finally, on the third day, he agreed to bring Mai's body to An Duong Dia in Phu Lam for cremation.

On the day after Mai's sacrifice, many newspapers carried blank spaces where the news of her act had been censored. Word of her death traveled only by friends, but even so, on the day of the cremation, a huge crowd came to the ceremony. When the funeral car reached Phu Lam Bridge, the crowd behind it stretched more than five kilometers, all the way back to the Tu Nghiêm Pagoda. Students and teachers, merchants and vendors, politicians and priests were all present. I was surprised to see so many wealthy men and women who, until then, had accused us of being under the control of the communists.

There was a fine, cool rain. The white dresses of young women students, the black shirts of poor workers, the monks' and nuns' robes, the simple rags of our street vendor friends from the markets, and the fine clothes of the well-to-do were all moistened by the gentle rain. My younger sister Thanh, with her gift for lightening even the saddest moments, whispered in my ear, "Sister, do you see Mai? She is sitting on the funeral car looking back at us, her face bright, saying, 'Oh, Phuong and Thanh, I feel very joyful. There really are a lot of people here, aren't there?'" I had been walking in the rain, immersed in my sadness, when I heard Thanh imitate Mai's special accent, and I had to smile. She was right. It was exactly what Mai would have said.

When you want something ordinary, you can just go out and buy it, but when you want something extraordinary, like love, understanding, and peace for a whole nation, you have to pay for it with something much more precious than money. My sister, Nhat Chi Mai, did not commit suicide. She loved life. She had a good education, and the conditions to live comfortably, even in the midst of the war. She sacrificed her life because, more than anything, she wanted the killing to stop. She tried to bring peace to Vietnam by paying for it with her life.

I remember Thay's poem, "Recommendation," that she read again and again just before she immolated herself:

Promise me,
promise me this day,
promise me now,
while the sun is overhead
exactly at the zenith,
promise me:

Even as they
strike you down
with a mountain of hate and violence;
even as they step on you and crush you
like a worm,
even as they dismember and disembowel you,
remember, brother,
remember:
man is not our enemy.

The only act worthy of you is compassion—
invincible, limitless, unconditional.
Hatred will never let you face
the beast in man.

One day, when you face this beast alone,
with your courage intact, your eyes kind,
untroubled,
(even as no one sees them),
out of your smile
will bloom a flower.
And those who love you
will behold you
across ten thousand worlds of birth and dying.

Alone again,
I will go on with bent head,
knowing that love has become eternal.
On the long, rough road,
the sun and the moon
will continue to shine.

After Nhat Chi Mai immolated herself for peace on May 16, 1967, I became ever more determined to find ways to end the suffering of Vietnam.

GARY SNYDER

Buddhism and the Possibilities of a Planetary Culture

1988

B UDDHISM HOLDS THAT the universe and all creatures in it are intrinsically in a state of complete wisdom, love, and compassion, acting in natural response and mutual interdependence. The personal realization of this from-the-beginning state cannot be had for and by one "self,"—because it is not fully realized unless one has given the self up and away.

In the Buddhist view, that which obstructs the effortless manifestation of this is ignorance, which projects into fear and needless craving. Historically, Buddhist philosophers have failed to analyze out the degree to which ignorance and suffering are caused or encouraged by social factors, considering fear-and-desire to be given facts of the human condition. Consequently the major concern of Buddhist philosophy is epistemology and "psychology" with no attention paid to historical or sociological problems. Although Mahayana Buddhism has a grand vision of universal salvation, the actual achievement of Buddhism has been the development of practical systems of meditation toward the end of liberating a few dedicated individuals from psychological hang-ups and cultural conditionings. Institutional Buddhism has been conspicuously ready to accept or ignore the inequalities and tyrannies of whatever political system it found itself under. This

can be death to Buddhism, because it is death to any meaningful function of compassion. Wisdom without compassion feels
no pain.

No one today can afford to be innocent, or to indulge themselves in ignorance of the nature of contemporary governments,
politics, and social orders. The national polities of the modern
world are "states" which maintain their existence by deliberately
fostered craving and fear: monstrous protection rackets. The
"free world" has become economically dependent on a fantastic
system of stimulation of greed which cannot be fulfilled, sexual
desire which cannot be satiated, and hatred which has no outlet
except against oneself, the persons one is supposed to love, or
the revolutionary aspirations of pitiful, poverty-stricken mar-
ginal societies. The conditions of the Cold War have fumed most
modern societies—both communist and capitalist—into vicious
distorters of true human potential. They try to create populations
of *preta*—hungry ghosts, with giant appetites and throats no bigger than needles. The soil, the forests, and all animal life are being
consumed by these cancerous collectivities; the air and water of
the planet is being fouled by them.

There is nothing in human nature or the requirements of
human social organization which intrinsically requires that a society be contradictory, repressive, and productive of violent and
frustrated personalities. Findings in anthropology and psychology make this more and more evident. One can prove it for oneself by taking a good look at Original Nature through meditation.
Once a person has this much faith and insight, one will be led to
a deep concern with the need for radical social change through a
variety of nonviolent means.

The joyous and voluntary poverty of Buddhism becomes a
positive force. The traditional harmlessness and avoidance of

taking life in any form has nation-shaking implications. The practice of meditation, for which one needs only "the ground beneath one's feet," wipes out mountains of junk being pumped into the mind by the mass media and supermarket universities. The belief in a serene and generous fulfillment of natural loving desires destroys ideologies which blind, maim, and repress—and points the way to a kind of community which would amaze "moralists" and transform armies of men who are fighters because they cannot be lovers.

Avatamsaka (Kegon or *Hua-yen)* Buddhist philosophy sees the world as a vast, interrelated network in which all objects and creatures are necessary and illuminated. From one standpoint, governments, wars, or all that we consider "evil" are uncompromisingly contained in this totalistic realm. The hawk, the swoop, and the hare are one. From the "human" standpoint we cannot live in those terms unless all beings see with the same enlightened eye. The Bodhisattva lives by the sufferer's standard, and he or she must be effective in aiding those who suffer.

The mercy of the West has been social revolution; the mercy of the East has been individual insight into the basic self/void. We need both. They are both contained in the traditional three aspects of the Dharma path: wisdom *(prajña),* meditation *(dhyana),* and morality *(shila).* Wisdom is intuitive knowledge of the mind of love and clarity that lies beneath one's ego-driven anxieties and aggressions. Meditation is going into the mind to see this for yourself—over and over again, until it becomes the mind you live in. Morality is bringing it back out in the way you live, through personal example and responsible action, ultimately toward the true community *(sangha)* of "all beings." This last aspect means, for me, supporting any cultural and economic revolution that moves clearly toward a truly free world. It means using such means as civil disobedience, outspoken criticism, protest, pacifism, voluntary poverty, and even gentle violence if it comes to a matter of restraining some impetuous crazy. It means affirming the widest possible spectrum of non-harmful individual behavior—defending the right of individuals to smoke hemp, eat peyote, be polygamous, polyandrous, or homosexual. Worlds of behavior and custom long banned by the Judaeo-Capitalist-Christian-Marxist West. It means respecting intelligence and learning, but not as greed or means to personal power. Working on one's own responsibility, but willing to work with a group. "Forming the new society within the shell of the old"—the I.W.W. slogan of 70 years ago.

The traditional, vernacular, primitive, and village cultures may appear to be doomed. We must defend and support them as we would the diversity of ecosystems; they are all manifestations of Mind. Some of the elder societies accomplished a condition of Sangha, with not a little of Buddha and Dharma as well. We touch base with the deep mind of peoples of all times and places in our meditation practice, and this is an amazing revolutionary aspect of the Buddhadharma. By a "planetary culture" I mean the kind of societies that would follow on a new understanding of that relatively recent institution, the National State, an understanding that might enable us to leave it behind. The State is greed made legal, with a monopoly on violence; a natural society is familial and cautionary. A natural society is one which "Follows the Way," imperfectly but authentically.

Such an understanding will close the circle and link us in many ways with the most creative aspects of our archaic past. If we are lucky, we may eventually arrive at a world of relatively mutually tolerant small societies attuned to their local natural region and united overall by a profound respect and love for the mind and nature of the universe.

I can imagine further virtues in a world sponsoring societies with matrilineal descent, free-form marriage, "natural credit" economics, far less population, and much more wilderness.

Genuine Compassion
1992

I REALLY ADMIRE bees' sense of common responsibility. When you watch a beehive, you see that those small insects come from far away, take a few seconds' rest, go inside, and then hurriedly fly away. They are faithful to their responsibility. Although sometimes individual bees fight, basically there is a strong sense of unity and cooperation. We human beings are supposed to be much more advanced, but sometimes we lag behind even small insects.

We are social animals. If we were by nature solitary, there would be no towns or cities. Because of our nature, we have to live in a cooperative setting. People who have no sense of responsibility for the society or the common good are acting against human nature. For human survival, we need genuine cooperation, based on the sense of brotherhood and sisterhood.

Friends make us feel secure. Without friends, we feel a great loneliness. Sometimes, there is no proper person with whom we can communicate and share affection, so we prefer an animal, such as a dog or a cat. This shows that even those people who lose their trusted friends need someone to communicate and share affection with. I myself like my wristwatch, even though it never shows me any affection! In order to get mental satisfaction, as a human being, it is best to love another human being, and, if that is not possible, then some animal. If you show sincere affection, you will receive a response, and you will feel satisfaction. We all need friends.

There are different approaches to friendship. At times we may think that we need money and power to have friends, but that is not correct. When our fortune is intact, those kinds of friends may appear loyal, but when our fortune disappears, they will leave us. They are not true friends; they are friends of money or power. Alcohol is another unreliable friend. If you drink too much, you may collapse. Even your dreams will be unpleasant.

But there are other kinds of friends who, no matter what the situation, remain true. When our fortunes rise, even without friends, we can manage. But when they go down, we need true friends. In order to make genuine friends, we ourselves must create an environment that is pleasant. If we just have a lot of anger, not many people will be drawn close to us. Compassion or altruism draws friends. It is very simple.

All of the world's religions emphasize the importance of compassion, love, and forgiveness. Each may have a different interpretation but, broadly speaking, everyone bases their understanding on the basis of brotherhood, sisterhood, and compassion. Those who believe in God usually see their love for their fellow human beings as an expression of their love for God. But if someone says, "I love God," and does not show sincere love toward his fellow human beings, I think that is not following God's teaching. Many religions emphasize forgiveness. Love and compassion are the basis of true forgiveness. Without them, it is difficult to develop forgiveness.

Love and compassion are basic human qualities. From a Buddhist point of view, love is an attitude of wanting to help other sentient beings enjoy happiness, and compassion is the wish for other sentient beings to be free from suffering. Compassion is not a selfish attitude, such as, "These are my friends, and therefore I want them to be free of suffering." Genuine compassion can be extended even toward one's enemies, because the very basis for generating compassion is seeing suffering in other living creatures, and that includes your enemies. When you see that your enemies are suffering, you are able to develop genuine compassion even toward those who have injured you.

Usual compassion and love give rise to a very close feeling, but it is essentially attachment. With usual love, as long as the other person appears to you as beautiful or good, love remains, but as soon as he or she appears to you as less beautiful or good, your love completely changes. Even though someone appears to you as a dear friend and you love him very much, the next morning the situation may completely change. Even though he is the same person, he feels more like an enemy. Instead of feeling compassion and love, you now feel hostility. With genuine love and compassion, another person's appearance or behavior has no effect on your attitude.

Real compassion comes from seeing the other's suffering. You feel a sense of responsibility, and you want to do something for him or her. There are three types of compassion. The first is a spontaneous wish for other sentient beings to be free of suffering. You find their suffering unbearable and you wish to relieve them of it. The second is not just a wish for their well-being, but a real sense of responsibility, a commitment to relieve their suffering and remove them from their undesirable circumstances. This type of compassion is reinforced by the realization that all sentient beings are impermanent, but because they grasp at the permanence of their identity, they experience confusion and suffering. A genuine sense of compassion generates a spontaneous sense of responsibility to work for the benefit of others, encouraging us to take this responsibility upon ourselves. The third type of compassion is reinforced by the wisdom that although all sentient beings have interdependent natures and no inherent existence, they still grasp at the existence of inherent nature. Compassion accompanied by such an insight is the highest level of compassion.

In order to cultivate and develop genuine compassion within yourself, you need to identify the nature of suffering and the state of suffering that sentient beings are in. Because you want sentient beings to be free from their suffering, first of all you have to identify what suffering is. When Buddha taught the Four Noble Truths, he spoke of three types of suffering: suffering that is obvious and acute, like physical pain; the suffering of change, such as pleasurable experiences that have the potential to turn into suffering; and pervasive suffering, which is the basic fact of conditioned existence. To cultivate compassion, first of all, you have to reflect on suffering and identify suffering as suffering. When reflecting in depth on the nature of suffering, it is always beneficial to search for an alternative—to see whether it is possible to ever get rid of suffering. If there is no way out, just reflecting on suffering will make you feel depressed, and that is not helpful. If there is no possibility of getting rid of the suffering, then it is better to not think about it at all.

After describing the origin of suffering, the Buddha spoke of the cessation of suffering and the path that leads to the cessation. When you realize that it *is* possible to eliminate the root that gives rise to suffering, that awareness will increase your determination to identify and reflect on suffering at all different levels, and that will inspire you to seek liberation.

After reflecting on the nature of suffering and feeling convinced that there is a path that leads to the cessation of suffering, then it is important to see that all sentient beings do not want suffering and do want happiness. Everyone has the right to be happy, to overcome suffering. When reflecting on ourselves, we find that we have a natural desire to be happy and to overcome suffering, and that this desire is just and valid. When we see that all living creatures have the natural right to be happy and overcome suffering and fulfill their wishes, we ourselves have a spontaneous feeling of self-worth.

The only difference between us and others is in number. We are just one individual among infinite others. No matter how important we are, we are just one sentient being, one single self, while others are infinite. But there is a close relationship of interdependence. Our suffering or happiness is very much related with others. That is also reality. Under these circumstances, if, in order to save one finger, the other nine fingers are sacrificed, that is foolish. But if, in order to save nine fingers, one finger is sacrificed, it may be worth it. So you see the importance of others' rights and your own rights, and others' welfare and your own welfare. Because of numbers, the infinite numbers of others' rights and welfare naturally become most important. The welfare of others is important not only because of the sheer number, but also if you were to sacrifice the infinite others for your own happiness, eventually you will lose. If you think more of others, taking care of others' rights, and serving others, ultimately you will gain.

Not only when you are engaging in the meditative practices of the bodhisattva path is it harmful to sacrifice the welfare and happiness of infinite others for your own happiness, as it prevents you from making progress in the spiritual path, but if you were to sacrifice the benefit and welfare of infinite others for the sake of your own happiness and welfare in your daily life, you are the one who ultimately will lose and suffer the consequences.

If you want to be selfish, you should be selfish-with-wisdom, rather than with foolishness. If you help others with sincere motivation and sincere concern, that will bring you more fortune, more friends, more smiles, and more success. If you forget about others' rights and neglect others' welfare, ultimately you will be very lonely.

Even our enemy is very useful to us because, in order to practice compassion, we need to practice tolerance, forgiveness, and patience, the antidotes to anger. In order to learn tolerance, forgiveness, and patience, we need someone to create some trouble. From this point of view, there is no need to feel anger toward the enemy or the person who creates the problem for us. In fact, we should feel gratitude for the opportunity he provides us. Regardless of whether he intended to benefit us, whenever we find anything that is helpful, we can utilize the opportunity. Of course, one might argue that the enemy has no conscious intention to be of help but, on the contrary, has a strong conscious intention to cause harm and, therefore, anger is justified. This is true. We categorize someone as an enemy because he has the intention to harm us. Even if a surgeon has to amputate our limb, because surgeons do not generally have the intention to harm us, we don't classify them as our enemy. Since our enemy has the intention to be harmful to us, we classify and identify him as an enemy, and therefore we have this opportunity to practice patience and tolerance toward that person.

In order to practice compassion toward all living beings, it is important to be able to generate a genuine sense of patience and tolerance toward our enemies. In order to cultivate genuine patience toward our enemy, there are certain types of mental trainings. For instance, if you have been injured by gunfire, if you feel angry, you should analyze the situation and think, what is it that I am angry at? If I am angry at the thing that injured me, I should be angry at the direct cause of my injury, which is the bullet. If I should feel anger toward the ultimate cause of my injury, I should feel anger toward the anger within the person who shot at me. But that is not the case. I don't feel angry at the bullet or the other person's anger; I feel angry at the person, who is just the medium. Under different circumstances, that person could change into a good friend.

As long as that negative emotion is there, it acts like an enemy. But when a positive motivation develops, that person becomes our friend. The person himself can be changed under different circumstances, dominated by different factors of the mind. So, logically speaking, if we are to feel anger toward the thing that harmed us, it is the anger within that person that we should feel angry at. So, just as we see how destructive is the anger generated within us, how it destroys our peace of mind, mental balance, and so forth, so it is in the case of the anger generated within the enemy's mind. It affects his mind and his happiness.

Therefore, when someone dominated by anger harms you, instead of feeling angry toward him, you should feel a sense of compassion and pity because that person is suffering himself. When you reflect in this way, it will help reduce the force of your anger. When you train your mind in this way, gradually you will be able to extend your compassion toward all living creatures, including your enemy.

I myself, as a Buddhist monk who is supposedly a practitioner—although my practice is very lazy and not at all satisfying to myself—even a lazy practitioner with not enough time, step by step, little by little, can change. I can change my own mental attitude, and it brings me some real joy and inner strength. Brothers and sisters, please think along these lines. If you feel you can practice at a certain point, please try to carry it out as a kind of experiment. As time goes on, you may get some benefit. But if you feel it isn't working, don't worry. Don't be concerned at all.

Compassion, or altruistic motivation, is really wonderful. Sometimes I feel a sense of wonder that we human beings can develop such altruism. It is really a precious source of inner strength, happiness, and future success.

ℭβ

PART IV

THE GREENING OF THE SELF

THICH NHAT HANH

The Bells of Mindfulness
2004

T HE BELLS OF mindfulness are sounding. All over the Earth, we are experiencing floods, drought, and massive wildfires. Sea ice is melting in the Arctic, and hurricanes and heat waves are killing thousands. The forests are fast disappearing, the deserts are growing, species are becoming extinct every day, and yet we continue to consume, ignoring the ringing bells.

All of us know that our beautiful green planet is in danger. Our way of walking on the Earth has a great influence on animals and plants. Yet we act as if our daily lives have nothing to do with the condition of the world. We are like sleepwalkers, not knowing what we are doing or where we are heading. Whether we can wake up or not depends on whether we can walk mindfully on our Mother Earth. The future of all life, including our own, depends on our mindful steps. We have to hear the bells of mindfulness that are sounding all across our planet. We have to start learning how to live in such a way that a future will be possible for our children and our grandchildren.

I have sat with the Buddha for a long time and consulted him about the issue of global warming, and the teaching of the Buddha is very clear. If we continue to live as we have been living, consuming without a thought of the future, destroying our forests and emitting dangerous amounts of carbon dioxide, then devastating climate change is inevitable. Much of our ecosystem will be destroyed. Sea levels will rise and coastal cities will be inundated, forcing hundreds of millions of refugees from their homes, creating wars and outbreaks of infectious disease.

We need a kind of collective awakening. There are among us men and women who are awakened, but it's not enough; most people are still sleeping. We have constructed a system we can't control. It imposes itself on us, and we become its slaves and victims. For most of us who want to have a house, a car, a refrigerator, a television, and so on, we must sacrifice our time and our lives in exchange. We are constantly under the pressure of time. In former times, we could afford three hours to drink one cup of tea, enjoying the company of our friends in a serene and spiritual atmosphere. We could organize a party to celebrate the blossoming of one orchid in our garden. But today we can no longer afford these things. We say that time is money. We have created a society in which the rich become richer and the poor become poorer, and in which we are so caught up in our own immediate problems that we cannot afford to be aware of what is going on with the rest of the human family or our planet Earth. In my mind I see a group of chickens in a cage disputing over a few seeds of grain, unaware that in a few hours they will all be killed.

People in China, India, Vietnam, and other developing countries are still dreaming the "American dream," as if that dream were the ultimate goal of mankind—everyone has to have a car, a bank account, a cell phone, a television set of their own. In twenty-five years the population of China will be 1.5 billion people, and if each of them wants to drive their own private car, China will need 99 million barrels of oil every day. But world production today is only 84 million barrels per day. So the American dream is not possible for the people of China, India, or Vietnam. The American dream is no longer possible even for the Americans. We can't continue to live like this. It's not a sustainable economy.

We have to have another dream: the dream of brotherhood and sisterhood, of loving-kindness and compassion. That dream is possible right here and now. We have the Dharma, we have the means, and we have enough wisdom to be able to live this dream. Mindfulness is at the heart of awakening, of enlightenment. We practice breathing to be able to be here in the present moment so that we can recognize what is happening in us and around us. If what's happening inside us is despair, we have to recognize that and act right away. We may not want to confront that mental formation, but it's a reality, and we have to recognize it in order to transform it.

We don't have to sink into despair about global warming; we can act. If we just sign a petition and forget about it, it won't help much. Urgent action must be taken at the individual and collective levels. We all have a great desire to be able to live in peace and to have environmental sustainability. What most of us don't yet have are concrete ways of making our commitment to sustainable living a reality in our daily lives. We haven't organized ourselves. We can't simply blame our governments and corporations for the chemicals that pollute our drinking water, for the violence in our neighborhoods, for the wars that destroy so many lives. It's time for each of us to wake up and take action in our own lives.

We witness violence, corruption, and destruction all around us. We all know that the laws we have in place aren't strong enough to control the superstition, cruelty, and abuses of power that we see daily. Only faith and determination can keep us from falling into deep despair.

Buddhism is the strongest form of humanism we have. It can help us learn to live with responsibility, compassion, and loving-kindness. Every Buddhist practitioner should be a protector of the environment. We have the power to decide the destiny of our planet. If we awaken to our true situation, there will be a change in our collective consciousness. We have to do something to wake people up. We have to help the Buddha to wake up the people who are living in a dream.

Reflections on the Fire Sermon
2012

F ROM THE WINDOW of my second-floor apartment at Chuang Yen Monastery, I can see below a pageant of colors celebrating the splendor of this mild October day in upstate New York. It's nine in the morning. Leaves of red, yellow, orange, purple, and brown flare up like brilliant flames against a background that stubbornly insists on preserving the green shades of summer. Across the road the surface of the Seven Jewels Lake is lightly rippled by soft breezes, forming an exquisite background to the large statue of Guan Yin, the bodhisattva of compassion, which juts out above the water. Her elegant figure conveys a feeling of peace, harmony, and gentleness. The surrounding paths are empty, and the scene before me seems the epitome of beauty and tranquility. I could not imagine a more perfect world. How could the Buddha say that everything is burning?

Yet I don't remain content admiring the scenery. Before long, curiosity gets the better of me, and I feel compelled to find out what's going on in the world beyond the gates of this monastery. With a few clicks of the mouse on my computer, I conjure up the morning's news. The home page springs up and the headlines immediately jump off the screen: "Libyan fighters seize Bani Walid," "Kenya sends troops to attack al-Shabab," "Fighting erupts in Yemeni capital," "UN Rights head warns of 'civil war' in Syria." I don't need the Internet to know what is taking place on Wall Street and in other cities around the world. I have visited the *Occupy Wall Street* and the *Stop the Machine* occupations in New York and Washington, respectively. I know that these campaigns were triggered by episodes of financial profligacy that have pushed millions into unemployment, home foreclosures, hunger, and escalating debt.

So, while the scene outside my window bears testimony to the unspeakable beauty of the world, it does not tell the whole story. It does not tell the story of what happens when human beings, driven by very ordinary human motives, prey on one another and on the natural world. It does not reveal how the primal impulses of the undisciplined mind can wreak havoc on populations spread out across the planet, even rocking the foundations of civilization itself.

The most ominous threat we face is almost too pervasive to be discerned, too slow and gradual in its incremental growth to capture our attention, and thus it remains virtually imperceptible. The threat comes from the changes being wrought upon our climate, from the slow warming of the Earth's atmosphere and oceans. The danger posed by climate change consists not only in forests turned into tinder, nor in accelerating loss of biodiversity— the decimation of countless species of birds, animals, insects, and plants. The danger is not only the vanishing of the glaciers that supply water to the great rivers of China, South Asia, and South America, or more violent wildfires, droughts, floods, hurricanes, and cyclones. The biggest danger is a diminished food supply. At the same time that crop yields decline due to higher temperatures and the assaults of industrial agriculture, the world's population is rising, driving up demand and pushing food prices beyond the reach of the poor. As the disparity between supply and demand widens, almost inevitably the result will be state failures and social unrest, exploding in regional conflict, violence, and war. Tens of millions will die.

Yet how are we to address this formidable situation? The news outlets report on the flames and the fuel, not on the sparks that ignite the fires. Even the most penetrating analyses of the causes and possible consequences of our current dilemmas sometimes conceal as much as they reveal, leaving the underlying causation on the sidelines. Could a clearer diagnosis be found in an ancient sermon spoken by the Buddha to a group of monks five hundred years before the Common Era?

We shouldn't be too quick to mock this suggestion. The Fire Sermon is one of the starkest, bluntest, and most powerful expressions of spiritual truth ever uttered. Though spoken long before the Industrial Revolution, before the rise of corporate capitalism and the global financial system, before modern technologies of war emerged, the discourse is astoundingly prescient in its diagnosis of the human condition. The text startles us, sounds a stern warning, wakes us up.

The Buddha begins straight off by declaring that everything is burning. And without any apologies he takes us straight to the heart of the matter: the world is burning with the fires of greed, hatred, and delusion. From the dawn of history, these primal motives have been at the root of all misery. Yet today they have acquired a potency that in the Buddha's time would have been unthinkable. In earlier eras, greed, hatred, and delusion were viewed as dangerous because of their impact on the individual mind and on the people with whom one directly interacted. Today, however, these three "roots of the unwholesome" have acquired a global reach. They've taken on systemic embodiments—in organizations and institutions, in the formulation of policies, in the rules and protocols by which political and economic objectives are pursued. They exist not only as motives in individual minds but as forces that energize colossal social systems spread out over the world, touching virtually everyone. Thus, they are now much more malignant than ever before.

The manifestation of greed that should concern us most is not the yearning for simple sensual pleasures but the lust for power, control, and domination. Greed drives the expansion of financial institutions to the point where they become "too big to fail." It underlies the race for corporate dominance at the risk of people's health and at the cost of a viable environment. It widens the divide between the rich and the multitudes, who are cast down into poverty without social safety nets to catch them. Greed invades our political systems, turning those who should lead into accessories of the corporate interests that finance their campaigns. Greed propels a gargantuan economy that goes on devouring ever-diminishing stocks of fossil fuels and other finite resources. Our collective greed blinds us to the future, so that we are willing to bequeath to later generations the task of revitalizing a planet that may be damaged beyond repair.

Hatred today still erupts in persistent wars and violence against those of different nationalities, ethnicities, and religious beliefs. But its most insidious manifestation is callous indifference, a disregard for everyone and everything beyond our own narrow interests. When our hearts are closed, we objectify others by reducing them to mere statistics. We turn a blind eye to the plight of the billion people afflicted with chronic hunger and malnutrition. We ignore the small-scale farmers who helplessly look on when their land is gobbled up by giant agro-industrial firms. We dismiss the killing of innocent civilians as "collateral damage."

In a similar way, we commodify the natural world so that animals become machines whose sole function is to supply meat and dairy products. We regard forests as nothing more than stocks of wood and paper. We grab hold of land and treat it solely as a source of coal, precious metals, petroleum, and gems. We strip people of their personhood, so that they are no longer dignified bearers of a hidden divinity but mere customers and clients whose being is to be *for us*. Isn't this, in a way, just a more polite and refined expression of hatred?

Delusion does not only mean sheer ignorance and wrong views. It also means distraction and self-deception. I often wonder whether we refuse to look at our global crises because they are too overwhelming or because other things with more glitter capture our attention. While I don't discount the former explanation, I'm often amazed to observe, even in myself, how trivial matters deflect us from the critical questions with which we should be grappling, how they shield from view the challenges on which our very survival depends. Is it possible that we are literally "amusing ourselves to death," letting a flood of hollow forms of entertainment sweep us toward a waterfall?

But distraction is not the only way that we succumb to delusion. We also engage in deliberate deception, and often we let ourselves be deceived. How do we account for the fact that, when 97 percent of climate scientists say that climate change is real and that it's caused by human activity, almost 40 percent of the U.S. population refuses to believe them? Fires rage in California and Texas; tornados strike in the Midwest and deep in the South; fierce hurricanes sweep across the country. And still the commentators don't connect the dots, don't dare tell us that these are heralds of even greater calamities to come, that the planet is getting hotter and we're the ones who have turned up the thermostat. While climate scientists almost unanimously warn us that global warming is real, their warnings are mocked and their motives slandered. Politicians beholden to the oil industry even hold a vote on the question whether climate change is genuine, and by majority opinion determine it's a hoax. Can a thicker cataract of self-delusion be imagined?

In the Fire Sermon, the Buddha says that the way to win release from the fires that devour us is by extinguishing them at their point of origin. This means extinguishing them in the mind, by putting out the fires of greed, hatred, and delusion. The specific method the discourse recommends is inevitably framed against the spiritual backdrop of early Buddhism, which stresses personal responsibility for suffering and sees release as an individual attainment. Hence liberation comes about through meditative insight, disenchantment, and detachment. However, given the global and systemic embodiments of greed, hatred, and delusion that today jeopardize humanity's future, I wonder whether a project aimed at individual emancipation alone is adequate for our needs.

As I see it, there are two trajectories along which human life is moving, and both need to be steered in a different direction. One is the *moral trajectory*, the other *the trajectory of sustainability*. The moral trajectory is currently being driven by lust for profit and power, which is ravaging the finite resources of the Earth and filling its sinks with toxic waste. The trajectory of sustainability is being propelled by an expanding population expected to increase to nine billion by 2050. At the same time, rising living standards in developing countries like China, India, and Brazil increase the pressure on the planet to provide the resources needed to satisfy the expectations of their newly affluent elites. If these two trajectories continue on their present course, they are bound to converge and plunge us into unthinkable calamity.

In my understanding, the only prospect for human flourishing lies in altering these trajectories, a task that requires collective action rather than merely a personal effort. To emerge intact, we have to work in unison to devise ways of mitigating the fires presently consuming our world. While rooted in the same essential insights enunciated in the Fire Sermon, the approach that I see as mandatory must match the global dimensions of our current crisis. If the fires that are burning up our world today are fueled by the systemic expressions of greed, hatred, and delusion, it seems that the imperative laid on us is to confront these collective expressions head on and curb the commanding roles they play in the systems they dominate. This would mean that our endeavor should not simply be to attain personal insight in order to break the bonds that individually tie us to suffering, but to reshape the structures themselves so that they provide everyone with opportunities for a more dignified and fulfilling life.

If we accept this imperative as our personal mission, it means that we apply the ideal of "the removal and abandoning of greed, hatred, and delusion" to the operation of collective systems. The solution becomes not merely a matter of economics and politics but a deeply moral and spiritual transformation that overturns our fundamental values. The moral trajectory must be bent in the direction of greater social and economic justice. The trajectory of sustainability must be bent away from infinite expansion toward a principle of sufficiency. This entails containing population growth, protecting biodiversity, expediting the transition to renewable sources of energy, and adopting effective strategies of climate mitigation and adaptation. But it also entails adopting new standards of the good life that emphasize contentment rather than consumption, expansion, and novelty.

Such a project would revisit the assumptions that underlie the prevailing model of a growth economy, which sees the increase of output as the principal rationale for economic policy. Instead of aiming at quantitative expansion, we must make our social institutions more equitable, generous, and compassionate, so that we can provide all the Earth's denizens with the material and social supports of a decent life. We must also learn to respect the rights of other sentient beings and acknowledge the inescapable finitude of the biosphere. At the deepest level, we are called upon to re-envisage life's ultimate purpose, seeing it as the actualization of truth, goodness, and beauty rather than the achievement of wealth, power, and domination. This amounts to nothing less than a complete revaluation of our collective goals, but if we want to survive and flourish as a species, in the end we probably have no alternative.

It is mid-afternoon now. I look out my window and, apart from the interplay of light and shadow, I see that not much has changed since this morning. The sun now illuminates the colored leaves more brightly than it did in the morning. The sunlight shines on the front of the Guan Yin statue, accentuating its delicate features. The paths are still empty, and the same peace and quiet prevails. But I ask myself: "Does there have to be an irreconcilable duality between the quiet of the monastery and the commotion, upheaval, and turmoil I discover when I pass beyond its gates? Can't we extinguish the grosser fires of greed, hatred, and delusion, so that the world need not be a blazing cauldron? Is it possible to persuade people to live together peacefully and harmoniously, to know simple joys, to treat one another with generosity and kindness?"

As long as life continues, inevitably the "fires of birth, old age, and death" will burn. Thus, liberation from the cycle of repeated existence, the attainment of the deathless, still reigns as the final goal. But, I ask myself, can't we draw a distinction between those fires that are intrinsic to life itself and those that are parasitic on the life process, the fires ignited and fueled by greed, hatred, and delusion? I myself draw such a distinction. Thus, in my own small way, I aspire to help reduce the global and systemic fires of greed, hatred, and delusion, to usher in a world in which justice, love, and generosity will finally prevail.

PETER MATTHIESSEN

Watering the Seed of Mindfulness
1994

IN LATE MARCH of 1991, on the way to a retreat for environmentalists to be led by the eminent Vietnamese Zen master, poet, and peace activist Thich Nhat Hanh, I took time for a walk up Malibu Creek, in the Malibu Canyon State Park. Spring songbirds were numerous, and a golden eagle sailed high overhead, crossing the Santa Catalina Mountains of the Coast Range, and from a bridge over the creek I saw a heavy brown-furred animal half-hidden behind rocks close to the bank. From its striped ears, I knew it was a bobcat, stalking three coot that had come ashore into the sedges. So intent was it upon its prey that, moving out into the open, it looked back just once, the sun catching the oval of light fur around the lynxish eyes. However, the coot, sensing danger, swam away from shore, and as the bobcat made its way downstream, striped bobbed tail twitching in frustration, the slate gray birds with their ivory bills followed along, just off the bank, peering and craning to see where the wildcat had got to.

The bobcat or bay lynx is not uncommon, but it is elusive, difficult to see; I have crossed paths with it perhaps eight times in fifty years of wildlife observation, usually as it crossed a trail or a night road. This was the first one I had ever watched for minutes at a time—ten minutes at the least—in open sunlight of mid-afternoon, scarcely fifty feet away, a stirring event that seemed to me an auspicious sign for the environmentalists' retreat that would begin that evening.

Originally the retreat was to take place at Ojai, but in recent weeks, due to housing complications, it had been shifted to Camp Sholom, a Jewish retreat in the Santa Catalinas, perhaps five miles inland from the coast; the camp lies in a hollow in the dry chaparral hills, in a grove of sycamore and live oak where two brooks come together. The hills were green and the brooks rushing from the heavy rains, which muddied the ground beneath the huge white tent and moved the whole retreat indoors.

My host was James Soshin Thornton, a student of Maezumi Roshi and the founding lawyer of the Los Angeles office of the Natural Resources Defense Council, which together with the Nathan Cummings Foundation, the Ojai Foundation, and the Community of Mindful Living, had sponsored the retreat. One of my own Zen students, Dennis Snyder, was also present, and so were several environmental acquaintances and friends-of-friends.

Zazen, seated meditation on the floor, which took place in the meeting hall on the first evening after some welcoming remarks by Thich Nhat Hanh, Joan Halifax of Ojai, and James Thornton, was a new experience for most of the environmentalists among the 225 retreatants, some of whom were later obliged to move to chairs, but they persevered bravely and by the week's end, were sitting as assiduously as all the rest.

"When you take care of the environmentalist," said Thich Nhat Hanh, urging the use of a gentle smile to help us pay attention to each moment, "you take care of the environment." This remark might have been the theme of the whole retreat.

Thich Nhat Hanh, called "Thay" by his students, is a small, large-toothed man with a broad smile and kind, smiling eyes, so youthful in appearance that one scarcely believes he was nominated in 1968 (by Martin Luther King) for the Nobel Peace Prize.

In his first Dharma talk next morning (on breathing meditation: "When I breathe in, I am aware of my eyes . . . of the lovely morning . . . of my heart. . . .") he stood in brown robes in the early sun that shimmered from the small hard shiny leaves of live oak and poured through the windowed wall behind him, filtered by a lovely wooden screen of six carved panels that Joan Halifax believes came originally from China. Like chinks of sun through the brown rosettes of the screen, Thay's white teeth glinted in that childlike wide-eyed smile.

"Sometimes we believe we would like to be someone else, but of course we cannot be someone else, we can only be ourselves, and even that is very difficult. . . . To be ourselves, we must be in the present moment, and to be in the present moment we must follow our breath, be one with our breath, for otherwise we are overtaken by emotions and events. . . ."

Thay's daily talks were pointed up by intermittent bell notes rung by his attendant Therese Fitzgerald (formerly of San Francisco Zen Center), and all meals, eaten in silence, were also punctuated by a bell, to remind retreatants to pay attention to this present moment.

Insight depends upon awareness of this moment, according to Thay's teaching, which leads inevitably to compassion and a natural state of being. His teaching returns again and again to the soft image of a flower, "showing its heart" as it opens to the sun. The mudra of gassho he likens to a closed lotus, the hands opening outward in gratitude and thanks for this extraordinary existence, in the way that a bean sprout opens, smiling, to the sun and wind. That half-smile on the lips will lead to an unforced well-being, contributing to a sincere joy in one's practice. "If your practice is not pleasurable," then some other practice might be more suitable, says Thay.

On the first evening, an informal panel—Thay's associate, the Vietnamese nun Sister Chan Khong, James Thornton, and Randy Hayes of the Rainforest Action Network, also Joan Halifax and myself—took questions from the gathering of perhaps 225 persons that filled the meeting hall right to the walls. Sister Chan Khong, a small dynamic person who administers one hundred social workers in Vietnam (all unknown to one another, since they may be harassed by the government), was articulate and eloquent; like Thich Nhat Hanh, she counseled returning to the breath as the foundation of this moment, of our very being. And the panel agreed that in time of distress, we must go into that distress, deeper and deeper, become one with it.

On other occasions, in a sweet voice, Sister Chan Khong burst into song, manifesting the joy in this moment that Thay talks about. Discussing the anger she sometimes feels, seeing the waste of water and materials in our bathrooms and kitchens, she says she cures this by singing aloud, "When I go to the bathroom (kitchen, etc.), I feel happy, because I have learned to breathe deeply. . . ." (After Thay's Dharma talk on the precepts, she remarked, "When you are truly mindful, you don't need the precepts.")

Each day began with two early periods of strong zazen, followed by recitation from the sutras or, on one occasion, a fine letter to Thay from an environmental lawyer in the group who stressed the need for the spiritual base for environmental work that has been sadly lacking in most organizations. After silent breakfast in the dining hall, down along the creek, Thay would talk to us again, in a Dharma talk that one day ran close to two hours.

"We are only real when we are one with our breathing—our walking, our eating—and it is then that everything around us becomes real. . . . Eating a bean, be conscious of the true nature of that bean, the structure, all the non-bean elements that make up that bean, and permit it to exist. If you look into a flower penetratingly, you will see the sun, the minerals, the water that make up the flower, which contains all the non-flower elements in the world, just as a Buddhist contains all the non-Buddhist elements."

Thay's eyes sometimes remain sad even when he is smiling, and more than once during the week he expressed distress over the actions of President Bush in the Gulf War, which had almost deterred him from making his annual visit to this country. He spoke to us of "sowing the seed of peace in our land," and attending to "the President Bush within ourselves . . . " as we might attend to our greed, ignorance, and anger.

"Take tender care of your anger, with mindfulness . . . don't suppress it . . . it is you. You have been watering the seed of your anger rather than the seed of your mindfulness; the anger comes from lack of understanding, and it comes very easily. . . . If mindfulness is there, you are protected from anger and from fear."

And he spoke to us strongly against "sowing the seed of suffering" in our speech and actions. Another day, he pointed out our compulsive behavior, our inability to stop: the more we eat (sleep, telephone, watch television, drive in our car)—the more we fill the emptiness, in short—the hungrier we become. We must fill every moment, we cannot just be. "How can we stop the arms race when we cannot stop ourselves?"

Following the Dharma talk came walking meditation in the hills, then lunch, then afternoon meetings with various leaders, late afternoon zazen, supper, and more evening meetings, followed by a last period of formal zazen. All of these events except zazen were interspersed with semi-spiritual musical presentations by two guitarist-singers, an evening of entertainment, and even a

Passover supper, or seder. At times, Thay appeared vaguely mystified by these secular events, which were not, however, permitted to alter the warm and yet serious tone of the retreat.

Despite his gentle manner, Thich Nhat Hanh is a strict teacher with a strong adherence to the precepts. Talking informally one evening over green tea in his room, we discussed the fact that many if not most Zen teachers transgress the precepts in one way or another, and he said wryly, "They have the idea that this is all right for enlightened people."

He went on to describe his Rinzai training in Vietnam, where he became a monk in 1942 and founded the Tiep Hien Order in 1964; I had not realized that Rinzai Zen, which traveled eastward from China to Korea and Japan, then the United States, had also made its way south into Southeast Asia, where Theravadin Buddhism had held sway for centuries.

As the days passed and the rain ceased and concentration deepened, Thich Nhat Hanh's mild tones came and went like some wonderful soft voice from faraway in the mysterious stacks of a huge library. At times the whole brown-robed being seemed to shine, as if he and the sun-filled screen, the mountain light, were now all one. "We have to be a little bit mindful just to notice the moon, but we don't appreciate the intensity, the beauty of our life, until we are truly mindful in each moment."

The Sun My Heart
1993

W HEN I FIRST left Vietnam, I had a dream in which I
was a young boy, smiling and at ease, in my own land, surrounded by my own people, in a time of peace. There was a beautiful hillside, lush with trees and flowers, and on it was a little house.
But each time I approached the hillside, obstacles prevented me
from climbing it, and then I woke up.

The dream recurred many times. I continued to do my work
and to practice mindfulness, trying to be in touch with the beautiful trees, people, flowers, and sunshine that surrounded me
in Europe and North America. I looked deeply at these things,
and I played under the trees with the children exactly as I had in
Vietnam. After a year, the dream stopped. Seeds of acceptance
and joy had been planted in me, and I began to look at Europe,
America, and other countries in Asia as also my home. I realized
that my home is the Earth. Whenever I felt homesick for Vietnam,
I went outside into a backyard or a park, and found a place to practice breathing, walking, and smiling among the trees.

But some cities had very few trees, even then. I can imagine someday soon a city with no trees in it at all. Imagine a city
that has only one tree left. People there are mentally disturbed,
because they are so alienated from nature. Then one doctor in the
city sees why people are getting sick, and he offers each person

who comes to him this prescription: "You are sick because you are cut off from Mother Nature. Every morning, take a bus, go to the tree in the center of the city, and hug it for fifteen minutes. Look at the beautiful green tree and smell its fragrant bark."

After three months of practicing this, the patient will feel much better. But because many people suffer from the same malady and the doctor always gives the same prescription, after a short time, the line of people waiting their turn to embrace the tree gets to be very long, more than a mile, and people begin to get impatient. Fifteen minutes is now too long for each person to hug the tree, so the city council legislates a five-minute maximum. Then they have to shorten it to one minute, and then only a few seconds. Finally, there is no remedy at all for the sickness.

If we are not mindful, we might be in that situation soon. We have to remember that our body is not limited to what lies within the boundary of our skin. Our body is much more immense. We know that if our heart stops beating, the flow of our life will stop, but we do not take the time to notice the many things outside of our bodies that are equally essential for our survival. If the ozone layer around our Earth were to disappear for even an instant, we would die. If the sun were to stop shining, the flow of our life would stop. The sun is our second heart, our heart outside of our body. It gives all life on Earth the warmth necessary for existence. Plants live thanks to the sun. Their leaves absorb the sun's energy, along with carbon dioxide from the air, to produce food for the tree, the flower, the plankton. And thanks to plants, we and other animals can live. All of us—people, animals, plants, and minerals—"consume" the sun, directly and indirectly. We cannot begin to describe all the effects of the sun, that great heart outside of our body.

When we look at green vegetables, we should know that it is the sun that is green and not just the vegetables. The green color in the leaves of the vegetables is due to the presence of the sun. Without the sun, no living being could survive. Without sun, water, air, and soil, there would be no vegetables. The vegetables are the coming-together of many conditions near and far.

There is no phenomenon in the universe that does not intimately concern us, from a pebble resting at the bottom of the ocean, to the movement of a galaxy millions of light years away. Walt Whitman said, "I believe a blade of grass is no less than the journey-work of the stars. . . ." These words are not philosophy. They come from the depths of his soul. He also said, "I am large, I contain multitudes."

This might be called a meditation on "interbeing endlessly interwoven." All phenomena are interdependent. When we think of a speck of dust, a flower, or a human being, our thinking cannot break loose from the idea of unity, of one, of calculation. We see a line drawn between one and many, one and not one. But if we truly realize the interdependent nature of the dust, the flower, and the human being, we see that unity cannot exist without diversity. Unity and diversity interpenetrate each other freely. Unity is diversity, and diversity is unity. This is the principle of interbeing.

If you are a mountain climber or someone who enjoys the countryside or the forest, you know that forests are our lungs outside of our bodies. Yet we have been acting in a way that has allowed millions of square miles of land to be deforested, and we have also destroyed the air, the rivers, and parts of the ozone layer. We are imprisoned in our small selves, thinking only of some comfortable conditions for this small self, while we destroy our large self.

If we want to change the situation, we must begin by being our true selves. To be our true selves means we have to be the forest, the river, and the ozone layer. If we visualize ourselves as the forest, we will experience the hopes and fears of the trees. If we don't do this, the forests will die, and we will lose our chance for peace. When we understand that we inter-are with the trees, we will know that it is up to us to make an effort to keep the trees alive. In the last twenty years, our cars and factories have created acid rain that has destroyed so many trees. Because we inter-are with the trees, we know that if they do not live, we too will disappear very soon.

We humans think we are smart, but an orchid, for example, knows how to produce noble, symmetrical flowers, and a snail knows how to make a beautiful, well-proportioned shell. Compared with their knowledge, ours is not worth much at all. We should bow deeply before the orchid and the snail and join our palms reverently before the monarch butterfly and the magnolia tree. The feeling of respect for all species will help us recognize the noblest nature in ourselves.

An oak tree is an oak tree. That is all an oak tree needs to do. If an oak tree is less than an oak tree, we will all be in trouble. In our former lives, we were rocks, clouds, and trees. We have also been an oak tree. This is not just Buddhist; it is scientific. We humans are a young species. We were plants, we were trees, and now we have become humans. We have to remember our past existences and be humble. We can learn a lot from an oak tree.

All life is impermanent. We are all children of the Earth, and, at some time, she will take us back to herself again. We are continually arising from Mother Earth, being nurtured by her, and then returning to her. Like us, plants are born, live for a period of time, and then return to the Earth. When they decompose, they fertilize our gardens. Living vegetables and decomposing vegetables are part of the same reality. Without one, the other cannot be. After six months, compost becomes fresh vegetables again. Plants and the Earth rely on each other. Whether the Earth is fresh, beautiful, and green, or arid and parched depends on the plants.

It also depends on us. Our way of walking on the Earth has a great influence on animals and plants. We have killed so many animals and plants and destroyed their environments. Many are now extinct. In turn, our environment is now harming us. We are like sleepwalkers, not knowing what we are doing or where we are heading. Whether we can wake up or not depends on whether we can walk mindfully on our Mother Earth. The future of all life, including our own, depends on our mindful steps.

Birds' songs express joy, beauty, and purity, and evoke in us vitality and love. So many beings in the universe love us unconditionally. The trees, the water, and the air don't ask anything of us; they just love us. Even though we need this kind of love, we continue to destroy them. By destroying the animals, the air, and the trees, we are destroying ourselves. We must learn to practice unconditional love for all beings so that the animals, the air, the trees, and the minerals can continue to be themselves.

Our ecology should be a deep ecology—not only deep, but universal. There is pollution in our consciousness. Television, films, and newspapers are forms of pollution for us and our children. They sow seeds of violence and anxiety in us and pollute our consciousness, just as we destroy our environment by farming with chemicals, clear-cutting the trees, and polluting the water. We need to protect the ecology of the Earth and the ecology of the mind, or this kind of violence and recklessness will spill over into even more areas of life.

Our Earth, our beautiful blue planet is in danger, and all of us know it. Yet we act as if our daily lives have nothing to do with the situation of the world. If the Earth were your body, you would be able to feel many areas where she is suffering. Many people are aware of the world's suffering, and their hearts are filled with compassion. They know what needs to be done, and they engage in political, social, and environmental work to try to change things.

But after a period of intense involvement, they become discouraged, because they lack the strength needed to sustain a life of action. Real strength is not in power, money, or weapons, but in deep, inner peace. If we change our daily lives—the way we think, speak, and act—we change the world. The best way to take care of the environment is to take care of the environmentalist.

Many Buddhist teachings help us understand our interconnectedness with our Mother, the Earth. One of the deepest is *The Diamond Sutra,* which is written in the form of a dialogue between the Buddha and his senior disciple, Subhuti. It begins with this question by Subhuti: "If sons and daughters of good families want to give rise to the highest, most fulfilled, awakened mind, what should they rely on and what should they do to master their thinking?" This is the same as asking, "If I want to use my whole being to protect life, what methods and principles should I use?"

The Buddha answers, "We have to do our best to help every living being cross the ocean of suffering. But after all beings have arrived at the shore of liberation, no being at all has been carried to the other shore. If you are still caught up in the idea of a self, a person, a living being, or a life span, you are not an authentic bodhisattva." Self, person, living being, and life span are four notions that prevent us from seeing reality.

Life is one. We do not need to slice it into pieces and call this or that piece a "self." What we call a self is made only of non-self elements. When we look at a flower, for example, we may think that it is different from "non-flower" things. But when we look more deeply, we see that everything in the cosmos is in that flower. Without all of the non-flower elements—sunshine, clouds, earth, minerals, heat, rivers, and consciousness—a flower cannot be. That is why the Buddha teaches that the self does not exist. We have to discard all distinctions between self and non-self. How can anyone work to protect the environment without this insight?

The second notion that prevents us from seeing reality is the notion of a person, a human being. We usually discriminate between humans and non-humans, thinking that we are more important than other species. But since we humans are made of non-human elements, to protect ourselves we have to protect all of the non-human elements. There is no other way. If you think, "God created man in His own image and He created other things for man to use," you are already making the discrimination that man is more important than other things. When we see that humans have no self, we see that to take care of the environment (the non-human elements) is to take care of humanity. The best way to take good care of men and women so that they can be truly healthy and happy is to take care of the environment. I know ecologists who are not happy in their families. They work hard to improve the environment, partly to escape family life. If someone is not happy within himself, how can he help the environment? That is why the Buddha teaches that to protect the non-human elements is to protect humans, and to protect humans is to protect non-human elements.

The third notion we have to break through is the notion of a living being. We think that we living beings are different from inanimate objects, but according to the principle of interbeing, living beings are comprised of non-living-being elements. When we look into ourselves, we see minerals and all other non-living-being elements. Why discriminate against what we call inanimate? To protect living beings, we must protect the stones, the soil, and the oceans. Before the atomic bomb was dropped on Hiroshima, there were many beautiful stone benches in the parks. As the Japanese were rebuilding their city, they discovered that these stones were dead, so they carried them away and buried them. Then they brought in live stones. Do not think these things are not alive. Atoms are always moving. Electrons move at nearly the speed of light. According to the teaching of Buddhism, these atoms and stones are consciousness itself. That is why discrimination by living beings against non-living beings should be discarded.

The last notion is that of a life span. We think that we have been alive since a certain point in time and that prior to that moment, our life did not exist. This distinction between life and non-life is not correct. Life is made of death, and death is made of life. We have to accept death; it makes life possible. The cells in our body are dying every day, but we never think to organize funerals for them. The death of one cell allows for the birth of another. Life and death are two aspects of the same reality. We must learn to die peacefully so that others may live. This deep meditation brings forth non-fear, non-anger, and non-despair, the strengths we need for our work. With non-fear, even when we see that a problem is huge, we will not burn out. We will know how to make small, steady steps. If those who work to protect the environment contemplate these four notions, they will know how to be and how to act.

In another Buddhist text, *The Avatamsaka (Adorning the Buddha with Flowers) Sutra,* the Buddha further elaborates his insights concerning our "interpenetration" with our environment. Please meditate with me on the "Ten Penetrations":

The first is, "All worlds penetrate a single pore. A single pore penetrates all worlds." Look deeply at a flower. It may be tiny, but the sun, the clouds, and everything else in the cosmos penetrates it. Nuclear physicists say very much the same thing: one electron is made by all electrons; one electron is in all electrons.

The second penetration is, "All living beings penetrate one body. One body penetrates all living beings." When you kill a living being, you kill yourself and everyone else as well.

The third is, "Infinite time penetrates one second. One second penetrates infinite time." A *ksana* is the shortest period of time, actually much shorter than a second.

The fourth penetration is, "All Buddhist teachings penetrate one teaching. One teaching penetrates all Buddhist teachings." As a young monk, I had the opportunity to learn that Buddhism is made of non-Buddhist elements. So, whenever I study Christianity or Judaism, I find the Buddhist elements in them, and vice versa. I always respect non-Buddhist teachings. All Buddhist teachings penetrate one teaching, and one teaching penetrates all Buddhist teachings. We are free.

The fifth penetration is, "Innumerable spheres enter one sphere. One sphere enters innumerable spheres." A sphere is a geographical space. Innumerable spheres penetrate into one particular area, and one particular area enters into innumerable spheres. It means that when you destroy one area, you destroy every area. When you save one area, you save all areas. A student asked me, "Thay, there are so many urgent problems, what should I do?" I said, "Take one thing and do it very deeply and carefully, and you will be doing everything at the same time."

The sixth penetration is, "All sense organs penetrate one organ. One organ penetrates all sense organs"—eye, ear, nose, tongue, body, and mind. To take care of one means to take care of many. To take care of your eyes means to take care of the eyes of innumerable living beings.

The seventh penetration is, "All sense organs penetrate non-sense organs. Non-sense organs penetrate all sense organs." Not only do non-sense organs penetrate sense organs, they also penetrate non-sense organs. There is no discrimination. Sense organs are made of non-sense-organ elements. That is why they penetrate non-sense organs. This helps us remember the teaching of *The Diamond Sutra*.

The eighth penetration is, "One perception penetrates all perceptions. All perceptions penetrate one perception." If your perception is not accurate, it will influence all other perceptions in yourself and others. Suppose a bus driver has an incorrect perception. We know what may happen. One perception penetrates all perceptions.

The ninth penetration is, "Every sound penetrates one sound. One sound penetrates every sound." This is a very deep teaching. If we understand one sound or one word, we can understand all.

The tenth penetration is, "All times penetrate one time. One time penetrates all times—past, present, and future. In one second, you can find the past, present, and future." In the past, you can see the present and the future. In the present, you can find the past and future. In the future, you can find the past and present. They "inter-contain" each other. Space contains time, time contains space. In the teaching of interpenetration, one determines the other, the other determines this one. When we realize our nature of interbeing, we will stop blaming and killing, because we know that we inter-are.

Interpenetration is an important teaching, but it still suggests that things outside of one another penetrate into each other. Interbeing is a step forward. We are already inside, so we don't have to enter. In contemporary nuclear physics, people talk about implicit order and explicit order. In the explicit order, things exist outside of each other—the table outside of the flower, the sunshine outside of the cypress tree. In the implicit order, we see that they are inside each other—the sunshine inside the cypress tree.

Interbeing is the implicit order. To practice mindfulness and to look deeply into the nature of things is to discover the true nature of interbeing. There we find peace and develop the strength to be in touch with everything. With this understanding, we can easily sustain the work of loving and caring for the Earth and for each other for a long time.

Reflections on the Paris Climate Conference 2016

O NCE AGAIN, A generation is called to stop, reflect, and take action for the collective, for our common home.

The 2015 Paris Climate Conference was an opportunity for our human family to pause and look at the reality of the situation, and to discover whether or not we can unite around a common cause. The conference aimed to achieve, for the first time in twenty years, a legally binding, universal agreement of 195 countries to keep global warming below 2°C and protect the Earth from dangerous climate change.

To help realize this aspiration, faith communities and indigenous communities were encouraged to contribute their voices. Plum Village was one of the groups invited to participate.

Some people in our community questioned why we should get involved in a conference that might contain more politics and rhetoric than action. Others questioned whether our participation was just a symbolic, superficial gesture with little real impact. And still others wondered what spirituality, and specifically Buddhist practice, has to offer to a problem that appears by nature economic, political, and diplomatic.

For our delegation of monastics, and for our wider community, this has been a chance to find ways to engage with this issue and to look deeply at where we are, both personally and collectively, and to see clearly our direction going forward.

On our first day in Paris we were on familiar spiritual ground. We gathered together with faith leaders from around the world in the huge Cathedral of Saint Denis to offer our spiritual practice, prayers, and insights on the theme of protecting the Earth. The kinship of our hearts was palpable. There were Hindu prayers and a Muslim chant, and a group of passionate young pilgrims from the Philippines offered a song. From our delegation, Sister Giac Nghiem led a moving guided meditation, from time to time inviting a small bell, and Sister Dao Nghiem read selections from Thay's books, chosen by the organizers.

Numerous faith leaders made heartfelt appeals for climate justice. Through their compassionate testimony, we learned about the people most vulnerable to ecological destruction and climate change: people with no other power than their voice and spirit.

Christiana Figueres, the convener and chairperson of the Paris Conference, is a student of Thay's and finds solace in his insights and teachings. In fact, it was she who invited faith leaders and spiritual communities to contribute their voices, both in Paris and around the world. "I don't think that I would have had the inner stamina, the depth of optimism, the depth of commitment, the depth of the inspiration if I had not been accompanied by the teachings of Thich Nhat Hanh," she said in an interview after the conference. She has shared that to keep herself grounded and inspired in her work, she takes *Love Letters to the Earth* with her wherever she goes.

At the interfaith event, Christiana gave a speech centered on the theme of walking the path of climate action with love and awareness. Speaking to the crowd of faith leaders, politicians, and journalists, she shared how the acronym WALK has guided her in her work.

For Christiana, "W" is for Wakening, "A" is for Affirmation (of our capacity to make a difference), "L" is for Love, and "K" is for Knowledge. She spoke with love, insight, and faith, and her powerful speech felt like a Dharma talk with the energy of Manjushri, right in the heart of the conference.

The next day, our delegation took our mindful steps into the deserted Place de la République in central Paris to bear witness to what should have been a day of climate action by the people. Over 70,000 people had been expected to gather in the square for a "People's Climate March" calling on governments to take ambitious action to safeguard our future. But after the Paris terrorist attacks three weeks earlier, the government decided to ban the march rather than protect it, causing great disappointment to hundreds of thousands around the world.

The thousands of people who would have marched were represented by thousands of pairs of empty shoes—including a pair of plain black shoes sent by Pope Francis. A few people gathered to contemplate the shoes in silence, and to show their defiance. Our delegation came to offer our presence, our love, and our peace.

We walked in silence around the carpet of shoes at the center of the plaza and around the colossal monument now covered with candles, pictures, and messages in memory of the 130 young victims who were killed in the terrorist attacks. It was no coincidence that the demonstration for climate action and the memorial for the victims of terrorism shared the same space. By looking deeply, the common conditions of the climate crisis and terrorism become clear: human avarice, hatred, and wrong views.

Journalists stopped us to ask questions: Why are you here? What does spirituality have to do with any of this? How can prayer or spiritual energy ever make a difference? We could not help but remember our teacher's reminder that *there is no way to peace, peace is the way.*

Every breath and step we make in Paris and on our planet needs to contain healing and peace. Our actions and efforts for a more peaceful and harmonious future need to be sustained by a deep spiritual practice that can help us overcome what Martin Luther King calls "our finite disappointments" and never lose our "infinite hope."

We were challenged to reflect: Where do we stand as a community? Do we need to protest? That morning in the Place de la République we smiled at passersby, joined in some chalk art on the pavement, and shared tea, chocolate, and tangerines with strangers on a bench.

Does the peace we generate have any relevance to the violence? Can small acts of peace and compassion in our daily life ever challenge the powerful structures of governments, the military-industrial complex, and mass media? How can current events inform each step of our walking meditation in the monastery?

We were present at the conference not just as participants or as observers, but as practitioners. We remembered Thay's teaching that our presence *is* our message: the way we look and walk can show the depth of our participation.

With our long robes, shaved heads, and gentle pace, we stood out among the sharp suits and high heels: occupied people, striding in haste, hands on cellphones. This contrast challenged us and reminded us of our purpose: not to get some kind of outcome, not to lose our self or our contact with the Earth, but to love the

Earth in each step. We tried our best to be aware and hear the cry of Mother Earth when we walked, and to be grateful to Mother Earth when we sat down to eat our lunch.

Our delegation was a catalyst for connection. People smiled, approached us, sat down with us, and many wanted to ask us questions. Who are you? What are you asking for? Everyone's here to hash out a political deal—what do *you* have to contribute? We also asked ourselves: can we *really* help? Do the people here need more views and ideas from us? Or something else?

Thay has taught us that this is not just a technological, economic, or political crisis, but a spiritual crisis. What spiritual medicine can we offer, and how? How can we be the voice of Mother Earth in each interview? How can we bear witness to her not just as inanimate planet, but as living spirit? We remembered the image of a monk sitting in the temple while bombs are falling outside. What does being a monastic today have to do with the climate crisis?

The Paris conference was a microcosm of the whole planet: each country had its own pavilion, furnished with beautiful photographs and presentations. Each country was making its request for help, partnership, and collaboration: for their community, their trees and animals, their mountains and rivers, their land. We could see the diversity of our human family and our deep interconnection. So many nations gathered around *one* concern.

It was humbling to see the Herculean efforts of the United Nations to gather 195 cultures together under one roof in order to come to a harmonious resolution. The conference had the flavor of a Biblical Noah's Ark. We couldn't help but imagine the Earth as a kind of boat, our only spaceship, sailing through the cosmos. And on this boat, the only kinds of solutions now are those that must include all of humanity, as well as the entire atmosphere and biosphere of plants, animals, and minerals.

Thay has said that we need more than just new technology to protect the planet: we need real community and cooperation. In this new millennia, we now have the ability to gather as a global family, to communicate, and to hear each other's concerns and values. We have enough scientific knowledge to know the state of our planet and what is in store for us if we do not change course. And we know that this is not something any nation can solve alone.

We already have the technology. What we need now is cooperation, collaboration, mutual understanding, and generosity, at an international level. The way forward is *as a global community*. It is the greatest challenge for our generation, no matter what part of this Earth-boat we're dwelling on.

In the fall of 2015, we had a chance to work with a diverse group of Buddhist traditions from all over the world to issue an *International Buddhist Declaration on Climate Change*. It was challenging to cultivate mutual cooperation, compassion, trust, and collective insight across our different cultures and Buddhist traditions.

We learned to open up and to allow ourselves to be affected by the values of others. We learned that none of us can define what is most important for others; that nobody has the "right" answer; that no community has the perfect way of living; and, most crucially, that everyone is trying their best.

What was unusual about the Paris Conference was the role of a collective grassroots movement from the people, rising up around the world. We could feel our affinity with the calls for a people's movement. As Bill McKibben says, such a people's movement calls for not one leader with a capital L, but for all of us to empower ourselves and become leaders in our local community.

What did the final Paris Agreement mean for the world and for us? It raises our awareness that in the centuries to come, there is a strong need for collective cooperation. It is the only option. Much like when the world witnessed and felt the collective horror of the atomic bombs dropped on Hiroshima and Nagasaki at the end of the Second World War, whatever one country does (or does not do) now will impact us all.

Just as global warfare was changed forever by the invention of the atomic bomb, the climate crisis has changed international development. We can no longer have infinite growth on a finite planet. We cannot progress as a nation at the expense of other nations, or to the detriment of our planet. The Paris Agreement is a text that affirms that restraint and moderation are now needed, and that each nation can no longer pursue economic growth and advancement without consideration of the rest of the world. It is a kind of *vinaya* (an ethical code) for the planet.

Compromise and restraint will be the ultimate challenge for our generation. As leading climate scientists have written in an open letter: "People wanted to hear that an agreement had been reached on climate change that would save the world *while leaving lifestyles and aspirations unchanged.*" But the reality is that lifestyles and aspirations *will* have to change.

The perennial challenge for our species has always been to balance our individual pursuits with the interests of the collective. That challenge is ever more pertinent now as we grapple with the survival of our planet as we know it.

Fortunately, in our community we have methods and practices that bring these two fronts together: addressing both collective global issues and our individual choices and lifestyles. Before participating in the Paris conference, we called on members of our Plum Village community to practice five specific actions in support of the conference and the delegates.

The first practice was to fast from meat and dairy products for the duration of the conference from November 30 to December 11 as a prayer for the environment.

Second, we asked everyone to make at least one commitment of action in their daily life from our list of actions to protect the environment.

Third, we encouraged people to come together in their families, communities, or Sanghas to support each other and to share about ways to help the climate crisis.

The fourth practice was to join the "People's March" in their local city as part of the global people's movement for climate change.

Lastly, we asked people to wear a green ribbon as a reminder for themselves and to raise awareness with those around them.

There were those who discounted these actions as merely symbolic expressions of personal concern; as tokenistic gestures that distract us from engaging in campaigns and actions in the public arena that challenge and disrupt the *systems* responsible for the crisis.

These five actions invited people to look deeply at the way they were living and affecting the climate. Like the robes or shaved head of a monastic, they are both a symbol *and* an action of resistance to the system: an alternative choice of lifestyle that is more harmonious with the state of the world and less impactful to the environment.

Our action is not to retreat from society and the world. When we practice walking meditation, it is not symbolic. We practice walking meditation not only for our personal enjoyment and spiritual growth, but as an action of resistance against the speed of our consumption society. And when we choose to move toward a vegan diet, it is the most practical action we can take, at least three times a day, to nourish our personal commitment and to reduce damage to the planet. Not only are we choosing to *not support* the system of mass industrial agriculture or the meat industry; we're choosing *to support* our reverence for life.

In one corner of the Paris conference, there was a giant art sculpture of the Eiffel Tower made of red patio chairs screwed together—red, as a symbol of the terrorist attacks on their city, and patio chairs as a symbol of the common life found in the Parisian streets and the cafes that were attacked.

We could not help but remember the gift of the Statue of Liberty that France made to America in 1886 as a symbol of their alliance and their common ideal of life, liberty, and the pursuit of happiness. We recall how Thay also once suggested that what America and the world need now is a Statue of Responsibility. He proposed that it could be erected in the San Francisco Bay, on the West Coast of the United States.

When we returned to the monastery, our delegation gave a presentation about what we'd learned from the conference and how we see our community's contribution and engagement. We learned that the nuns from our hamlets got together to look deeply at what further changes they could make in their hamlet to save water, electricity, and be more efficient and less wasteful.

People have expressed their wonder at why, in recent years, Thay has not been as politically active as he was during the Vietnam War. Why hasn't he spoken out more publicly on current social conflicts and issues? Why is he just teaching how to breathe and smile, leading mindfulness retreats for the general public?

Thay has taught us that when a person is able to stop, silence their mind, and see clearly the root of their suffering and take care of it, they have a chance to touch true happiness. It is from this personal insight that they will heal and transform, and thus have the energy to aspire to help and be of benefit to others. Only once we have developed such a practice that helps us to slow down and to touch peace and happiness right in the present moment, will we have the time and space in our mind to look deeply at the state of the world and our responsibility in it.

This is what we have witnessed over and over again at all our retreats and at our practice centers. After just five days or a week of mindfulness practice and community living, people aspire to commit to the ethical guidelines of the Five Mindfulness Trainings.[1] They are motivated and determined to return home to reconcile with their loved ones and find a lifestyle that is more happy, healthy, and responsible.

Thay has always emphasized the importance of practicing the Trainings and cultivating mindfulness in our everyday actions. When we are mindful, we can see that by refraining from doing one thing, we can prevent another thing from happening. We arrive at our own unique insight. It is not something imposed on us by an outside authority. We renew our hope for the future and realize our common aspiration.

The twentieth century saw the liberation of many peoples and countries from oppression and exploitation. In India, Gandhi led his people in a nonviolent revolution to free his country from British rule. In the United States, Dr. Martin Luther King, Jr., led African Americans in a nonviolent movement for civil and racial justice, and Susan B. Anthony led the battle for women's suffrage. In Vietnam and other developing countries, the common people rose up to free themselves from colonial rule and exploitation. And in other affluent countries, the poor and people subject to discrimination also rose in protest for rights and equality.

---

1 See the last chapter in this book for the Five Mindfulness Trainings.

As this century unfolds, there is a need for awareness that freedom must go hand in hand with responsibility. The pursuit of liberty and happiness should not infringe on the right to life of other species, and of our planet. The Paris Climate Conference has made our inseparable connection to one another clear to the world—whether we choose to accept it or not. It is not a matter of belief or philosophy. It is an evident scientific truth. It is now our practice to be more aware and mindful of this interconnection and the responsibility that this entails for our own generation and many generations to come.

JOANNA MACY

The Greening of the Self
1991

S OMETHING IMPORTANT IS happening in our world that you are not going to read about in the newspapers. I consider it the most fascinating and hopeful development of our time, and it is one of the reasons I am so glad to be alive today. It has to do with what is occurring to the notion of the *self*.

The self is the metaphoric construct of identity and agency, the hypothetical piece of turf on which we construct our strategies for survival, the notion around which we focus our instincts for self-preservation, our needs for self-approval, and the boundaries of our self-interest. Something is happening to the self!

The conventional notion of the self with which we have been raised and to which we have been conditioned by mainstream culture is being undermined. What Alan Watts called "the skin-encapsulated ego" and Gregory Bateson referred to as "the epistemological error of Occidental civilization" is being unhinged, peeled off. It is being replaced by wider constructs of identity and self-interest—by what you might call the ecological self or the eco-self, co-extensive with other beings and the life of our planet. It is what I will call "the greening of the self."

At a recent lecture on a college campus, I gave the students examples of activities that are currently being undertaken in defense of life on Earth—actions in which people risk their comfort and even their lives to protect other species. In the Chipko, or tree-hugging, movement in North India, for example, villagers fight the deforestation of their remaining woodlands. On the open seas, Greenpeace activists are intervening to protect marine mammals from slaughter. After that talk, I received a letter from a student I'll call Michael. He wrote:

> I think of the tree-huggers hugging my trunk, blocking
> the chain saws with their bodies. I feel their fingers
> digging into my bark to stop the steel and let me
> breathe. I hear the bodhisattvas in their rubber boats as
> they put themselves between the harpoons and me, so
> I can escape to the depths of the sea. I give thanks for
> your life and mine, and for life itself. I give thanks for
> realizing that I too have the powers of the tree-huggers
> and the bodhisattvas.

What is striking about Michael's words is the shift in identification. Michael is able to extend his sense of self to encompass the self of the tree and of the whale. Tree and whale are no longer removed, separate, disposable objects pertaining to a world "out there"; they are intrinsic to his own vitality. Through the power of his caring, his experience of self is expanded far beyond that skin-encapsulated ego. I quote Michael's words not because they are unusual, but to the contrary, because they express a desire and a capacity that is being released from the prison-cell of old constructs of self. This desire and capacity are arising in more and more people today as, out of deep concern for what is happening to our world, they begin to speak and act on its behalf.

Among those who are shedding these old constructs of self, like old skin or a confining shell, is John Seed, director of the

Rainforest Information Center in Australia. One day we were walking through the rainforest in New South Wales, where he has his office, and I asked him, "You talk about the struggle against the lumbering interests and politicians to save the remaining rainforest in Australia. How do you deal with the despair?"

He replied, "I try to remember that it's not me, John Seed, trying to protect the rainforest. Rather I'm part of the rainforest protecting myself. I am that part of the rainforest recently emerged into human thinking." This is what I mean by the greening of the self. It involves a combining of the mystical with the practical and the pragmatic, transcending separateness, alienation, and fragmentation. It is a shift that Seed himself calls "a spiritual change," generating a sense of profound interconnectedness with all life.

This is hardly new to our species. In the past poets and mystics have been speaking and writing about these ideas, but not people on the barricades agitating for social change. Now the sense of an encompassing self, that deep identity with the wider reaches of life, is a motivation for action. It is a source of courage that helps us stand up to the powers that are still, through force of inertia, working for the destruction of our world. I am convinced that this expanded sense of self is the *only* basis for adequate and effective action.

When you look at what is happening to our world—and it is hard to look at what's happening to our water, our air, our trees, our fellow species—it becomes clear that unless you have some roots in a spiritual practice that holds life sacred and encourages joyful communion with all your fellow beings, facing the enormous challenges ahead becomes nearly impossible.

Robert Bellah's book *Habits of the Heart* is not a place where you are going to read about the greening of the self. But it is where you will read *why* there has to be a greening of the self, because it describes the cramp that our society has gotten itself into with its rampant, indeed pathological, individualism. Bellah points out that the individualism that sprang from the Romantic movement of the eighteenth and nineteenth centuries (the seeds of which were planted even earlier than that) is accelerating and causing great suffering, alienation and fragmentation in our century. Bellah calls for a moral ecology which he defines as a moral connectedness or interdependence. He says, "We have to treat others as part of who we are, rather than as a 'them' with whom we are in constant competition."

To Robert Bellah, I respond, "It is happening." It is happening in the arising of the ecological self. And it is happening because of three converging developments. First, the conventional small self, or ego-self is being impinged upon by the psychological and spiritual effects we are suffering from facing the dangers of mass annihilation. The second thing working to dismantle the ego-self is a way of seeing that has arisen out of science itself. It is called the systems view, cybernetics, or new paradigm science. From this perspective, life is seen as dynamically composed of self-organizing systems, patterns that are sustained in and by their relationships. The third force is the resurgence in our time of non-dualistic spiritualities. Here I am speaking from my own experience with Buddhism, but it is also happening in other faith-systems and religions, such as "creation spirituality" in Christianity. These developments are impinging on the self in ways that are undermining it, or helping it to break out of its boundaries and old definitions. Instead of ego-self, we witness the emergence of an eco-self!

The move to a wider ecological sense of self is in large part a function of the dangers that are threatening to overwhelm us. Given nuclear proliferation and the progressive destruction of our biosphere, polls show that people today are aware that the world, as they know it, may come to an end. I am convinced that this loss of certainty that there will be a future is the pivotal psychological reality of our time. The fact that it is not talked about very much makes it all the more pivotal, because nothing is more preoccupying or energy-draining than that which we repress.

Why do I claim that this erodes the old sense of self? Because once we stop denying the crises of our time and let ourselves experience the depth of our own responses to the pain of our world—whether it is the burning of the Amazon rainforest, the famines of Africa, or the homeless in our own cities—the grief or anger or fear we experience cannot be reduced to concerns for our own individual skin. It can never be the same.

When we mourn over the destruction of our biosphere, it is categorically distinct from mourning over our own death. We suffer with our world—that is the literal meaning of compassion. It isn't some private craziness. Yet, when I was weeping over the napalming of villages in Vietnam twenty years ago, I was told that I was suffering from a hangover of Puritan guilt. When I expressed myself against President Reagan, they said I had unresolved problems regarding my own father. How often have you had your concerns for political and ecological realities subjected to reductionist pop-therapy? How often have you heard, "What are you running away from in your life that you are letting yourself get so concerned about those homeless people? Perhaps you have some unresolved issues? Maybe you're sexually unfulfilled?" It can go on and on. But increasingly it is being recognized that a compassionate response is neither craziness nor a dodge. It is the opposite; it is a signal of our own evolution, a measure of our humanity. We are capable of suffering with our world, and that is the true meaning of compassion. It enables us to recognize our profound interconnectedness with all beings. Don't ever apologize for crying for the trees burning in the Amazon or over the waters polluted from mines in the Rockies. Don't apologize for the sorrow, grief, and rage you feel. It is a measure of your humanity and your maturity. It is a measure of your open heart, and as your heart breaks open there will be room for the world to heal. That is what is happening as we see people honestly confronting the sorrows of our time. And it is an adaptive response.

The crisis that threatens our planet, whether seen from its military, ecological, or social aspect, derives from a dysfunctional and pathological notion of the self. It derives from a mistake about our place in the order of things. It is a delusion that the self is so separate and fragile that we must delineate and defend its boundaries, that it is so small and so needy that we must endlessly acquire and endlessly consume, and that it is so aloof that as individuals, corporations, nation-states, or species, we can be immune to what we do to other beings.

This view of human nature is not new, of course. Many have felt the imperative to extend self-interest to embrace the whole. What is notable in our situation is that this extension of identity can come not through an effort to be noble or good or altruistic, but simply to be present and own our pain. And that is why this shift in the sense of self is credible to people. As the poet Theodore Roethke said, "I believe my pain."

This "despair and empowerment" work derives from two other forces I mentioned earlier: systems theory, or cybernetics, and nondualistic spirituality, particularly Buddhism. I will now turn to what we could call the cybernetics of the self.

The findings of twentieth-century science undermine the notion of a separate self, distinct from the world it observes and acts upon. Einstein showed that the self's perceptions are shaped by its changing position in relation to other phenomena. And

Heisenberg, in his uncertainty principle, demonstrated that the very act of observation changes what is observed.

Contemporary science, and systems science in particular, goes farther in challenging old assumptions about a distinct, separate, continuous self, by showing that there is no logical or scientific basis for construing one part of the experienced world as "me" and the rest as "other." That is so because as open, self-organizing systems, our very breathing, acting, and thinking arise in interaction with our shared world through the currents of matter, energy, and information that move through us and sustain us. In the web of relationships that sustain these activities there is no clear line demarcating a separate, continuous self.

As postmodern systems theorists say, "There is no categorical 'I' set over against a categorical 'you' or 'it.'" One of the clearer expositions of this is found in the teachings and writings of Gregory Bateson, whom I earlier quoted as saying that the abstraction of a separate "I" is the epistemological fallacy of Western civilization. He says that the process that decides and acts cannot be neatly identified with the isolated subjectivity of the individual or located within the confines of the skin. He contends that "the total self-corrective unit that processes information is a system whose boundaries do not at all coincide with the boundaries either of the body or what is popularly called 'self' or 'consciousness.'" He goes on to say, "The self is ordinarily understood as only a small part of a much larger trial-and-error system which does the thinking, acting, and deciding." Bateson offers two helpful examples. One is the woodcutter, about to fell a tree. His hands grip the handle of the axe, there is the head of the axe, the trunk of the tree. Whump, he makes a cut, and then whump, another cut. What is the feedback circuit, where is the information that is guiding that cutting down of the tree? It is a whole circle; you can begin at any point. It moves from the eye of the woodcutter, to the hand, to the axe, and back to the cut in the tree. That is the self-correcting unit, that is what is doing the chopping down of the tree.

In another illustration, a blind person with a cane is walking along the sidewalk. Tap, tap, whoops, there's a fire hydrant, there's a curb. What is doing the walking? Where is the self then of the blind person? What is doing the perceiving and deciding? That self-corrective feedback circuit is the arm, the hand, the cane, the curb, the ear. At that moment that is the self that is walking. Bateson's point is that the self is a false reification of an improperly delimited part of a much larger field of interlocking processes. And he goes on to maintain that:

> this false reification of the self is basic to the planetary
> ecological crisis in which we find ourselves. We have
> imagined that we are a unit of survival and we have to
> see to our own survival, and we imagine that the unit of
> survival is the separate individual or a separate species,
> whereas in reality through the history of evolution, it is
> the individual plus the environment, the species plus
> the environment, for they are essentially symbiotic.

The self is a metaphor. We can decide to limit it to our skin, our person, our family, our organization, or our species. We can select its boundaries in objective reality. As the systems theorists see it, our consciousness illuminates a small arc in the wider currents and loops of knowing that interconnect us. It is just as plausible to conceive of mind as coexistent with these larger circuits, the entire "pattern that connects," as Bateson said.

Do not think that to broaden the construct of self this way involves an eclipse of one's distinctiveness. Do not think that you will lose your identity like a drop in the ocean merging into the oneness of Brahman. From the systems perspective this interaction, creating larger wholes and patterns, allows for and even requires diversity. You become more yourself. Integration and differentiation go hand in hand.

The third factor that is aiding in the dismantling of the ego-self and the creation of the eco-self is the resurgence of nondualistic spiritualities. Buddhism is distinctive in the clarity and sophistication with which it deals with the constructs and the dynamics of self. In much the same way as systems theory does, Buddhism undermines categorical distinctions between self and other and belies the concept of a continuous, self-existent entity. It then goes farther than systems theory in showing the pathogenic character of any reifications of the self. It goes farther still in offering methods for transcending these difficulties and healing this suffering. What the Buddha woke up to under the Bodhi tree was the *paticca samuppada,* the co-arising of phenomena, in which you cannot isolate a separate, continuous self.

We think, "What do we do with the self, this clamorous 'I,' always wanting attention, always wanting its goodies? Do we crucify it, sacrifice it, mortify it, punish it, or do we make it noble?" Upon awaking we realize, "Oh, it just isn't there." It's a convention, just a convenient convention. When you take it too seriously, when you suppose that it is something enduring which you have to defend and promote, it becomes the foundation of delusion, the motive behind our attachments and our aversions.

For a beautiful illustration of a deviation-amplifying feedback loop, consider *Yama* holding the wheel of life. There are the domains, the various realms of beings, and at the center of that wheel of suffering are three figures: the snake, the rooster, and the pig—delusion, greed, and aversion—and they just chase each other around and around. The linchpin is the notion of our self, the notion that we have to protect that self or punish it or do *something* with it.

Oh, the sweetness of being able to realize: I am my experience. I am this breathing. I am this moment, and it is changing, continually arising in the fountain of life. We do not need to be doomed to the perpetual rat-race. The vicious circle can be broken by the wisdom, *prajña,* that arises when we see that "self" is just an idea; by the practice of meditation, *dhyana;* and by the practice of morality, *shila,* where attention to our experience and to our actions reveals that they do not need to be in bondage to a separate self.

Far from the nihilism and escapism that is often imputed to the Buddhist path, this liberation, this awakening puts one *into* the world with a livelier, more caring sense of social engagement. The sense of interconnectedness that can then arise, is imaged—one of the most beautiful images coming out of the Mahayana—as the jeweled net of Indra. It is a vision of reality structured very much like the holographic view of the universe, so that each being is at each node of the net, each jewel reflects all the others, reflecting back and catching the reflection, just as systems theory sees that the part contains the whole.

The awakening to our true self is the awakening to that entirety, breaking out of the prison-self of separate ego. The one who perceives this is the bodhisattva—and we are all bodhisattvas because we are all capable of experiencing that—it is our true nature. We are profoundly interconnected and therefore we are all able to recognize and act upon our deep, intricate, and intimate inter-existence with each other and all beings. That true nature of ours is already present in our pain for the world.

When we turn our eyes away from that homeless figure, are we indifferent or is the pain of seeing him or her too great? Do not be easily duped about the apparent indifference of those around you.

What looks like apathy is really the fear of suffering. But the bodhisattva knows that to experience the pain of all beings is necessary to experience their joy. It says in *The Lotus Sutra* that the bodhisattva hears the music of the spheres, and understands the language of the birds, while hearing the cries in the deepest levels of hell.

One of the things I like best about the green self, the ecological self that is arising in our time, is that it is making moral exhortation irrelevant. Sermonizing is both boring and ineffective. This is pointed out by Arne Naess, the Norwegian philosopher who coined the phrase "deep ecology." This great systems view of the world helps us recognize our embeddedness in nature, overcomes our alienation from the rest of creation, and changes the way we can experience our self through an ever-widening process of identification.

Naess calls this self-realization, a progression "where the self to be realized extends further and further beyond the separate ego and includes more and more of the phenomenal world." And he says,

> In this process, notions such as altruism and moral duty are left behind. It is tacitly based on the Latin term "ego" which has as its opposite the "alter." Altruism implies that the ego sacrifices its interests in favor of the other, the alter. The motivation is primarily that of duty. It is said we *ought* to love others as strongly as we love our self. There are, however, very limited numbers among humanity capable of loving from mere duty or from moral exhortation.

Unfortunately, the extensive moralizing within the ecological movement has given the public the false impression that they are being asked to make a sacrifice—to show more responsibility, more concern, and a nicer moral standard. But all of that would flow naturally and easily if the self were widened and deepened so that the protection of nature was felt and perceived as protection of our very selves.

Please note this important point: virtue is *not* required for the greening of the self or the emergence of the ecological self. The shift in identification at this point in our history is required precisely *because* moral exhortation doesn't work, and because sermons seldom hinder us from following our self-interest as we conceive it.

The obvious choice, then, is to extend our notions of self-interest. For example, it would not occur to me to plead with you, "Oh, don't saw off your leg. That would be an act of violence." It wouldn't occur to me because your leg is part of your body. Well, so are the trees in the Amazon rain basin. They are our external lungs. And we are beginning to realize that the world is our body.

This ecological self, like any notion of selfhood, is a metaphoric construct and a dynamic one. It involves choice; choices can be made to identify at different moments, with different dimensions or aspects of our systemically interrelated existence—be they hunted whales or homeless humans or the planet itself. In doing this the extended self brings into play wider resources—courage, endurance, ingenuity—like a nerve cell in a neural net opening to the charge of the other neurons.

There is the sense of being acted through and sustained by those very beings on whose behalf one acts. This is very close to the religious concept of grace. In systems language we can talk about it as a synergy. But with this extension, this greening of the self, we can find a sense of buoyancy and resilience that comes from letting flow through us strengths and resources that come to us with continuous surprise and sense of blessing.

We know that we are not limited by the accident of our birth or the timing of it, and we recognize the truth that we have always been around. We can reinhabit time and own our story as a species. We were present back there in the fireball and the rains that streamed down on this still molten planet, and in the primordial seas. We remember that in our mother's womb, where we wear vestigial gills and tail and fins for hands. We remember that. That information is in us and there is a deep, deep kinship in us, beneath the outer layers of our neocortex or what we learned in school. There is a deep wisdom, a bondedness with our creation, and an ingenuity far beyond what we think we have. And when we expand our notions of what we are to include in this story, we will have a wonderful time and we will survive.

PART V

COMMUNITY

THICH NHAT HANH

Community as a Resource
1994

O NE TIME THE Buddha visited a small community of three monks in a bamboo forest near Kosambi. Anuruddha, Nandiya, and Kimbila were extremely happy to see the Buddha— Nandiya took the Buddha's bowl, Kimbila took his outer robe, and they cleared a place for him to sit next to a yellow bamboo thicket. With their palms joined, the three monks bowed to the Buddha, and the Buddha invited them to sit down. "How is your practice going?" he asked. "Are you content here? Do you encounter difficulties while begging for alms or sharing the teachings?"

Anuruddha answered, "Lord, we are most content here. It is calm and peaceful. We receive ample food offerings, we are able to share the Dharma, and we are making progress in our practice."

The Buddha then asked, "Do you live in harmony?"

Anuruddha replied, "Lord, we do live in harmony, like milk and honey. Living with Nandiya and Kimbila is a great blessing. I treasure their friendship. Before saying or doing anything, I always reflect on whether my words or actions will be helpful for my brothers. If I feel any doubt, I refrain from speaking or acting. Lord, we are three, but we are also one."

The Buddha nodded in assent and looked at the other two monks. Kimbila said, "Anuruddha speaks the truth. We live in harmony and care deeply for each other." Nandiya added, "We share all things—our food, our insight, and our experience."

The Buddha praised them, "Excellent! I am most pleased to hear how you live. A community is truly a community when there is harmony. You demonstrate real awakening."

The Buddha stayed with the monks for a month, and he observed the way they went begging each morning after meditation. Whoever returned first prepared a place for the other two, gathered water for washing, and set out an empty bowl, into which he would place some food in case one of his brothers did not receive enough offerings. After all three monks finished eating, they placed their leftover food on the ground or in the stream, careful not to harm any of the creatures who lived there. Then they washed their bowls together. When one of them noticed something that needed tending, he did it at once, and all of them worked together on tasks that required more than one person. And they sat together regularly to share their insights and experiences.

Before leaving the Bamboo Forest, the Buddha told the three monks, "The nature of a community is harmony, and harmony can be realized by following the Six Concords: sharing space, sharing the essentials of daily life, observing the same precepts, using only words that contribute to harmony, sharing insights and understanding, and respecting each other's viewpoints. A community that follows these principles will live happily and in peace. Monks, please continue to practice this way." The monks were overjoyed to spend a month with the Buddha and to receive such encouragement from him.

When we were in our mother's womb, we felt secure—protected from heat, cold, and hunger. But the moment we were born and came into contact with the world's suffering, we began to cry. Since then, we have yearned to return to the security of our mother's womb. We long for permanence, but everything is changing. We desire an absolute, but even what we call our "self" is impermanent. We seek a place where we can feel safe and secure, a place we can rely on for a long time.

When we touch the ground, we feel the stability of the earth and feel confident. When we observe the steadiness of the sunshine, the air, and the trees, we know that we can count on the sun to rise each day and the air and the trees to be there tomorrow. When we build a house, we build it on ground that is solid. Before putting our trust in others, we need to choose friends who are stable, on whom we can rely. "Taking refuge" is not based on blind faith or wishful thinking. It is gauged by our real experience.

We all need something good, beautiful, and true to take refuge in. To take refuge in mindfulness, our capacity of being aware of what is going on in the present moment, is safe and not at all abstract. When we drink a glass of water and know we are drinking a glass of water, that is mindfulness. When we sit, walk, stand, or breathe and know that we are sitting, walking, standing, or breathing, we touch the seed of mindfulness in us, and, after a few days, our mindfulness will grow stronger. Mindfulness is the light that shows us the way. It is the living Buddha inside of us. Mindfulness gives rise to insight, awakening, and love. We all have the seed of mindfulness within us and, through the practice of conscious breathing, we can learn to touch it.

Taking refuge in our capacity to wake up is a daily practice. If we wait for difficulties to arise before we begin to practice, it will be too late. When the bad news arrives, we will not know how to cope. If we cultivate our own strengths and abilities by taking refuge in our breathing and our mindfulness every day, several times a day, we will be solid and will know what to do and what not to do to help the situation.

When we cut our skin, our body has the capacity to heal itself. We only need to wash the wound, and our body will do the rest. The same is true of our consciousness. When we feel anger, distress, or despair, if we breathe consciously and recognize the feeling, our consciousness will know what to do to heal these wounds. To practice mindful living is to take refuge in our body, and also in our mind.

> I take refuge in the Buddha,
> the one who shows me the way in this life.
> I take refuge in the Dharma,
> the way of understanding and love.
> I take refuge in the Sangha,
> the community that lives in harmony and awareness.

Taking refuge in the Three Jewels is a very deep practice. It means, first of all, to take refuge in ourselves. Taking refuge in the Buddha in myself, I vow to realize the Great Way in order to give rise to the highest mind. Taking refuge in the Dharma in myself, I vow to attain understanding and wisdom as immense as the ocean. Taking refuge in the Sangha in myself, I vow to build a community without obstacles.

If, for example, you are a single parent and think that you need to be married in order to have stability, please reconsider. You may have more stability right now than with another person. Taking refuge in yourself protects the stability you already have. Taking refuge in what is solid helps you become more solid and develop yourself into a ground of refuge for your child and your friends. Please make yourself into someone we can rely on. We need you—the children need you, the trees and the birds also need you. Please practice going back to yourself, living each moment of your life fully, in mindfulness. Walking, breathing, sitting, eating, and drinking tea in mindfulness are all ways of taking refuge.

Taking refuge in a Sangha means putting your trust in a community of solid members who practice mindfulness together. It is difficult if not impossible to practice mindfulness without a Sangha. Teachers and teachings are important for the practice, but a community of friends is the most essential ingredient. We need a Sangha to support our practice.

When we practice breathing, smiling, and living mindfully with our family, our family becomes our Sangha. If there is a bell at home, the bell is also part of the Sangha, because the bell helps us to practice. Our meditation cushion is a part of our Sangha, too. Many elements help us practice.

We can begin our Sangha-building by inviting one friend to come over for tea meditation, sitting meditation, walking meditation, precept recitation, or Dharma discussion. These are all efforts to establish a Sangha at home. Later, when others wish to join, we can form a small group and meet weekly or monthly. Someday in the future we may even wish to set up a country retreat center. But the practice is not to seclude ourselves for many years in order to attain enlightenment. Real transformation, real enlightenment, is possible only when we stay in touch.

Every Sangha has its problems. It is natural. If you suffer because you do not have confidence in your Sangha and feel on the verge of leaving, I hope you will make the effort to continue. You do not need a perfect Sangha. An imperfect one is good enough. We do our best to transform the Sangha by transforming ourselves into a positive element of the Sangha, accepting the Sangha, and building on it. The principle is to organize the Sangha in a way that is enjoyable for everyone.

Siddhartha, the Buddha-to-be, invited the children of Uruvela village, the water of the Neranjara River, the Bodhi tree, the kusha grass, and many birds and flowers into his Sangha. We have more possibilities available in each moment than we may realize. I know of people who have been in prisons or in reeducation camps in Vietnam who were able to practice walking meditation in their cells. We should not miss the opportunity to set up a Sangha. The Sangha is a jewel.

Ditthadhamma sukhavihari means "dwelling happily in the present moment." We don't rush to the future, because we know that everything is here in the present moment. We know that we have arrived. Walking meditation can help a lot. We walk and touch our deepest happiness. In Plum Village, we always walk mindfully, and we are a bell of mindfulness for others. I practice for you, and you practice for me. Other people are very important.

We do not have to practice intensively. If we allow ourselves to be in a good Sangha, transformation will come naturally. Just being in a Sangha where people are happy, living deeply the moments of their days, is enough. Transformation will happen without effort. The most important thing a Dharma teacher can offer his or her students is the art of Sangha-building. Knowing the sutras is not enough. The main concern is building a happy Sangha—taking care of each person, looking into his pain, her difficulties, his aspirations, her fear, his hopes in order to make everyone comfortable and happy. This takes time and energy.

When the Buddha was eighty years old, King Prasenajit, who was also eighty, told him, "My Lord, when I look at your Sangha, I feel confidence in the Lord." When the king observed the Buddha's community of monks and nuns and saw the peace and joy emanating from them, he felt great confidence in the Buddha. When we see a Sangha whose practice reveals peace, calm, and happiness, confidence is born in us right away. Through the Sangha, you see the teacher. A teacher without a Sangha is not effective enough. The value of a doctor, a psychotherapist, or a Dharma teacher can be seen in the Sangha around her. Looking at the Sangha, we can see her capacity for helping people.

It is a joy to be in the midst of a Sangha where people are practicing well together. Each person's way of walking, eating, and smiling can be a source of inspiration. If we just put someone who needs to be helped in the midst of such a Sangha, even if that person does not practice, he will be transformed. The only thing he has to do is allow himself to be there. As a teacher, I am always nourished by my Sangha. Any achievement in the Sangha supports me and gives me strength. It is so important to build a Sangha that is happy, where communication is open.

If you don't have a good Sangha yet, please spend your time and energy building one. If you are a psychotherapist, a doctor, a social worker, a peace worker, or an environmentalist, you need a Sangha. Without a Sangha, you will burn out very soon. A psychotherapist can choose among his clients who have overcome their difficulties, who recognize him as a friend or a brother in order to form a group. We need brothers and sisters in the practice in order to continue. In Vietnam we say, "When a tiger leaves his mountain and goes to the lowlands, he will be caught by humans and killed." When a practitioner leaves her Sangha, at some time she will abandon her practice. She will not be able to continue practicing very long without a Sangha. Sangha-building is a crucial element of the practice.

If there is no Sangha in your area, try to identify elements for a future Sangha—your children, your partner, a path in the woods, the blue sky, some beautiful trees—and use your creative talents to develop a Sangha for your own support and practice. We need you to water the seeds of peace, joy, and loving kindness in yourself and others so that all of us will blossom.

Every time I see someone without roots, I see him or her as a hungry ghost. In Buddhist mythology, a hungry ghost is a wandering soul whose throat is too narrow for food or drink to pass through. Hungry ghosts need love, but they do not have the capacity to receive it. They understand in principle that there is beauty in life, but they are not capable of touching it. Something is preventing them from touching the refreshing and healing elements of life. They want to forget life, and they turn to all kinds of intoxicants to help them forget. If we tell them not to, they will not listen. They have heard enough. What they need is something to take refuge in, something that proves to them that life is meaningful. To help a hungry ghost, first of all we have to listen deeply to him or her, to provide an atmosphere of family, and to help him or her experience something beautiful and true to believe in.

Our society produces millions of hungry ghosts, people of all ages. I have seen children just ten years old who have no roots at all, who have never experienced happiness at home and have nothing to believe in or belong to. This is the main sickness of our time. With nothing to believe in, how can a person survive? How can he find the energy to smile or touch the linden tree or the beautiful sky? He is lost, living with no sense of responsibility. Alcohol, drugs, and craving are destroying his body and soul, but he has nowhere to turn. The availability of drugs is only a secondary cause of the problem. The primary cause is the lack of meaning in people's lives. Those who abuse drugs or alcohol are unhappy; they do not accept themselves, their families, their society, or their traditions. They have renounced them all.

We cannot be by ourselves alone, we can only "inter-be" with everyone else, including our ancestors and future generations. Our "self" is made only of non-self elements. Our sorrow and suffering, our joy and peace have their roots in society, nature, and those with whom we live. When we practice mindful living and deep looking, we see the truth of interbeing.

I hope communities of practice will organize themselves in warm, friendly ways, as families. We need to create environments in which people can succeed easily in the practice. If each person is an island, not communicating with others, transformation and healing cannot be obtained. To practice meditation, we must be rooted. Buddhism helps us get rooted again in our society, culture, and family. The Buddha never suggested that we abandon our own roots in order to embrace something else.

Interpersonal relationships are the key to the practice. With the support of even one person, you develop stability, and later you can reach out to others. In Asian Buddhist communities, we address one another as Dharma brother, Dharma sister, Dharma uncle, or Dharma aunt, and we call our teacher Dharma father or Dharma mother. A practice center needs to possess that kind of familial brotherhood and sisterhood for us to be nourished. Aware that we are seeking love, Sangha members will treat us in a way that helps us get rooted. In a spiritual family, we have a second chance to get rooted.

In the past, we lived in extended families. Our houses were surrounded by trees and hammocks, and people had time to relax together. The nuclear family is a recent invention. Besides mother and father, there are just one or two children. When the parents have a problem, the atmosphere at home is heavy and there is nowhere to escape, not even enough air to breathe. Even if the child goes into the bathroom to hide, the heaviness pervades the bathroom. The children of today are growing up with many seeds of suffering. Unless we intervene, they will transmit those seeds to their children.

At Plum Village, children are at the center of attention. Each adult is responsible for helping the children feel happy and secure. We know that if the children are happy, the adults will be happy, too.

I hope that communities of practice will take this kind of shape in the West, with the warmth and flavor of an extended family. I have seen some practice centers where children are regarded as obstacles to the practice. We have to form communities where children are viewed as the children of everyone. If a child is hitting another child, his parents are not the only ones responsible. Everyone in the community has to work together to find ways to help the children. One adult might try holding the child back, not as a policeman, but as an uncle or aunt. Of course, the parents should prevent their child from hitting others, but if they cannot discipline their child, they have to let an uncle or an aunt do it. In the practice center, there should be a garden where the children can play, and there should be people skillful in helping children. If we can do that, everyone—parents and non-parents—will enjoy the practice. If we form practice communities as extended families, the elderly will not have to live apart from the rest of society. Grandparents love to hold children in their arms and tell them fairy tales. If we can do that, everyone will be very happy.

Nowadays, when things become difficult, couples think of divorce. In traditional cultures, the whole community worked together to help the couple find ways to live in harmony and understanding together. Some people today divorce three, four, or five times. This is an issue that Buddhist practice has to address. How can we create a community that supports couples? How can we support single parents? How can we bring the practice community into the family and the family into the practice community?

If you are a single parent raising your child alone, you have to be both a mother and a father. You have to let go of the idea that you will not be complete unless that "someone" or "something" is with you. You yourself are enough. You can transform yourself into a cozy, stable hermitage, filled with light, air, and order, and you will begin to feel great peace and joy.

It is not easy for a single mother to also be a father, but with a good Sangha helping by being uncles and aunts, you can do your best to play both roles. One day the Abbot of Kim Son Monastery in California said to me, "Thay, you are our mother." Something in me has the manner of being a mother. When I am with children, I can play the role of a mother as well as a father.

Single parenting is widespread in the West. If you succeed in bringing your child up happily, then you can share the fruit of your practice with many people. Single parenting is a Dharma door. Parenting is a Dharma door. We need retreats and seminars to discuss the best ways to raise our children. We do not accept the ancient ways of parenting, but we have not fully developed modern ways of doing so. We need to draw on our practice and our experience to bring new dimensions to family life. Combining the nuclear family with the practice community may be a successful model. We bring our children to the practice center, and all of us benefit. When the children are happy, the adults will be happy also, and everyone will enjoy the practice.

Many people were abused or beaten by their parents, and many more were severely criticized or rejected by them. These people have so many seeds of unhappiness in their consciousness that they do not even want to hear their father's or mother's name. When I meet someone like this, I usually suggest that he or she practice the meditation on the five-year-old child. It is a kind of mindfulness massage.

"Breathing in, I see myself as a five-year-old child. Breathing out, I smile to the five-year-old child in me." During the meditation, you try to see yourself as a five-year-old child. If you look deeply at that child, you see that you are vulnerable and can be easily hurt. A stern look or a shout can cause internal formations in your store consciousness. When your parents fight, your five-year-old receives many seeds of suffering. I have heard young people say, "The most precious gift my parents can give is their own happiness." Because he himself was unhappy, your father made you suffer a lot. Now you visualize yourself as a five-year-old child. Smiling at that child in yourself, you experience real compassion. "I was so young and tender, and I received so much pain."

The next day, I would advise you to practice, "Breathing in, I see my father as a five-year-old child. Breathing out, I smile to that child with compassion." We are not accustomed to thinking of our father as a child. We picture him as having always been an adult—stern and with great authority. We do not take the time to see our father as a tender, young boy who was easily wounded by others. To help you visualize your father as a young boy, you can peruse the family album and study images of your father when he was young. When you are able to see him as fragile and vulnerable, you may realize that he must have been the victim of someone also, perhaps his father. If he received too many seeds of suffering from his father, it is natural that he will not know how to treat his own son properly. He made you suffer, and the circle of samsara continues. Unless you practice mindfulness, you will probably behave exactly the same way towards your children. But if you see your father as himself a victim, compassion will be born in your heart and you will smile. By bringing mindfulness and insight into your pain, your anger toward him will begin to dissolve, and one day, you will be able to say, "Dad, I understand you. You suffered very much during your childhood."

One fourteen-year-old boy who practices at Plum Village told me this story. He said that every time he fell down and hurt himself, his father would shout at him. The boy vowed that when he grew up, he would not act that way. But one time his little sister was playing with other children and she fell off a swing and scraped her knee, and the boy became very angry. His sister's knee was bleeding and he wanted to shout at her, "How can you be so stupid! Why did you do that?" But he caught himself. Because he had been practicing breathing and mindfulness, he was able to recognize his anger and not act on it.

While the adults were taking care of his sister, washing her wound and putting a bandage on it, he walked away slowly and meditated on his anger. Suddenly he saw that he was exactly the same as his father. He told me, "I realized that if I did not do something about the anger in me, I would transmit it to my children." He saw that the seeds of his father's anger must have been transmitted by his grandparents. This was a remarkable insight for a fourteen-year-old boy. Because he had been practicing, he could see clearly like that.

It is important that we realize that we are the continuation of our ancestors through our parents. By making peace with our parents *in us,* we have a chance to make real peace with our real parents.

For those who are alienated from their families, their culture, or their society, it is sometimes difficult to practice. Even if they meditate intensively for many years, it is hard for them to be transformed as long as they remain isolated. We have to establish links with others. Buddhist practice should help us return home and accept the best things in our culture. Reconnecting with our roots, we can learn deep looking and compassionate understanding. Practice is not an individual matter. We practice with our parents, our ancestors, our children, and their children.

There are gems in our own tradition that have come down to us, and we cannot ignore them. Even the food we eat has our ancestors in it. How can we believe that we can cut ourselves off from our culture? We must honor our tradition. It is in us. Meditation shows us the way to do so. Whether we are Christian, Jewish, Muslim, Buddhist, or something else, we have to study the ways of our ancestors and find the best elements of the tradition. We have to allow the ancestors in us to be liberated. The moment we can offer them joy, peace, and freedom, we offer joy, peace, and freedom to ourselves, our children, and their children at the same time. Doing so, we remove all limits and discrimination and create a world in which all traditions are honored.

Some of us do not like to talk or think about our roots, because we have suffered so much. We want something new, but our ancestors in us are urging us to come back and connect with them—their joy and their pain. The moment we accept this, transformation will take place right away, and our pain will begin to dissolve. We realize that we are a continuation of our ancestors and that we are the ancestors of all future generations. It is crucial for us to "return home" and make peace with ourselves and our society.

There is no need to be afraid of going home. It is at home that we touch the most beautiful things. Home is in the present moment, which is the only moment we can touch life. If we do not go back to the present moment, how can we touch the beautiful sunset or the eyes of our dear child? Without going home, how can we touch our heart, our lungs, our liver, or our eyes to give them a chance to be healthy? At home, we can touch the refreshing, beautiful, and healing elements of life.

When we touch the present moment deeply, we also touch the past, and all the damage that was done in the past can be repaired. The way to take care of the future is also to take good care of the present moment.

One Frenchwoman I know left home at the age of seventeen to live in England, because she was so angry at her mother. Thirty years later, after reading a book on Buddhism, she felt the desire to reconcile with her mother, and her mother felt the same. But every time the two of them met, there was a kind of explosion. Their seeds of suffering had been cultivated over many years, and there was a lot of habit energy. The willingness to make peace is not enough. We also need to practice.

I invited her to come to Plum Village to practice sitting, walking, breathing, eating, and drinking tea in mindfulness, and through that daily practice, she was able to touch the seeds of her anger. After practicing for several weeks, she wrote a letter of reconciliation to her mother. Without her mother present, it was easier to write such a letter. When her mother read it, she tasted the fruit of her daughter's flower watering, and peace was finally possible.

If you love someone, the greatest gift you can give is your presence. The most meaningful declaration we can offer is, "Darling, I am here for you." Without your attention, the person you love may die slowly. When she is suffering, you have to make yourself available right away: "Darling, I know that you are suffering. I am here for you." This is the practice of mindfulness. If you yourself suffer, you have to go to the person you love and tell him, "Darling, I am suffering. Please help." If you cannot say that, something is wrong in your relationship. Pride does not have a place in true love. Pride should not prevent you from going to him and saying that you suffer and need his help. We need each other.

One day in Plum Village, I saw a young woman walking who looked like a hungry ghost. The flowers were blooming everywhere, but she could not touch them. She seemed to be dying of loneliness. She had come to Plum Village to be with others, but when she was there, she was not able to be with anyone. I thought she must come from a broken family, from a society that does not appreciate her, and from a tradition not capable of nourishing her. I have met many people without roots. They want to leave their parents, their society, and their nation behind and find something that is good, beautiful, and true to believe in. People like that come to meditation centers, but without roots, they cannot absorb the teaching. They do not trust easily, so the first thing we have to do is earn their trust.

In Asian countries, we have an ancestors' altar in each home and offer flowers, fruits, and drink to them. We feel that our ancestors are with us. But, at the same time, we are aware that many hungry ghosts have nowhere to go. So once a year we set up a special table and offer them food and drink. Hungry ghosts are hungry for love, understanding, and something to believe in. They have not received love, and no one understands them. It is difficult for them to receive food, water, or love. Our society produces thousands of hungry ghosts every day. We have to look deeply to understand them.

We need two families—blood and spiritual—to be stable and happy. If our parents are happy together, they will transmit the love, trust, and the values of our ancestors to us. When we are on good terms with our parents, we are connected with our blood ancestors through them. But when we are not, we can become rootless, like a hungry ghost.

Transmission has three components: the one who transmits, the object transmitted, and the receiver. Our body and our consciousness have been transmitted to us by our parents, and we are the receiver. When we look deeply, we can see that the three components are one. In Buddhism, we call this the "emptiness of transmission." Our parents did not transmit anything less than themselves—their seeds of suffering, happiness, and talent, which they received, at least in part, from their ancestors. We are very much a continuation of our parents and our ancestors. To be angry at our parents is to be angry at ourselves. To reconcile with our parents is to make peace with ourselves.

An American young man who came to Plum Village told me that he was extremely angry at his father even after his father had passed away. So the young man put a photo of his father on his desk, and practiced looking into the eyes of his father. Doing this, he was able to see his father's suffering and he realized that his father had been incapable of transmitting seeds of love and trust, because he had not touched these seeds in himself. When the young man became aware of that, he was able to forgive his father. He also realized that if he did not practice mindfulness, the seeds of love and trust in him would remain buried. He made peace with his parents, and through this act, reconnected with all of his blood ancestors.

In our spiritual family, we have ancestors, too, those who represent the tradition. But if they were not happy, if they were not lucky enough to receive the jewels of the tradition, they will not be able to transmit them to us. If we do not respect our pastor, our rabbi, our priest, we may decide to leave the tradition. Disconnected from our spiritual ancestors, we suffer, and our children suffer, too. We have to look deeply to see what is wrong. When those who represent our tradition do not embody the best values of the tradition, there must be causes, and when we see the causes, insight and acceptance arise. Then we are able to return home, reconnect with our spiritual mentors, and help them.

Through the practice of mindfulness, we can discover the jewels of our spiritual traditions. In Christianity, for example, Holy Communion is an act of mindfulness—eating our bread deeply in order to touch the entire cosmos. In Judaism, mindfulness is there when you set the table or light the Sabbath candles. Everything is done in the presence of God. The equivalents of the Three Jewels can be found in Christianity, Judaism, Islam, and other great traditions. After practicing mindfulness, you will be able to return to your spiritual home and discover the jewels of your own tradition. I hope you will do so, for your nourishment and the nourishment of your children. Without roots, we cannot be happy and our children cannot be happy. Returning home and touching the wondrous jewels of our blood and spiritual traditions, we become whole.

We need to establish retreat centers where we can go from time to time to renew ourselves. The features of the landscape, the buildings, even the sound of the bell can be designed to remind us to return to awareness. The residential community there does not need to be large. Ten or fifteen people who emanate freshness and peace, the fruits of living in awareness, are enough. When we are there, they care for us, console us, support us, and help us heal our wounds. Even when we cannot actually go there, just thinking of the center makes us smile and feel more at peace.

The residents can organize larger retreats occasionally to teach the art of enjoying life and taking care of each other. Mindful living is an art, and a retreat center can be a place where joy and happiness are authentic. The community can also offer Days of Mindfulness for people to come and live happily together for one day, and they can organize study courses on mindfulness, conscious breathing, Buddhist psychology, and transformation. We must work together with everyone in peace and harmony. Using each person's talents and ideas, we can organize retreats and Days of Mindfulness that children and adults love and want to practice more.

Most of the retreats can be for preventive practice, developing the habit of practicing mindfulness before things get too bad. But some retreats should be for those who are undergoing extreme suffering, although even then two-thirds of the retreatants should be healthy and stable for the practice to succeed. The depth and substance of the practice are the most important. The forms can be adapted.

At the retreat center, we can enjoy doing everything in mindfulness, and our friends will see the value of the practice through us—not through what we say, but through our being. We can also enjoy the practice at home, at work, or at school. For the practice to succeed, we have to find ways to incorporate it into our daily lives. Going to a retreat center from time to time can help a lot. Forming a Sangha at home is crucial.

Two thousand, five hundred years ago, the Buddha Shakyamuni predicted that the next Buddha will be named Maitreya, the "Buddha of Love." I think the Buddha of Love may be born as a community and not just as an individual.

Communities of mindful living are crucial for our survival and the survival of our planet. A good Sangha can help us resist the speed, violence, and unwholesome ways of our time. Mindfulness protects us and keeps us going in the direction of harmony and awareness. We need the support of friends in the practice. You are my Sangha. Let us take good care of each other

MUSHIM PATRICIA IKEDA

I Vow Not to Burn Out
2017

AT THE END of January, one of my close spiritual friends died. A queer Black man, a Sufi imam "scholartivist" (scholar–artist–activist) and professor of ministry students, Baba Ibrahim Farajajé died of a massive heart attack. He was sixty-three, and I'm guessing he had been carrying too much. It was only six months earlier that Baba and I had sat together on a stage in downtown Oakland, California, under a large hand-painted banner that read #BlackLivesMatter. A brilliant, transgressive bodhisattva, Baba had been targeted for multiple forms of oppression throughout his life and had not been silent about it. When he died, I was sad and angry. I took to staying up all night, chanting and meditating; during my daytime work, I was exhausted.

How many of us who have taken the bodhisattva vow are on a similar path toward burnout? Is it possible for us, as disciples of the Buddha, to engage with systemic change, grow and deepen our spiritual practice, and, if we're laypeople, also care for our families? How can we do all of this without collapsing? In my world, there always seems to be way too much to do, along with too much suffering and societal corruption and not enough spaces of deep rest and regeneration.

When I get desperate, which is pretty often, I ask myself how to not be overwhelmed by despair or cynicism. For my own sake, for my family, and for my sangha, I need to vow to not burn out. And I ask others to vow similarly so they'll be around when I need them for support. In fact, I've formulated a "Great Vow for Mindful Activists":

> Aware of suffering and injustice, I, _____, am working to create a more just, peaceful, and sustainable world. I promise, for the benefit of all, to practice self-care, mindfulness, healing, and joy. *I vow to not burn out.*

It's the first thing I give to students in my yearlong program of secular mindfulness for social justice activists. I ask them to sign and date it, because each of them, through their work as community leaders and agents of change, is a precious resource.

The cosmic bodhisattvas like Sadaparibhuta and Avalokiteshvara and the rest of the gang don't burn out. Maybe they have big muscles from continuously rowing suffering beings to the farther shore. They are willing to take abuse while demonstrating unfailing respect and love toward sentient beings. When something bad happens, they immediately absorb the blame. They vow to return, lifetime after lifetime, until the great work is fully accomplished, and until that probably distant time they remain upbeat, serene, and self-sacrificing.

I love this section from the poem "Bodhisattva Vows" by Albert Saijo:

> . . . YOU'RE SPENDING ALL YOUR TIME &
> ENERGY GETTING OTHER PEOPLE OFF THE
> SINKING SHIP INTO LIFEBOATS BOUND
> GAILY FOR NIRVANA WHILE THERE YOU ARE
> SINKING—& OF COURSE YOU HAD TO GO &

GIVE YOUR LIFEJACKET AWAY—SO NOW LET US BE CHEERFUL AS WE SINK—OUR SPIRIT EVER BUOYANT AS WE SINK

This poem never fails to give me a refreshing laugh; the archetype of bodhisattva activity it presents resonates with my early Buddhist training. But I have changed. In the social justice activist circles I travel in, giving your lifejacket away and going down with the sinking ship is now understood as a well-intentioned but mistaken old-school gesture—right now, the sinking ship is our entire planet, and there are no lifeboats. As the people with disabilities in my sangha have said, in order to practice universal access, there needs to be a radical shift toward an embodied practice of "All of us or none of us." In other words, no one can be left behind on the sinking ship, not even those who want to self-martyr. Why? Because self-martyrdom is bad role modeling. Burnout and self-sacrifice, the paradigm of the lone hero who takes nothing for herself and gives everything to others, injure all of us who are trying to bring the dharma into everyday lay life through communities of transformative well-being, where the exchange of self for other is reenvisioned as the care of self in service to the community. The longer we live, the healthier we are; the happier we feel, the more we can gain the experience and wisdom needed to contribute toward a collective reimagining of relationships, education, work, and play.

Here in Oakland, I don't think it's melodramatic or inaccurate to say that we now live in the midst of multiple ongoing crises. Thich Nhat Hanh has said that the future Buddha, Maitreya, may be a community, not an individual. Perhaps your community, like mine, is in need of inventive ways to carve out spaces for what some are now calling "radical rest."

I advocate for more forgiving and spacious schedules of spiritual practice that value being well-rested and that move toward honoring the body-mind's need for enough sleep and downtime. Social justice activist Angela Davis, in an interview in *YES! Magazine*, says:

I think our notions of what counts as radical have changed over time. Self-care and healing and attention to the body and the spiritual dimension—all of this is now a part of radical social justice struggles. This wasn't the case before. And I think that now we're thinking deeply about the connection between interior life and what happens in the social world. Even those who are fighting against state violence often incorporate impulses that are based on state violence in their relations with other people.

Healing. Rest. Self-care. Restorative justice. Restorative yoga. Trauma-informed dynamic mindfulness. Compassion. Love. Community healing. These are words I hear every day within spiritual activist forums, from "scholartivists" and from people embodying the bodhisattva vow to save all beings.

Dr. Martin Luther King, Jr., and his fellow organizers sometimes planned protests to occur at around eleven in the morning, because then the people who were arrested would get lunch in jail and wouldn't have to wait many hours to eat. For those of you who may feel that social-change work isn't your thing, or that it's too big to take on, it may help you, as it helped me, to know that it often comes down to these little details. Every movement is made of real people, and every action is broken down into separate tasks. This is work we need to do and can do together.

How can you make your life sustainable—physically, emotionally, financially, intellectually, spiritually? Are you helping create communities rooted in values of sustainability, including environmental and cultural sustainability? Do you feel that you have enough time and space to take in thoughts and images and experiences of things that are joyful and nourishing? What are your resources when you feel isolated or powerless?

Samsara is burning down all of our houses. We need a path of radical transformation, and there's no question in my mind that the bodhisattva path is it. Speaking as a mother and a woman of color, I think we're all going to need to be braver than some of us have been prepared to be. But brave in a sustainable way— remaining with our children, our families, and our communities. We need to build this new "woke" way of living together—how it functions, handles conflict, makes decisions, eats and loves, grieves and plays. And we can't do that by burning out.

SISTER ANNABEL LAITY

The Six Principles of Harmony
2019

T HE MOST NOBLE task is to build Sangha, the community
that lives in harmony and awareness. As Dr. Martin Luther
King, Jr., saw, being able to live in harmony in a community (what
he called the Beloved Community) is the way ahead for our civilization. When we live together, we share our resources and consume much less. We have an opportunity to let go of our idea of
being a separate self and realize that our suffering and our happiness are not different from the suffering and happiness of those
with whom we live. Seeing that we are not a separate self, we gain
freedom from the prison of grasping to a separate self; we do not
have to be in charge and make the decisions. The community is
like an orchestra without a conductor, like a hive of bees where
decisions are made collectively. Maybe the greatest advantage of
living in community or having a local Sangha is that with the six
principles of harmony we can produce a collective energy that is
a very strong contribution for the good in whatever activity we
engage. The collective energy becomes much greater than simply
the sum of the individual energies.

Our community can be a community of peace activists, of
artists, of monks and nuns, or your own family. There are six principles of living together in harmony that have been practiced since
the time of the Buddha. They are particularly useful for those of

us living in community and can also be used in the family and the workplace. Since they are not devotional practices, they can be used by any community, whether it is Buddhist or not.

Although they are six principles, if we practice one principle well, we are practicing all six. These six principles are essential for our being able to live together happily. By practicing them, we learn how to be both individuals and community members at the same time. At Plum Village, the practice of the Six Principles of Living in Harmony helps us to diminish our individualism and at the same time to practice in a way that nurtures creativity in each one of us.

The first principle of harmony is the body. In Chinese it is 身和同住, "harmony of the body while staying together." In order to practice, we stay in the same place and practice acts of loving kindness for each other with actions done by our body. We may be practicing nonviolent resistance and staying in a camp to oppose armaments coming out of a base or to stop fracking trucks. We may be living with our partner and children, or in a monastery, or lay practice center. Whatever form our community may take, we need to practice bodily acts of kindness for each other.

In the family, the mother and father take care of the children, but the children also learn how to perform acts of kindness for their parents and siblings. As a peace activist, or a monk or nun, we do not have our family nearby, so we need to take care of each other as if we were family members. Even if we only come together in our local Sangha for a few hours each week, we take care of each other. If one of our local Sangha members is sick in the hospital we take turns to go and visit him or her. The Buddha said that when we take care of each other, we are taking care of the Buddha.

Breathing together is also practicing harmony of the body. When we come into the place where our community is sitting in meditation, we may like to take our first breaths: "Breathing in, I am breathing for my Sangha. Breathing out, I am nourishing my Sangha. Breathing in, the Sangha is breathing for me. Breathing out, the Sangha is nourishing me." Sometimes, rather than talking to someone, we just breathe together. When someone is suffering, we just use our body to sit near them and breathe. This can be a wonderful practice where no one needs to say or think anything. Our mindful presence at Sangha activities, whether in the practice center or in our local Sangha, is already practicing harmony of the body.

The second principle of harmony is 利和同均, "harmony of sharing benefits." It is about sharing material things with the community. Some of us may have more of something than others. It is a principle of community living that we have as few personal material items as possible. If we receive gifts or offerings, we are happy to share them with others. It is a great happiness to share and be generous. Even very young children find happiness in sharing.

Many local Sanghas practice the "pot-luck" meal. We also learn to share our time and energy with others. Sometimes our Sangha will decide together to support a certain project to alleviate the suffering of others: being present at a soup kitchen, supporting a demonstration for peace, human rights, or protecting Mother Earth. To support such initiatives as a Sangha is so much more effective than as an individual. We are sharing our time with our Sangha and at the same time with those outside our Sangha.

The third principle of harmony is practicing the same precepts or trainings, 戒和同修, "The harmony of practicing the Trainings together." Living together we need to share ethical principles and do our best to follow the principles laid down for our community. Our practice of the trainings includes recitations and

Dharma sharings about the trainings. No one is perfect in their practice of the trainings but we do our very best. When we recite the Five Trainings we expect everyone in our local community to be there.[1] If, for reasons of ill-health or a special task, someone cannot be present, he or she sends a note asking to be represented.

Reciting the Trainings gives a chance to look deeply into how we have practiced the Trainings since the last time we recited them. When we are asked whether we have practiced them during the past month, we do not answer "yes" or "no" but silently look deeply into how we have practiced. Dharma sharing is another important aspect of the harmony of Mindfulness Trainings. We share openly with each other about the practical ways we have of bringing the Trainings into our daily life and if we are having difficulties, we also share these. We learn from each other how to practice the Trainings more effectively in order to lessen our suffering and the suffering in the world.

The fourth principle of harmony has speech as its basis: 口和無爭, "the harmony of speech without disputes." Much of our speech is habitual—it comes from things we have said before or have heard others say. When we were children, our parents repeated certain things, and their habits have become a part of our own way of speaking. We need to develop new harmonious patterns of speech. This means being mindful of what we are saying or are about to say. If we are not sure that what we are about to say is helpful, we stop and ask ourselves, "If I say this, will it make my sisters and brothers happy? Will it help the other members of the community?" If we stop and follow our breathing before we speak, there is a renewal, and a new kind of speaking comes out from us.

1　See the last chapter in this book for the Five Trainings.

Listening deeply is an important aspect of the harmony of speech. If we do not listen deeply to what others have to say, how can we reply compassionately? Listening deeply, we hear not just the words the other person is saying but also what lies underneath the words: the fear, the wounds, and the hurts. Speaking unkindly about someone who is not present is a way of creating division in our community. If we are involved in a conversation that is denigrating other members of our community or workplace, we should say clearly that we do not wish to participate in such a conversation.

The fifth principle of harmony has the mind as its basis: 意和同悦, "the harmony of thought for common joy." The harmony of mind is important in helping us practice the harmony of speech. If we think unkindly about another person, sooner or later it will come out in our speech. We use our mind, our thinking, to understand others.

With a mind of loving kindness and the eyes of loving kindness, we want to learn about our brothers and sisters: what are their skills and talents, what are the wounds, what brings them joy and so on. It is as if we keep a dossier on them. If someone has some physical suffering, we keep that in our mind. If they tell us a story about their past, that becomes part of our understanding about that person. Gradually we learn more and more about each person, and with this understanding we are able to love them more. If our mind has a tendency to think in negative ways about a certain person, we need to recognize that, and as soon as we recognize that kind of thinking coming up in us, we should do our best to change it by giving our attention to the positive qualities of the other or by seeking to see the suffering that has led to the negative qualities, and to see that the other is suffering and needs our help not our blame.

The sixth principle is harmony of views. 見和同解 "harmony of views: resolving matters together," may be the most important principle. We think our viewpoints come from reason. Actually, they come from feelings and emotions. When we come to a meeting, of course we can have a viewpoint about matters on the agenda and we have a right or even a duty to express that viewpoint. Once we have stated our viewpoint, however, it is as if we have given it to the community. It is no longer ours, and now we must listen to everyone else's views. We may see very quickly that our view has inadequacies, or it may be that others support it.

When we hear someone else's viewpoint, we usually react, "That must be right" (because it's what I think), or "That must be wrong" (because it is not what I think). In a community, when someone offers an idea, we need to listen deeply and take what has been said seriously. We should never denigrate the views of another. A skillful facilitator can often find ways to synthesize differing points of view. Consensus is not the most important thing. Listening deeply to each other, and not being caught in our own view, come first. If we see that we our view is not held by a majority of 70 percent or more, we should let it go, unless we have some information that others do not have.

We can also make sure that everyone's views are heard. Young children have an intuitive understanding and we can always ask them for their opinion on matters that involve the whole family or community. In this way the children feel they are listened to and they learn how to express their views.

We can see how the harmony of views, of thinking, and speech support each other. If we do not know how to think and speak with loving kindness it will be difficult to harmonize our views with those of others.

If we want to engage in the noble task of building Sangha or the beloved community, it is important for us to practice the Six Principles of Living Together in Harmony and to share the practice with others, not just in words or teachings but in the way we live and engage with others in our daily life.

Where the Heart Lives
2018

*W*E ARE SPECKS *of dust on a strand of Mother Earth's hair. There is no need for us to "save" the Earth; we simply need to let her discard what has become stale. We need to release our planet of our wanting and begging, our ignorance and confusion, and be weaned from her breast, even when it feels we won't survive. When we stop exploiting the Earth, she will return to sustainability on her own and share her bounty generously.*

In November 2016, America and the rest of the world were stunned when a candidate whose platform included harming immigrants and discriminating against certain citizens won the presidency. When I learned he'd been voted in, my heart sank, realizing that America had become even less of a place I can call *home*. Many of us had been living under a constant threat of harm for decades. Now, the blatant hatred ignored by so many others could no longer go unacknowledged. Many would recognize and join a shared sense of homelessness.

In spiritual communities, especially in Buddhist ones, the teachings on finding home are profound, but they often leave out the experiences of those who are dehumanized in their own homeland. Spiritual teachings like, "Home is within the heart" can be off-putting when loss and disconnection aren't also acknowledged. Those who have such experiences can feel homeless spiritually and physically, and finding refuge, or sanctuary, from acts of hatred must be offered along the path of finding our true home.

My parents were born and raised in southern Louisiana at the turn of the twentieth century, not far from the plantations where their ancestors labored as slaves, and where lynching of their neighbors occurred often. While I'm certain they did not feel at home in that environment, there was sanctuary among others who embraced the black Creole culture. Because of *their* cultural sanctuary, they were able to experience a sense of home in their hearts. Although I wasn't born or raised in the homeplace of my parents, grandparents, and great-grandparents, the bayou, swamps, music, foods, and eloquent Creole language were transmitted in part to me through my parents' very being. The cultural, ecological, and social life of Louisiana is in my bones, and whenever I'm there, I feel a primal sense of home—despite having never lived there. In this case home is a matter of the heart. As a result, finding home, feeling home, and being at home are complex, multilayered, spiritual, and cultural experiences independent of the place we live. Where is home? When I don't feel at home, where can I find sanctuary? These questions become critical when our lives are under threat.

In the twenty-first century, groups are still being terrorized because of race, religious choice, physical ability, class, sexual orientation, and gender. Legendary radical feminist and academic Angela Davis points out that racism, Islamophobia, anti-Semitism, hetero-patriarchy, and xenophobia are, in fact, the ghosts of slavery. We have returned full circle to what catalyzed the Civil Rights Movement and forced the creation of political and spiritual sanctuaries for those who were hunted by people trying to maintain white supremacy. Finding Buddha's home of the heart can be a shallow quest without the exploration of homelessness, sanctuary, and refuge in the light of such terrorism and its impact on life, death, identity, and peace.

I was invited to teach at Deer Park Monastery in Escondido, California, where the Zen master is Thich Nhat Hanh. When I arrived, I saw a sign in the teacher's beautiful calligraphy that said, "I am home." When I saw it, the words vibrated through me as though I were hearing a temple bell. I felt relieved, and *my heart knew* I was home. I don't live at Deer Park, but reading the Zen master's words, I felt deeply at home. The home dwelled in my heart.

If the heart is at the center of our being home, what leads a person to homelessness? What happens when your home doesn't have the peace you'd hoped for? If we look at the impact of history, culture, and ancestry on finding home, we begin to understand the vastness of homelessness and what it would take to find home. When we recognize the profound influence of social factors upon homelessness, how do we find compassion, forgiveness, and similar virtues that can carry us home?

When I was eleven years old, my family was having a tough time. One evening at dinner, the meat was stringy, and I asked, "Daddy, what's this?" My father proudly answered, "Possum. I caught it in the backyard." I didn't know what a possum looked like. All I could think of was the blood that might still be behind the house. I dropped the meat from my fork. My father, from the back roads of Opelousas, was doing what he'd always done to survive hard times. It wouldn't be long before we received our first— and last—bag of groceries from the welfare office. We were too proud to continue.

I remember saying to myself, *I will never be as poor as my parents.* I wanted to feel that I could get what I needed. And I know that when my father promised each of his three daughters a Cadillac and a house, he meant for us to be better off than he was. First, second, and third-generation African Americans who migrated north were supposed to succeed, and our progress was measured by external appearances. Most important was to have a roof over our heads. When you lose your house, you feel like a failure—a disappointment to yourself and your family. When I grew older, the experience of compassion for my parents was to love them despite our hardships. I forgave them for the poverty they could not control. The compassion and forgiveness enabled me to feel at home with them regardless of living in a state of insecurity and distress.

What if those who have been pushed to the economic, political, and social margins were *seen* and their true histories revealed while presenting the teachings of finding one's true home? Would that help us understand the depth of our connections or disconnections to self and each other and facilitate the quest for an authentic home? Would it invite compassion and forgiveness?

As I explored the epidemic of homelessness and the urgent need for sanctuary historically and in our time, I tasted the tears of so many. How much longer will those who have been pushed out be able to survive? Is there too much water under the bridge to reconcile our disconnections from one another as people? If we are not paying attention to who and what is unacknowledged, we'll always have dangerous demagogues who shake us loose from the illusion that all is well. They are a curse and a blessing, as they help us remember what matters. Patience is more than waiting and hoping. Patience is taking the time to love what is difficult to love. This is the quest toward compassion and forgiveness in regard to finding home in a place that is foreign and difficult to fully live in freedom. The other quest has been creating sanctuary when one is marginalized and disenfranchised from the larger society.

Sanctuary is the place we can go when our lives are under

threat, where we can consider patience, compassion, forgiveness, and love in the midst of oppression. It's a place for those who feel differently than the dominant culture, a place where anyone can say, "I am home." Taking sanctuary can be an act of finding home or saving one's life.

At the core of sanctuary is the failed quest to find home in the places we live. For centuries sanctuaries have been the answer to finding home. Millions have sought refuge from genocide, violence, economic loss, and political oppression, forced to venture into unfamiliar places. Some have climbed mountains, some have swum the seven seas, others have crossed deserts to save their families and their communities' lives. Millions have been forced to leave when their ancestral lands were destroyed; others have fled refugee camps where it had become too dangerous to remain, leaving generations of descendants with an insatiable yearning to return home. Displacement is an embodied experience, imprinted on our bones. Since the advent of nations and boundaries, the discarded have left home and their descendants have sought to find it again.

Sanctuary is where you go when your soul cannot live in peace on the land that is your birthright. Maybe it is not a land that has been conquered by outside forces. Perhaps you've moved to an urban space where gentrification and the purchase of entire neighborhoods are displacing generations of those you know and love. Maybe your family home or farm had to be sold because of an unpayable mortgage or taxes or insurance. You began to question what you thought you knew about home.

When I came through many initiations of being unhoused, I discovered that homelessness is more than just the loss of a physical place. It is also the loss of culture, connection, identity, and affiliation. This hunger for home is deep and wide, touching the nerve of ancient displacement and dispossession. It feels ancient and visceral, a trauma that passes from generation to generation. In search of home, many of us stop off at a sanctuary to gain insight, to breathe, and feel as a person who belongs.

A friend who lives in Haiti told me that in the Haitian *Kreyól* language, the word for home is *lakay*, which literally means "being at home." This is significant because *having a home* and *being at home* can be entirely different experiences. Having a home conjures up a physical locale. We are born in a place, indigenous to some land, somewhere. We have residency, or citizenship. Among Haitian people, it is important to know exactly where you are from. When first meeting, Haitians try to situate you in relation to others. The question, "Where are you from?" literally means, "Where are you a person?" And if we are not *at* home, when homelessness is deep-seated and outside our control, where are you a person?

Sanctuary can be a refuge to reconcile the discord between not belonging and knowing oneself as a person. In this case, sanctuary is refuge.

"Taking refuge" is the English translation of *sarana-gamana*; *sarana* in Pali means shelter, protection, or sanctuary—a place where safety and peace are possible. To take refuge in the three treasures—Buddha, Dharma, Sangha—is to follow a path that leads us home to who we are, a path of awakening. In sanctuary, we can pause and discover the nature of this life.

Zen Master Shunryu Suzuki said, "We began to strive *for ourselves*, we strive for God." We reach out for love and acceptance and through practices like prayer and meditation, ceremony, drumming, and chanting, honoring ourselves, and evolving in a creative spiritual community. Revitalizing ourselves in community gives us the energy we need to shift our sense of who we are and transform the way we live. Taking refuge, we gain insight and see possibilities. With the support of others, we awaken to the conditions that cause us to suffer the suffering. When we say, "I take refuge," we're appealing to what brings us home to ourselves. This is the reason our spiritual communities must be sanctuaries that understand the depth at which people have been stripped of their culture for a more dominant one. In sanctuary, we recover from being lost and take refuge in shared community, the collective embodiment of all that symbolizes home.

Sanctuaries based on kinships, such as race, sexuality, gender, or any combination of factors is significant to feeling connected. If there is a spiritual aspect to a culturally-based sanctuary, the ceremonies and rituals help to create a sense of love and well-being around kinship and provide a place to attend to our own and others' suffering.

Creating a sanctuary takes imagination, trust, and determination—but first it takes the courageous thought that homelessness need not be endured. We begin by envisioning ways to foster resiliency and learn to be well while resisting injustice. We see and hear those around us who might need protective sanctuary.

When Dr. Martin Luther King, Jr., spoke of the "beloved community," it was not the first time I'd heard of such a thing. I was raised in one—the black church. Every Sunday morning, my family dressed in our finest, and we gathered with the tribe that had migrated to Los Angeles from Texas and Louisiana. We arrived in our Buicks, Lincolns, Fords, and Chevrolets. It was our time to see each other eye to eye, time to sing, to let loose from bearing yet another week of blatant discrimination.

I would be in the back seat of our Buick with my younger sister, feeling beautiful, my hair slick and wearing my shining shoes and a dress reserved for Sundays. I was headed to the beloved community where love was guaranteed.

To come to the beloved community was to head home, a place where you walk through the doors and are instantly hugged simply because you are alive. You might come to cry about what was lost or to eat homemade rolls or lemon meringue pie like they made back home. You might come to hear that song that lifts you from distress or just because you had nowhere else to go. There was nothing like listening to the old ones talk about the old times and their migration from the South in the 1940s for work. Of course, they didn't always have good times, but the joy of a life gone by lit up their eyes. The memories were what they had left.

On the day Dr. King was murdered, it was clear that his call for our human connection across cultural boundaries was more than a dream. It was a prophecy.

I was in high school and students were running in the hallway yelling about the assassination. As one of few youth of color, white students looked at me as if I might attack them for what had just happened. There was a feeling that African Americans had lost the race war, but it was clear that Dr. King's dream was as lucid and prophetic as the dreams the Buddha had, from which emerged the Four Noble Truths. It was more than a dream about whites and blacks holding hands and singing, eating at the local diner, living in shared neighborhoods, or desegregating schools.

The beloved community King spoke of was meant for an entire country, an entire world, not just the black community. He was encouraging a sanctuary within our country and our world that would be based on peace, so we might live in the magnificent oneness available to all beings.

Although he used the language of the day, speaking to the brotherhood of "man," the patriarchy of mostly white and black men in the movement, *excluding black women and black gays and lesbians,* the ultimate aim of King's Southern Christian Leadership

Conference was "to foster and create the 'beloved community' in America." At that time, like many times after, black people were under siege, so his language was pointedly addressed to white people, but his message—and his audience—was larger than we could imagine.

He was speaking about creating a community of peace within a country that was built on division and destruction. At the time, with Jim Crow laws in effect, the country was not safe for black people. When Dr. King called for a beloved community, he was envisioning a sanctuary for those who felt marginalized or displaced. King's sanctuary would reestablish a sense of personhood.

Although influenced by separate and unequal access to housing, education, and health care for black Americans, his call for integration was not of the relative kind. Dr. King did not imagine *only* a political and legislative response to his call for integration— he was calling for a larger and more powerful kind of integration, like Buddha's teachings of interrelationship, Thich Nhat Hanh's "interbeing," or Paramahansa Yogananda, who said, "May my love shine forever on the sanctuary of my devotion, and may I be able to awaken thy love in all hearts."

Dr. King said, "We are tied together in the single garment of destiny, caught in an inescapable network of mutuality." He was asking us to acknowledge that this destiny was, in fact, the very basis for our existence as a country. He was begging the nation to transform itself and begin anew.

The creation of the beloved community as a vision of sanctuary was both an action *and* a consciousness to be embodied across the globe. Beloved community as sanctuary was, for Dr. King, a heartfelt way to attend to those who did not feel at home in the U.S. and to prevent the continued killing of human life on this planet, especially black people. His call was an alarm going off, not a man dreaming in his sleep. *He felt we could not go on as a society without conscious love.*

In a beloved community, our sacred incarnation is honored and loved. In a beloved community, "unacceptable" embodiments of the larger society are accepted. The protection, refuge, healing, guidance, and companionship found in sanctuary are prerequisites for our happiness and well-being. Finding personhood, dignity, and respect are the soil in which we can plant our feet in a true home. Sanctuary is a place you create when you are "missing" in the scheme of humanity. Establishing sanctuary is critical to finding home.

What might happen if those in a sanctuary based on a shared history of atrocity begin to water a seed of freedom from the pain and suffering of having a lost feeling of home? The quality of the sanctuary would become the expression of a renewed consciousness for wellness. We can have a direct experience of our boundlessness, while still understanding the historical origin of our trauma. The sanctuary of freedom surfaces from an *awakened heart* that fully recognizes an historical experience *and* the absolute availability of peace. With freedom, we begin to participate in our destiny and not fear or live in reaction to the wrath of oppressors or dominant cultures. We bloom rather than wither away in our suffering. In this way home is sanctuary and sanctuary is home.

Is home a matter of the heart? Yes. When what has gone unacknowledged in our society surfaces, it feels like a new reality, but we know in our hearts it is not new. Our hearts say there can be no better answer to our meditations and prayers for dissolving hatred than for it to be placed front and center and exposed. What is our truth? Have our actions been ineffective? Have we relied *only* on prayer and meditation or *only* on social activism? When a shift in a system takes place, especially one that causes fear and discomfort, it allows for something strikingly different to appear, furthering our growth as individuals and as a community of people.

Many of us have been practicing Buddha's teachings or walking other spiritual paths for what feels like forever, preparing for major challenges. We've been waiting for this time to create a home that mirrors the compassion and freedom in our hearts. We are ready. Our rage, pain, and anger need to be exposed so we can transform and mature with them. Our heart-home is revealed when we come to know who we are, right where we are.

Finding Home

Enchanted are the souls of Africans whose bloody
feet cracked the seashells that lay beneath the sand on
the seashores of our beginnings. I call for the healing
of those feet, between my own toes, breathing wind
a million years old, left in foul marshes. Come my
ancestors to the table where I eat rice that you gave
3,000 years ago. Come feel the cotton clothes from
the crops you harvested. Let me kiss your hands that
swelled long after sunset each day. If only all that you
loved and lost came back from beneath the sea.

Walking sacred land where you withered and rose
again despite the horror, honor is given and survives
your invisibility, for the world shares in the abundance
created by you.

We remember you stained the sand that washes away, pushing us deeper into it, turning us into purple sand dunes in your honor. I lost sight of home, the trees planted in my name, ceremonies, waterfalls; and I have lost the smell of certain flowers and fruits. Rage stays a memory of you on this planet, a memory that will not pain us forever.

And now I'm finding home, close to the sacred earth your bones have settled, nestled close to each breath. I climbed the clouds and saw you there; your face alights from resting. Where the sea delivered you to this land is where you are too. I move on in your honor, your stories unburied, your spirit alive in everything. I go now speaking your names, finding home in the way I walk across the street. Being so close to home that one day, someone will yell out to me, "Hey, this isn't Africa." And I will respond, "It certainly isn't."

Precious Jewel
1994

EVERY NEW YEAR'S Day in some countries in Asia, monks and nuns write their last wills and testament. They light incense, sit quietly, following their breathing and looking deeply at birth and death, and think, soon it will be the New Year. What kind of will should I write?

What can we inherit? What can we pass on? What kind of treasure are we? Over time we receive many things, enjoy them, share them with others, and pass them on. We especially want to pass on what is most precious, so we look after those things most carefully. Whatever we receive, whatever we are—our robes, bowl, lamps, body, mind, feelings, emotions, understanding, love, and support—are all part and parcel of the precious jewel we want to pass on.

We want this heritage to go to its rightful heirs. Normally our family members are considered to be the rightful heirs, but what is it that makes an heir rightful? To me, one who is lacking in whatever is to be given is what makes him or her a rightful heir. There is a famous story about a shepherd in France who planted trees. He had lost his wife and son, and so he spent his time gathering the healthiest acorns in the forest and planting them in barren, deserted areas where nothing would grow and no one lived.

Carrying a stick with a metal point, he made little holes in the ground and planted an acorn in each one. As years passed, trees sprang up and soon the barren land was transformed into a green, fertile oasis that became a national park.

For the universe to be whole, no one should lack what is essential. If food is lacking, we give food. If shelter is lacking, we give shelter. If love is lacking, we give love.

It is easy to love someone lovable. He is lovable because he already has love. He is love. But those who do not have love are the ones who need it. They ought to be the rightful heirs of our love. Someone who has love and is happy is like a beautiful landscape that we enjoy entering. Someone who has no love, who is sad or angry, is like a barren landscape where nothing will grow and no one wants to enter. However, that barren land is like that because we are like this, because we turn away from it. Let us not turn away from it, but approach it, and plant acorns there so that it will transform itself into a fresh and fragrant oasis that offers peace and joy to all.

A tiny little acorn has the totality of the tree in it. The same is true of us. We inherited from our parents their whole being—including their parents, teachers, friends, and environment, everyone and everything that made them, as well as everyone and everything that made our parents' teachers, friends, and parents, and their parents, teachers, friends, and so on—and that jewel is in us in its totality. We are the receiver of the heritage of the whole universe, and we are also the one who passes it on, day and night, without stopping. When we transform something negative in us into something more wholesome, we do it for everyone, and we make everyone else's transformation easier.

Once we know who our heirs are, we naturally become mindful and take good care of our heritage, our universal jewel. Our parents, grandparents, ancestors, teachers, friends, and everything that was, is, and will be are in their totality in us, and we are in our totality in everything that ever was, is, and will be.

Mindfulness and the Police
2016

I WAS A police officer seven years into my career when I ended up at my first retreat with Thich Nhat Hanh. I had already noticed that with many police officers, three things start to happen over the course of their career and those had already happened to me.

Physiologically, many of you might be able to relate to this if you live very busy lives, multitasking and doing too much. Research has shown that we all have a certain amount of adrenaline. People who know how to be rather than do are probably in the normal range. What happens with police officers, and you can probably relate to this, is that adrenaline starts to shoot up because of hypervigilance—being worried about your own safety and the safety of everybody else. We're always taught about what can go wrong—not so much about what can go right, which is the majority of the time. The adrenaline shoots out of the normal range and peaks, then takes twenty-four hours to come back to normal, but people go back to work before that twenty-four hours is up. So adrenaline starts going up and down, above and below the normal range. When the adrenaline kicks in, people are fast on their feet, able to make command decisions, and they have a sense of humor. And then when they are at home, the adrenaline drops way down—no energy, listlessness, depression. There are usually four times as many police officers in the United States who take their own lives as are killed in the line of duty. This is a very real phenomenon.

Emotionally, what begins to happen is that the effects manifest as irritation and impatience and anger and depression. There's a very cynical sort of response that develops. Spiritually, the effects of doing the job manifest as an armoring and numbing of the heart. It's very hard to be compassionate when those things are going on.

The other thing that happens is you develop what is known as the "I used to" syndrome:

I used to know how to water the seeds of joy.
I used to bike.
I used to play sports.
I used to garden.
I used to write poetry.
I used to have hobbies.

All those things are gone, and your world becomes smaller and smaller because of shift work and odd hours. Thinking that people don't understand, you end up socializing only with other police officers, so all those things get reinforced.

That's how I showed up at my very first retreat with Thay (Vietnamese for "teacher," which Thich Nhat Hanh's students affectionately call him) in 1991. I came very armored and defended. I was ready for people to hate me because I was a police officer. That happens a lot, even among people who share my progressive politics. They'd see the uniform and immediately make a decision about who I was. That's the attitude I came there with, and what happened? Imagine a red dot on a whiteboard. That's where I was living, in the red dot. Meditation and mindfulness help you see the white space. Here we are with all this spaciousness available to us, and we hang on so tight to our little red dots: our thoughts and our emotions.

Out here, love is available, happiness is available. No coming, no going is available, the spaciousness of being everything and nothing at the same time. Even after that first retreat, I started to understand some of that intuitively. All I wanted to do was practice. I began to think of meditation as just resting my mind in open awareness, and at that retreat I touched peace in a really fabulous way.

Transformation on the Job

Many strange things happened after that retreat. I was working nights as a sergeant. I was going on calls and I couldn't understand why everybody around me had changed. They seemed to have gotten kinder in my absence, even people I was arresting! It didn't make any sense to me. I didn't know if somebody had gone around and sprayed Prozac or some other antidepressant while I was gone, but it took me a little while to see that it was my energy that was different, and people were responding to it. That was an incredible teaching for me because there it was, the proof in the pudding.

At that retreat, the Five Mindfulness Trainings came up, and of course the first one is Reverence for Life.[1] I said, "I can't take these, I carry a gun for a living, and I never know what's going to happen." To this day I can't remember if it was Thay or Sister Chan

---

1 See the last chapter in this book for the Five Trainings.

Khong who said to me, "Who else would we want to carry a gun except somebody who will do it mindfully?" It was a whole new way to look at things!

The changes were incremental, but I stopped doing my job in a mechanical way. What I started to see is what was right in front of me, which I seemed to have missed with the other attitude: a suffering human being who needed my help and often didn't have any place else to turn. So, I started taking my time on the calls I went on. I started trying to connect with people from a different space.

One of my favorite stories is an experience of going on a domestic violence call. We had a mandatory arrest policy in those days, so if anybody was threatening somebody in a physical way, you were supposed to arrest them. I went on this call, and I didn't have any backup, and a woman came running out and said, "My husband has my child and I'm really scared. We just broke up, and he won't let her out to come be with me. I'm picking her up. We have an agreement about who is supposed to have the child when, and now it's my turn."

I asked her to go wait in the car down the block, and I knocked on the door. I'm about five feet three inches, and this six-foot-four-inch man who looked very angry opened the door. I could just see the suffering. It was so obvious to me. In a very calm voice, I said, "May I come in? I'm just here to listen and to help." I came in and saw his daughter, and I said, "You know what, I see your little girl over here, and I know you love her, and I know how much you care about her, and I see that she's scared, and I know you don't want that to happen. So how about if we let her go out and be with her mother, and you and I talk." And he did.

Rather than escalating this situation to the point where an arrest had to be made, it was just a matter of being compassionate and mindful. I violated every policy in the book, and with my gun belt and my bulletproof vest I sat down next to this guy on the couch, which you're never supposed to do. And he started crying in my arms. That was an incredible experience for me in terms of what a little kindness and compassion can do, and that there are alternative ways to respond to people. Of course, when you're angry, irritated, and cynical yourself, it's really hard to see those possibilities.

I ran into this man three days later. I was walking down the street that I lived on and he came up behind me—you know, it's not good to come up behind a police officer. He picked me up off the ground and he said, "You! You! You saved my life that night." It was a wonderful experience.

Building Community, Engaged Practice

So, I emphasized two of the teachings of Thay and the Order of Interbeing. There's an emphasis on community. There's also an emphasis, not only on happiness in the present moment and having a foundational mindfulness practice, but also building community and engaged practice.

Those two things, building community (Sangha) and engaged practice, are not found in too many other Buddhist traditions. Those two things are just so special. I started thinking of Sangha as community. I joined a Sangha right after that retreat, but I started thinking of community as wherever I was. I started thinking of my workplace as a Sangha; I started thinking of my family as a Sangha.

In 2002, I came to Plum Village. Eleven years had passed, and I became a member of the Order of Interbeing. Thay transmitted the Fourteen Mindfulness Trainings to me and thirty-two other people when I was here for the twenty-one-day retreat.

In those days you wrote a letter to Thay. You still write a letter if you want to be ordained. I didn't think that he read these letters, but I put it in the bell in the meditation hall. My letter was about how I was still struggling with feeling like both the victim and oppressor in this job, bouncing back and forth between those. The next day Thay gave a Dharma talk on the different faces of love. I was sitting in the back, and he mentioned police officers. I had tears streaming down my face. Another big transition took place, more softness, more understanding of Thay's teaching that we're all victims and oppressors.

A Retreat for Police Officers

One of the ripple effects of this happened when we were doing working meditation and chopping vegetables. I said to the woman next to me, "I have this very ridiculous image in my head of police officers holding hands and doing walking meditation together, creating peaceful steps on the Earth." She looked at me and she said, "Cheri, you can make that happen!" Thursday there was a question-and-answer session, and I got up and asked Thay if he would come do a retreat for police officers. I was very worried about what the response would be, and much to my delight he looked up and said, "Yes, I think we'll do it next year."

There was a year to organize things and try to get police officers to come to a mindfulness retreat with a Buddhist teacher. It was very, very hard. There was a big reaction. I started getting hate emails. The separation of church and state, even though it was going to be a nonsectarian retreat, came up—and it was very challenging. But I had wonderful people in my own Sangha and had contacted people among the monastics. That helped a lot.

So, Thay came and we made this happen. I don't remember how many people there were. About sixteen officers from my own police department were there. Thay's first Dharma talk included a statement about how you cannot fight violence with violence. If you use violence, you are going to get violence in return. After that first talk, the police officers surrounded me and said, "Cheri, what are we supposed to do? What do you mean, you can't fight violence with violence? What does he mean by that? We want to talk to him." And I said, "Well, I've never had a personal talk myself with Thich Nhat Hanh, but I will see what I can do." Eventually Thay came and talked to just the police officers, and by the end of the hour that he spent with them, the whole room grew calm. It was just so beautiful, and after that there was never another problem or objection that entire week.

One of the things that affected me was that at the end of the retreat, Thay said, "Are we going to hear from the police officers?" The night before the retreat ended, the police officers gave a presentation. I have never heard police officers share like that, share what life is like for them as a police officer, and never before have I seen a community be so receptive to what they had to say. I could just see them lighting up; it was so meaningful that there were people who were willing to be receptive to this. At the end of that retreat, the officers from my department and I held hands and did walking meditation. You never know what the ripple effects of anything can be!

Transmission of the Lamp

Then all kinds of things happened once I got back to Madison out on the street. This is a story that I just love: one of the people who was at the retreat came up to me and said, "Cheri, I just saw two of your young officers who were at the retreat. They were arresting somebody, and they recognized me. They arrested the person, and they put him in the back of the car, and then they turned to me and they bowed." I said, "Well, when we bow to the person that we're arresting as well as to the community that we're doing it for, we will really have arrived."

Then in 2007, I went to Vietnam along with a big group of Westerners with Thay and the monastic community. That had a big impact on me. Toward the end of that, Sister Chan Khong delivered the message to me that Thay wanted to make me a Dharma teacher and to transmit the lamp to me. So, in 2008 the transmission of the lamp happened. When a person receives the lamp transmission and becomes a Dharma Teacher, they write a gatha poem for the ceremony. This is my gatha for Thay that I'd like to share with you:

> Breathing in, I know that mindfulness is the path
>   to peace.
> Breathing out, I know that peace is the path to
>   mindfulness.
> Breathing in, I know that peace is the path to justice.
> Breathing out, I know that justice is the path to peace.
> Breathing in, I know my duty is to provide safety and
>   protection to all beings.
> Breathing out, I am humbled and honored by my
>   duty as a peace officer.

Breathing in, I choose mindfulness as my armor and
    compassion as my weapon.
Breathing out, I aspire to bring love and
    understanding to all I serve.

Cornel West said something that is the epitome of how I think we should view policing: "Justice is what love looks like in public." How different would our system look if we adopted this definition of justice as the foundation for our whole system? It would just be incredible.

The Psychology of Mindfulness

There are three interrelated areas in my own personal work over the course of the years where the practice got deeper and deeper for me. The first was my own inner work, my meditation and mindfulness practice, which is of course the foundation for everything; the second area was relationships; and the third area was engaged practice.

The Buddha was so good at providing the architecture for our distress and also the architecture for our liberation. Thay is so wonderful at conveying the Buddhist teachings in a simple way that could be understood. One of the things that happened for me is what Thay describes as the psychology of mindfulness. In the psychology of mindfulness, there are two things that we are asked to be. One is a good curator of the museum of our past, and the other is a good gardener of our store consciousness. If we're a good curator of the museum of our past, we can reframe our past, we can understand it in the service of our own freedom. However, if we carry it too far, we get attached to the wounded self, because then we're constantly taking bus tickets back to our past.

We're also learning how to be a good gardener. We're learning what to incline our mind toward, how to water the seeds of joy and kindness and understanding and compassion. But in order to be able to do this, we have to understand how our experience is born moment to moment. If we can start to watch what arises and notice how our experience is born moment to moment, we can make conscious decisions about how to incline the heart and mind. And that is probably the most powerful thing that has happened to me over the years of this practice.

I can't tell you how many people come up to me and say: "Cheri, you've gotten so much softer." And I guess it's true! Those protective layers of armor are removed one at a time.

You learn about craving and aversion and how to work with both of them. A very subtle form of craving that I noticed was the craving to become. Unfortunately, in our society, success often gets equated with doing. One thing Thay has helped me understand is that the quality of your doing will always be dependent on the quality of your being. This requires a certain discipline, in that you cannot let the things that matter the most be at the mercy of the things that matter the least. So often we think, if I just get this done, and this done, and this done, then I'll focus on my practice. We become habitual "waiters." We become addicted to doing. As a result, in my culture anyway, we have many people who are tired and wired, which leads to a lot of contentious behavior.

Understanding is key to this practice. I want to tell you a little story that, when I think back on it, makes me smile so much. It was my first week of being a rookie police officer on the street. We had just come off all of our experiences with our field training officers, and we were now riding alone. We have these briefing sessions before every shift starts. One of the first things that happened to me is the lieutenant of my shift said to me, "Maples, there's a homeless guy down there in the basement, where our squad cars are and where our evidence room is. I want you to go down there and get him out of there and skip briefing to do it." I go down there and I make contact with this man, who proceeds to tell me he doesn't have to go anywhere because he's the president of the United States. Rather than understanding him and trying to put myself in his position, I argue with him that he's not the president of the United States. I'm getting more and more nervous because I know all these veteran police officers are going to be coming down the stairs, and I'm failing at my very first assignment. So this is not going well.

Finally, one of the veteran officers walked down. He said, "Hey, rookie, let me show you how it's done." He went and he got a key to the squad car closest to where this homeless man was standing. He opened the back door and said, "Mr. President, your limo awaits you." The guy got right in and off they went. So that taught me something about working for social change.

One of the things that I think is really important is that we have to learn the difference between self-esteem and self-compassion, because until we learn how to bring true self-compassion to ourselves, the practice doesn't really work well with other people. You can make a full-time job out of self-improvement, which leads to high self-esteem, and I guess that's better than low self-esteem. But the problem with high self-esteem is you're still comparing yourself to other people. In fact, sometimes you're competing with them and secretly hoping they do worse than you do. It's not a very good way to live a spiritual life.

With self-compassion, we're learning how to bring not just empathy to ourselves but goodwill to ourselves, in a phenomenal way. When I'm able to do that with the tools in the practice, the volume of "me" goes way down. I'm happiest when the volume of "me" is lowest. When the volume of "me" goes up, all those habit seeds are ready to spring into action.

Thomas Merton said this, and to me it is the epitome of Thay's teachings: "To allow ourselves to be carried away by a multitude of conflicting concerns, to surrender to too many demands, to commit oneself to too many projects, to want to help everyone and everything, is to succumb to violence. The frenzy of our activism neutralizes our work for peace; it destroys our own inner capacity for peace; it destroys the fruitfulness of our own work because it kills the root of inner wisdom, which makes work fruitful."

We have prison projects in Wisconsin now, which went from being in one prison to being in many prisons. I'm happy to say that we are about to start teaching mindfulness to the guards. With all the scientific research that's out there on mindfulness now, they are asking us to bring it, not just to the correctional officers but to probation and parole agents as well. That is huge.

It's so important to keep the energy of our practice alive; that's why we have sixty days of mindfulness a year as members of the Order of Interbeing. Have any of you heard of compassion fatigue, burnout? To me, burnout is a sign that we're violating our own nature in some way. It's usually regarded as a result of trying to give too much, but I think it could result from trying to give what we don't have, and this is the ultimate in giving too little. I think that's where compassion fatigue comes from. When the gift that we give is an integral and valued part of our own journey, when it comes from the organic reality of inner work, it's going to renew itself and be limitless in nature. But that means we have to keep our practice very strong and very alive.

Relationship as Spiritual Practice

To me, relationships are the litmus test of spirituality. If our practice doesn't show up in our relationships, then something is wrong. From a practice perspective, this is probably the single most important thing. As a cop who carried a gun on a daily basis, I started to experience the incredible healing power of nonaggression. What I learned to bring to any interaction was the intention not to cause more harm, and that included those times when I had to use force.

One of the other things that Thay taught me that was so valuable is that compassion can be gentle and compassion can be fierce. Wisdom is knowing when to employ the gentle compassion of understanding or the fierce compassion of good boundaries. How we talk and relate to others is probably the most important peace work that we can engage in.

At work when I was captain of personnel and training, I was in charge of training the whole department, so I could get some really good things done. I remember sitting at my computer, working on the curriculum for the Leadership Academy, when one of my young officers came in and said, "Captain, can I please talk to you?" Internally I went, "Argh!" because I didn't want to interrupt what was happening; I had to get this done. That was such a lesson to me. I immediately recognized what was happening and made a commitment that I was going to switch the foreground and the background. Relationships were going to be more important to me than tasks. That meant managing a to-do list. It meant some people would be upset because I didn't get as many things done as I did before. But what could be more important than giving my presence to another human being? The ripple effects of that, you can never know.

Reforming the Criminal Justice System

I want to talk to you about the current criminal justice system and what I think needs to change. I can't speak for what's going on in other countries, but I can speak about what's going on in the United States. Our current criminal justice system is based on a very faulty premise: the premise that the punishment of the perpetrator is going to heal the victim and rehabilitate the perpetrator.

What I found is that neither of those things is true. It seems to reflect a collective belief that contributes to all kinds of interpersonal and systemic dysfunction. What this premise fails to recognize is one of the basic premises of restorative justice: it's not the wrongdoer's repentance that creates forgiveness; it's the victim's forgiveness that creates repentance. I've seen this happen over and over again. So, what do we have to do to change the criminal justice system? I've been focusing on five things.

1. Teach mindfulness

We need to recognize the costs of working as a police officer. If you take soldiers or people that are on SWAT teams, or the ops-teams in policing, the effects that I talked about are much more intense. We teach them how to keep themselves and others physically safe by using force, and how to use force. But we don't teach them how to keep themselves emotionally safe.

It's important that we begin to provide criminal justice professionals with the training that will help them identify how their world works, especially in the emotional realm. It's important that we not just do stress reduction. The thing about mindfulness, and we know this from the mindfulness trainings, is that it brings a whole ethical framework along with it. What I can do, as a fellow police officer, is translate that language into language they understand. I don't talk to them about Buddhism. I know the language, I know the culture, and all of you know this same thing wherever you are; we have to figure out how to translate it. So, focusing on the emotional health of criminal justice professionals is very important.

2. Recognize biases in decision-making

The second thing is that we need to take seriously the conscious and unconscious biases that police officers and other criminal justice professionals carry that leads to racial profiling and the incredible racial disparities throughout our system. These unconscious biases show up, not just in the obvious ways of deadly force, but they also show up with coworkers and people we interact with. This builds resentments and fuels divisions and threatens our own safety as well as the safety of others.

With respect to racial disparities, I think police officers can be trained to slow down the decision-making process. I used to watch young officers stop a car, and I would say to them, "Okay, I want you to talk me through the reasons you made that stop and what was going on. And now I want you to talk me through where your reasonable suspicion was for having them get out of the car and for searching the car. I want you to talk me through the thought process that happened." There usually is an opportunity for me to make a difference.

There are decision-making points in any organization that can be identified where race can be a factor. It's important that every single one of us identifies those decision-making points in our own organizations. With respect to discrimination and oppression in our collective lives, activists face many challenges. For those of us who have experienced marginalization of some kind, how do we free ourselves from the adaptations that we've made to our oppression? For those of us who have unearthed the unearned assets of privileges, how do we cut through the sense of privilege in some areas of life and our inferior status in others? How do we get over our superiority, inferiority, and equality complexes?

3. Build the capacity of neighborhoods

The third thing that has to happen is coordinated community responses. We have to start taking seriously the proposition that public safety depends on the capacity of neighborhoods.

4. Rely on coordinated community responses

The fourth strategy is that we need to put a lot more effort into reducing environmental opportunities for crime. We could gather more data to notice what the patterns are, be proactive rather than reactive so that we don't keep responding to the same thing over and over. Rather than having officers tied to radio calls—"go here, go there"—they would be more connected to neighborhoods and technology and crime prevention resources. Police officers have to understand that in order to be effective, they can't rely on their authority. They have to rely on so much more, a much larger coordinated community effort.

5. Be wary of militarization

A fifth thing I want to address is that we should all be very, very concerned about the militarization of our police departments. The police mission is very different—to serve and protect our neighbors, our friends, our community residents. We don't do that by militarizing our departments and turning people into enemies. I think that's where communities really matter, because it's pressure on police departments to change that makes all the difference.

The last thing I would say is that police officers need your support. They need your understanding. I've seen what happens when they get it. They need to hear from you, they need to understand you. We need to put police officers and residents of communities into situations where they have the opportunity for dialogue. I think that makes all the difference in the world.

The Most Radical Political Act

One of the things that I committed to, as a result of my own engaged Buddhism, is noticing the unwritten and unconscious agreements that exist in the organization, in the culture of policing. Those things aren't in the policy manual.

The things we get socialized to in any community can be identified. Once you bring them into the conscious arena for discussion, more ethical behaviors start to happen just because people are examining and thinking about those behaviors. So often in the organizations and communities we're part of, we tend to think of ourselves as effect rather than cause. We seem to believe that someone or something else is the problem, and that someone needs to do something better for things to change. We forget that we're a member of this organization! People come out of a meeting and say, "Oh, that was a terrible meeting." And I say, "Were you there? It was a terrible meeting because we all made it a terrible meeting. What could you have done to improve it?" In authentic community membership, we're always holding ourselves accountable for the well-being of the larger community. We become more than just judging critics and consumers, and we start to believe that this world, this organization, this meeting, this gathering, is ours to construct together.

You can be the person who makes the difference in a contentious interaction; you can be the person who, because of your practice, pauses and refrains; you can be the person who, rather than exacerbating pain and violence, transforms it by the way you bear witness to it; you can be the person who, instead of telling people how it should be, brings those unconscious and unskillful ways into the conscious arena of dialogue; you can be the person who chooses not to gossip or to recruit others to your viewpoint behind closed doors in an organization.

Probably the most radical political act that any of us will engage in is to learn to live in more harmony with everyone and everything. To change the world or to love everybody is too big an ambition for any single person, but to respond to *this* moment with engagement and compassion is possible for each and every one of us. What Thich Nhat Hanh inspired in me was a strong belief that even something like carrying a gun for a living can be an act of love, if one is also armed with mindfulness and a compassionate intention.

❧

PART VI

FOR A FUTURE TO BE POSSIBLE

THICH NHAT HANH

Why We Need a Global Ethic
2012

T HE WORLD IN which we live is globalized. Economies halfway around the world affect our own. Our politics, education, and cultural consumption happen on a global scale. Our ethics and morality also need to be globalized. A new global order calls for a new global ethic. A global ethic is the key to addressing the true difficulties of our time.

Around the world, we are facing climate change, terrorism, and wars between people of different religions. Fanaticism, discrimination, division, violence, economic crises, and the destruction of the environment affect us all. We have to look deeply into these sufferings so we can make good decisions and conduct ourselves wisely. We have to sit down together, as people of many traditions, to find the causes of global suffering. If we look deeply with clarity, calm, and peace, we can see the causes of our suffering, uproot and transform them, and find a way out.

A Global Offering

We are many different cultures and nations, each with its own values, ways of behaving, and criteria for conduct. Every country and every culture can offer something beautiful. It will take all of our collective wisdom to make a global code of ethics. With insight from all the world's people and traditions, we can create a global ethic that has as its base mutual respect.

Some people base their ethics on their religion. If you believe there is a deity that decides what is right and wrong, regardless of what you observe, then you only need to follow the rules laid out by that religion to engage in right action. Others follow a scientific or utilitarian approach, looking only at what is a logical consequence of their actions. A Buddhist contribution to global ethics is different from both of these. It is based on observing and understanding the world with mindfulness, concentration, and insight. It begins with an awareness of the nonduality of subject and object, and the interconnectedness of all things. It is a practice that can be accepted by everyone, regardless of whether or not you believe in a god. When you train yourself in this practice, you will see that you have more freedom.

Applying Buddhist Ethics in Daily Life

The term "Engaged Buddhism" was created during the time of the Vietnam War. As monks, nuns, and laypeople during the war, many of us practiced sitting and walking meditation. But we would hear the bombs falling around us, and the cries of the children and adults who were wounded. To meditate is to be aware of what is going on. What was going on around us was the suffering of many people and the destruction of life. So we were motivated by the desire to do something to relieve the suffering in us and around us.

We wanted to serve, and we wanted to practice sitting and walking meditation to give us the stability and peace we needed to go out of the temple and help relieve this suffering. We walked mindfully right alongside suffering, in the places where people were still running under the bombs. We practiced mindful breathing as we cared for children wounded by guns or bombs. If we didn't practice while we served, we would lose ourselves, burn out, and not be able to help anyone.

Engaged Buddhism was born from this difficult situation; we wanted to maintain our practice while responding to the suffering. Engaged Buddhism isn't just Buddhism that's involved in social problems. Engaged Buddhism means we practice mindfulness wherever we are, whatever we are doing, at any time. When we are alone, walking, sitting, drinking our tea, or making our breakfast, that can also be engaged Buddhism. We practice this way not only for ourselves but to preserve ourselves so that we are able to help others and be connected with all life. Engaged Buddhism is not just self-help. It helps us feel more strong and stable and also more connected to others and committed to the happiness of all beings.

Engaged Buddhism is Buddhism that penetrates into life. The Chinese term is 入世佛教, meaning Buddhism that penetrates right into the world, into everyone's real everyday lives, at home, on the streets, in the city. In Vietnamese we use the phrase *Đạo phật đi vào cuộc đời,* literally meaning Buddhism entering into life, entering into society. We have translated that term into English as "engaged," giving us the phrase "Engaged Buddhism."

If Buddhism is not engaged, it's not real Buddhism. This is the attitude of the *bodhisattvas,* beings whose whole intention and actions are to relieve suffering. We practice meditation and mindfulness not only for ourselves; we practice to relieve the suffering of all beings and of the Earth. With the insight of interbeing—that we are elementally interconnected with all other beings—we know that when other people suffer less, we suffer less. And when we suffer less, other people suffer less.

Now, as well as Engaged Buddhism, we are using the term "Applied Buddhism." "Applied" is a word that is often used in science and we deliberately use it here as a way of saying that our understanding of reality can be used to help clarify and find a way to transform every situation. *In Buddhism, there is something that can be used in every circumstance to shed light on the situation and help solve the problem. There is a way to handle any situation with compassion and understanding so that suffering can be relieved.* That is the essence of Applied Buddhism.

The Starting Point for a Buddhist Ethic

Mindfulness is the starting point of Applied Buddhism and is the basis of a Buddhist Ethic. What does being mindful mean? It means, first of all, that we stop and observe deeply what is happening in the present moment. If we do this, we can see the suffering that is in us and around us. We can practice looking deeply with concentration in order to see the causes of this suffering. We need to understand suffering in order to know what kind of action we can take to relieve it. We can use the insight of others, the mindfulness of our Sangha—our larger community of practitioners—to share our insight and understand what kind of action can lead to the transformation of that suffering. When we have collective insight, that will help us see the mutually beneficial path that will lead to the cessation of suffering, not only for one person, but for all of us.

The Virtuous Path

In Vietnamese, we translate ethics as *đạo đức*, the virtuous path. *Đức* means virtue in the sense of honesty, integrity, and understanding. The word is small but it implies a lot—forgiveness, compassion, tolerance, and a sense of common humanity—all the good things that everyone needs. The path should be able to provide the kind of virtuous conduct that will help us to transform and to bring a happy life to everyone. When we have the characteristics of someone who is virtuous, we don't make people suffer. That virtue offers us a guideline, a way of behaving that doesn't cause suffering to others or to ourselves.

Another way to translate ethics is *luong li*, which means the behavior of humans to each other. *Luong* means the morality of humans and *li* means the basic principles that lead to correct behavior and correct action. When you put the two phrases together, you get *dao li luong thuong*, which means moral behavior that everyone agrees to. Usually *thuong* means common, ordinary, something everybody can accept, about which there's a consensus. Ethics are something consistent; they don't change from day to day. So this means a kind of permanent ethics, basic principles we can agree upon that lead to more understanding and acceptance.

Mindfulness, Concentration, and Insight

From the time of his first teaching delivered to his first disciples, the Buddha was very clear and practical about how we can transform our difficulties, both individually and collectively. He focused on how we put the teachings into practice in our everyday lives. That is ethics. Practice is key because practice generates mindfulness, concentration, and insight. These three energies are the foundation of all Buddhist practice and Buddhist ethics. We cannot speak about Buddhist ethics without speaking of these three energies. Mindfulness, concentration, and insight help us build a path that will lead to peace and happiness, transformation and healing. It is so important that we don't focus on ethics in the abstract. Our basic practice is the practice of generating the energy of mindfulness, concentration, and insight. We rely on our insight to guide us and help us bring compassion, love, harmony, and peace to ourselves and to the world.

Recently, a Christian theologian asked me how to bring about a global spirituality. The person who interviewed me seemed to distinguish between the spiritual and the ethical, but there is always a relationship between the two. Anything can be spiritual. When I pick up my tea in mindfulness, when I look at my tea mindfully, and begin to drink my tea in mindfulness, tea drinking becomes very spiritual. When I brush my teeth in mindfulness, aware that it's wonderful to have the time to enjoy brushing my teeth, aware that I'm alive, aware that the wonders of life are all around me, and aware that I can brush with love and joy, then tooth-brushing becomes spiritual. When you go to the toilet, defecating or urinating, if you are mindful, this can also be very spiritual. So there's a deep link between the ethical and the spiritual. If you can't see the spiritual in the ethical, your ethics may be empty. You may live by this ethical code but you don't know why, and so you can't enjoy it. If your ethical and spiritual practices are connected, you will not only follow your ethical path, you will be nourished by it.

The Buddha's First Teaching
Hundreds of years ago, under a sacred fig tree in Bodhgaya, India, the Buddha woke up; he realized deep awakening. His first thought upon awakening was the realization that every living being has this capacity to wake up. He wanted to figure out how he could create a path that would help others on this path toward insight and enlightenment. The Buddha did not want to create a religion. He thought of a path because to follow a path you don't have to believe in a particular creator.

After the Buddha was enlightened, he enjoyed sitting under the Bodhi tree, doing walking meditation along the banks of the Neranjara River, and visiting a nearby lotus pond. The children from nearby Uruvela village would come to visit him. He sat and ate fruit with them and gave them teachings in the form of stories. He wanted to share his experience of practice and awakening with his closest five friends and old partners in practice. He heard they were now living in the Deer Park near Benares. It took him about two weeks to walk from Bodhgaya to the Deer Park. I imagine that he enjoyed every step.

In his very first teaching to his five friends, the Buddha talked about the path of ethics. He said that the path to insight and enlightenment was the Eightfold Noble Path, also called the Eight Ways of Correct Practice. The Eightfold Path is the Fourth Noble Truth of the Buddha's Four Noble Truths. If we understand the Four Noble Truths and use their insight to inform our actions in our daily life, then we are on the path to peace and happiness.

Applied Ethics

The Five Mindfulness Trainings are a very concrete way to apply the teachings of the Four Noble Truths and the Noble Eightfold Path into our daily life. Today we have to call ill-being by its modern names.

The first of the Four Noble Truths is *dukkha*, ill-being, suffering. This ill-being is first of all the tension, stress, and pain in our body. We have to be aware that there is ill-being, there is *dukkha* in our body, in the form of tension, stress, and pain, and we have to apply the practice of mindfulness to try to remove, relieve, and transform these things in our body.

Then in the realm of our feelings, there is *dukkha* in terms of painful feelings and painful emotions like anger, fear, despair. Not only does the way we live make us suffer, it also makes others suffer too, even those very close to us, like our mother, our father, our son, our daughter, our partner. That is why communication between the two of us has become very difficult, and we can no longer talk to each other. So, one of the new names of ill-being is "difficult relationships," difficult communication. The practice is to find a way to restore communication and to reconcile with the other person.

The teaching and the practice that can help us to remove tension, stress, and pain; to transform anger, fear, and despair; and to overcome difficult relationships, restore communication, and reconcile—that teaching and practice is called "applied ethics." And since that teaching and practice can be used by anyone in our world, we can call it a *global* ethic.

We do not need to use Buddhist terms, even though the roots of this teaching and practice have come from the Buddhist tradition. Using this kind of language can help everyone practice. Anyone can feel comfortable with the teaching and practice, including those who are not Buddhist, but are Christian, Jewish, Muslim—even Communist. It's our responsibility to find secular words in order to translate the Dharma into the kind of language that can be accepted by everyone.

ROSHI JOAN HALIFAX

Hope at the Edge
2019

A GOOD PART of my life has been spent relating to situations that might be deemed hopeless—as an anti-war activist and civil rights worker in the 1960s, and as a caregiver for dying people and a teacher of clinicians in conventional medical centers for fifty years. I also worked as a volunteer with death row inmates for six years, continue to serve in medical clinics in remote areas of the Himalayas, and in Kathmandu served Rohingya refugees who have no status, anywhere. Feminism and ending gender violence have also been lifelong commitments of mine.

You might ask, why work in such hopeless situations? Why care about ending the direct and structural violence of war or injustice? Isn't violence a constant in our world? Why have hope for people who are dying, when death is inevitable; why work with those who are on death row, when redemption is unlikely; or why serve refugees fleeing from genocide, when no country seems to want these men, women, and children? Why work for women's rights? What does it mean to hope in our fraught world?

Wise Hope

I have long been troubled by the notion of hope. It just did not seem very Buddhist to hope. The Zen Master Shunryu Suzuki Roshi once said that life is "like stepping onto a boat which is about to sail out to sea and sink." That certainly brings conventional hope up short! But some time ago, in part because of the work of social critic Rebecca Solnit and her powerful book *Hope in the Dark*, I am opening to another view of hope—what I am calling "wise hope."

As Buddhists, we know that ordinary hope is based in desire, wanting an outcome that could well be different from what might actually happen. To make matters worse, not getting what we hoped for is often experienced as a misfortune. If we look deeply, we realize that anyone who is conventionally hopeful has an expectation that always hovers in the background, the shadow of fear that one's wishes will not be fulfilled. Ordinary hope, then, is a form of suffering. This kind of hope is a nemesis and a partner with fear.

We might then ask: what more specifically is hope? Let's begin by saying what hope is not: hope is not the belief that everything will turn out well. People die. Populations die out. Civilizations die. Planets die. Stars die. Recalling the words of Suzuki Roshi, the boat is going to sink! If we look, we see the evidence of suffering, of injustice, of futility, of desolation, of harm, of things ending all around us, and even within us. But we have to understand that hope is not a story based on optimism, that everything will be okay. Optimists imagine that everything will turn out positively. I consider this point of view dangerous; being an optimist means one doesn't have to bother; one doesn't have to act. Also, if things don't turn out well, cynicism or futility often follow. Hope, of course, is also opposed to the narrative that everything is getting worse, which is the position that pessimists take. Pessimists take refuge in depressive apathy or apathy driven by cynicism. And, as we might expect, both optimists and pessimists are excused from engagement.

So, what is it to be hopeful and not optimistic? The American novelist Barbara Kingsolver explains it this way:

> I have been thinking a lot lately about the difference between being optimistic and being hopeful. I would say that I'm a hopeful person, although not necessarily optimistic. Here's how I would describe it. The pessimist would say, "It's going to be a terrible winter; we're all going to die." The optimist would say, "Oh, it'll be all right; I don't think it'll be that bad." The hopeful person would say, "Maybe someone will still be alive in February, so I'm going to put some potatoes in the root cellar just in case. . . ." Hope is . . . a mode of resistance . . . a gift I can try to cultivate.

If we look at hope through the lens of Buddhism, we discover that wise hope is born of radical uncertainty, rooted in the unknown and the unknowable. How could we ever know what is really going to happen? Wise hope requires that we open ourselves to what we do not know, what we cannot know, that we open ourselves to being surprised, perpetually surprised. In fact, wise hope appears through the spaciousness of radical uncertainty, of surprise, and this is the space in which we can engage. This is what socially engaged Buddhist Joanna Macy calls "active hope," the engaged expression of wise hope.

It's when we discern courageously, and at the same time realize we don't know what will happen, that wise hope comes alive; in the midst of improbability and possibility is where the imperative to act rises up. Wise hope is not seeing things unrealistically but rather seeing things as they are, including the truth of impermanence, as well as the truth of suffering—both its existence and the possibility of its transformation, for better or for worse.

Through another Buddhist lens, we can see that wise hope reflects the understanding that what we do matters, even though how and when it may matter, who and what it may impact, are not things we can really know beforehand. Rebecca Solnit points out that truly, we cannot know what will unfold from our actions now or in the future; yet we can trust that things will change; they always do. But our vows, our actions, how we live, what we care about, what we care for, and how we care really do matter all the same.

Yet often we become paralyzed by the belief that there is nothing to hope for—that our patient's cancer diagnosis is a one-way street with no exit, that our political situation is beyond repair, that there is no way out of our climate crisis. We might feel that nothing makes sense anymore or that we have no power and there's no reason to act.

I often say that there should be just two words over the door of our Zen temple in Santa Fe: *Show up!* One might ask why would I want these words over the door of our temple, when despair, defeatism, cynicism, skepticism, and the apathy of for-getting are fed by the corroding effect of conventional hopeless-ness. Yes, suffering is present. We cannot deny it. There are 67.3 million refugees in the world today; only eleven countries are free from conflict; climate change is turning forests into deserts. Japan's population is declining. Suicide rates for children are up. Violence toward women is increasing. Many feel no connection to religion or spirituality, and countless people are deeply alien-ated and take refuge in their digital devices. We also see that economic injustice is driving people into greater and greater pov-erty. Racism and sexism remain rampant. Our medical system is deeply challenged. Globalization and neoliberalism are putting the planet at great risk.

The peacemaker Daniel Berrigan once remarked, "One cannot level one's moral lance at every evil in the universe. There are just too many of them. But you can do something; and the difference between doing something and doing nothing is everything." Berrigan understood that wise hope doesn't mean denying the realities that we are confronted with today. It means facing them, addressing them, and remembering what else is present, like the shifts in our values that allow us to recognize and move us to address suffering right now. Seven hundred years ago in Japan, Zen Master Keizan wrote: "Do not find fault with the present." He invites us to see it, not flee it!

Returning to the difference between hope and optimism and why hope makes sense in our fraught world, the Czech statesman Václav Havel said, "Hope is definitely not the same thing as optimism. It is not the conviction that something will turn out well but the certainty that something makes sense, regardless of how it turns out." For many of us, it is an imperative to march for peace, to work for the ending of nuclear proliferation, to put pressure on the U.S. government to re-sign the Paris Agreement on Climate Change. It makes sense to shelter the homeless, including those fleeing from war and climate devastation; it makes sense to support compassion and care in medicine in spite of the increasing presence of technology that stands between patients and clinicians. It makes sense to educate girls and vote for women. It makes sense to sit with dying people, take care of our elders, feed the hungry, love and educate our children. In truth, we can't know how things will turn out, but we can trust that there will be movement, there will be change. And at the same time, something deep inside us affirms what is good and right to do. So we move forward in our day and sit at the bedside of the dying grandmother or teach that third grade class of kids from the poor neighborhood. We bear witness to the young woman who wants to take her life. We hold our CEO's and politicians accountable. It is exactly at this point of not knowing, that our vows come alive, in the midst of seeming futility or meaninglessness.

The American Benedictine nun and social activist Sister Joan Chittister writes: "Everywhere I looked, hope existed—but only as some kind of green shoot in the midst of struggle. It was a theological concept, not a spiritual practice. Hope, I began to realize, was not a state of life. It was at best a gift of life."

This gift of life that I have called "wise hope" is rooted in our vows and is what Zen Master Dogen means when he admonishes us to "give life to life," even if it's just one dying person at a time, one refugee at a time, one prisoner at a time, one life at a time, one ecosystem at a time.

As Buddhists, we share a common aspiration to awaken from our own confusion, from greed, and from anger in order to free others from suffering. For many of us, this aspiration is not a "small self" improvement program. The Bodhisattva Vows at the heart of the Mahayana tradition are, if nothing else, a powerful expression of radical and wise hope and hope against all odds. This kind of hope is free of desire, free from any attachment to outcome; it is a species of hope that is victorious over fear. What else could be the case as we chant: "Creations are numberless, I vow to free them. Delusions are inexhaustible, I vow to transform them. Reality is boundless, I vow to perceive it. The awakened way is unsurpassable, I vow to embody it."

Our journey through life is one of peril and possibility—and sometimes both at once. How can we stand on the threshold between suffering and freedom, between futility and hope, and remain informed by both worlds? With our penchant for dualities, humans tend to identify either with the terrible truth of suffering or with freedom from suffering. But I believe that excluding any part of the larger landscape of our lives reduces the territory of our understanding. This includes the complex landscape of hope and futility.

When I began my work in the end-of-life care field nearly fifty years ago, dying in Western culture was often considered a failure of medicine, even a failure of life. At the time, I did not consider hope as anything relevant. What motivated me to do the work was that it felt like an imperative to do the best I could to address the deficits of compassion that I witnessed in modern medicine and to serve those who were suffering, including dying patients, family caregivers, and clinicians.

At the same time, I could not be attached to any outcome, as I intuitively knew that futility might paralyze me. I learned that in order to do my best I had to move away from the story that working for peace, justice, or an equitable and compassionate society, including medical culture, would turn out well, was too big a job, or was hopeless. I had to "just show up" and do what I felt was morally aligned with my values, my principles, my commitments, regardless of what might happen. Much later, I came to understand that this work was an outcome of the gift of wise hope, springing from not-knowing as well from the sense of meaning it gave my life.

I also somehow understood that being with dying was sacred work. For most people, confronting death brings into focus existential dimensions of our lives. I knew that I too was mortal; I too would face my death one day; I too would confront loss and sorrow. What happened was that I was unwittingly drawn into the strong current of the end-of-life care field without having the conscious intention to do this work. I only knew that I had to turn toward and serve dying people, because it felt aligned with who I was and who I was learning to be.

Living by Vow

In Zen, this is what I believe is called "living by vow." I have come to understand that wise hope is in fact living by vow, and a powerful expression of fundamental integrity and respect.

As my Zen practice matured over the years, I came to understand that living by vow reflects our ability to be guided by our deepest values, to be conscientious, and to connect to who we really are. Living by vow also points to our capacity for moral sensitivity, our ability to identify morally relevant features in our interaction with others, in how we choose to live our lives, in the organizations in which we work, and in those whom we serve. Living by vow reflects our capacity for insight and our ability to manifest moral nerve to deal with issues of harm, no matter how egregious or seemingly insignificant.

I came to see that our vows are a grammar of values reflected in our attitudes, in our thoughts, in our hopes, and in how we are in the world. The promises and commitments reflected in wise hope are fundamentally about how we are with each other and ourselves, how we connect, and how we meet the world. Practicing our vows and embodying them reflect our integrity and help give us ballast and meaning as we confront the inner and outer storms of being human. And what we come to realize is that our vows are a bigger landscape than most of us realize, and they support integrity in our lives, and protect our world, and give hope gravity and momentum.

The most powerful vows are those that point us toward living a larger identity, of being Buddha, of being a Buddha now. These vows support us in recognizing impermanence, interdependence, unselfishness, compassion, and wisdom. I believe that these kinds of vows are essential practices that support integrity and the development of moral character, and they are the fuel of wise hope.

Our vows are strengthened and actualized through the medium of wise hope. If wise hope is not present, we might be afraid to take a stand and choose to ignore or back away from situations of harm. We might be in denial or willfully ignorant over the suffering experienced by others when transgressive situations arise. We might be morally apathetic, or paralyzed by hopelessness, or living in a bubble of privilege and be blind to suffering. But if we aren't trapped by these defenses, we might step forward and meet harm with the determination to end suffering, even when our actions might appear futile; and we do so "with no gaining idea," to quote Suzuki Roshi.

I have learned from my long experience of being with dying that what keeps us upright in our aspirations and vows is our moral nerve, the courage to stand in principles of goodness and non-harming. What keeps our integrity on track is our moral sensitivity, our ability to see the contours of reality that make harm and futility visible and also point past suffering to a larger and deeper identity. As Brené Brown says, we need both a strong back and a soft front, lived equanimity and compassion, to keep ourselves aligned with our values and abiding in the strength of wise hope.

We also need to have the kind of heart that is wide enough to accept rejection, criticism, disparagement, anger, and blame, if our views, aspirations, and actions are against the mainstream and what we do are seen by others as without meaning or even a threat to the social order of the day. Furthermore, it is important to remember that our vows support us in staying aligned with our deepest values and remind us of who we really are.

We live in a time of rapid psychosocial change, a time of the normalization of disrespect, lying, violence, and worse. We live in a time when futility and hopelessness are all too common. We also live in an extraordinary time that could not be foreseen, in which we see the spread of socially engaged Buddhism in many parts of the world and in many sectors of society: Buddhist chaplains working in hospitals and prisons; Buddhists working to protect Central American immigrant mothers and children fleeing from violence; Buddhists in service to those who have fallen into despair and want to take their lives; socially engaged Buddhists serving food and providing shelter for the homeless; Buddhists working with refugees in Greece; Buddhists supporting medical care for Rohingya refugees in Kathmandu; socially engaged Buddhists bearing witness in Rohingya refugee camps in Bangladesh, bearing witness in Auschwitz, and in Native American lands; Buddhists working in medical projects in the high Himalayas; socially engaged Buddhists working as chaplains in schools and businesses; socially engaged Buddhists working to end nuclear proliferation; and socially engaged Buddhists politically and institutionally engaging in issues related to structural violence. It's a challenging and brave time in the history of our world. For us to be engaged requires that we perceive the whole spectrum of both suffering and freedom from suffering, both futility and hope, wise hope.

Edge States and Social Engagement

I want now to address recent work I have been doing around what I call "Edge States" and explore Edge States in relation to wise hope. Understanding Edge States can give our vows greater grounding, deepen our access to wise hope, and enhance resilience for those of us who are socially engaged Buddhists.

What are Edge States? Over the years, I slowly became aware of five internal and interpersonal qualities that are keys to a compassionate and courageous life, a life that is grounded in wise hope, and without which we cannot serve, nor can we survive. Yet if these internal and interpersonal resources deteriorate, they can manifest as dangerous landscapes that cause harm. I call these bivalent qualities *Edge States.*

The Edge States are altruism, empathy, integrity, respect, and engagement, assets of a mind and heart that exemplify caring, connection, virtue, strength, and wise hope. Yet we can also lose our firm footing on the high edge of any of these qualities and slide into a mire of suffering where we find ourselves caught in the toxic and chaotic waters of the harmful aspects of an Edge State.

For example, *altruism* can turn into *pathological altruism.* Selfless actions in service to others are essential to the well-being of society and the natural world. It is important to note that healthy and unconditional altruism is not based in conventional hope. It is a psychosocial imperative and arises naturally, like the right hand taking care of the left hand should the left hand be injured. But sometimes our seemingly altruistic acts harm us, harm those whom we are trying to serve, or harm the institutions we serve in. This is when altruism gets compromised—when small hope for an outcome or hope for recognition, or fear of failure drive us toward helping others at a cost to all. This is what social psychologists call pathological altruism.

A second Edge State is *empathy*, which can slide into *empathic distress.* When we expand our subjectivity to include the suffering of another person physically, emotionally, or cognitively, empathy can bring us closer to another's experience. This can inspire us to serve, and can enhance our understanding of others. But if we take on too much of the suffering of another, and identify too intensely with the suffering, we may become damaged and unable to serve. Wise hope allows us to see that impermanence will prevail. It also helps us understand that we cannot ever really know the experience of another. Thus, wise hope engenders humility through not knowing, and grounds our experience of empathy to keep it healthy and balanced.

A third Edge State is *integrity*, which points to having strong moral principles. But when we engage in or witness acts that violate our sense of integrity, justice, or beneficence, *moral suffering* can be the outcome. Moral suffering includes moral distress, moral injury, moral outrage, and moral apathy. We have to be aware that conventional hope can drive us to violate our integrity when we are a toy of our expectations or the expectations of others. On the other hand, integrity is founded on wise hope, the recognition of the basic goodness in others and ourselves.

The fourth Edge State is *respect*, a way we uphold beings and things in high regard. Respect can disappear into the swamp of disrespect, when we go against the grain of compassion-based values and principles of civility, and when we end up disparaging others or ourselves. Disrespect is an attitude that reflects cynicism and futility. Wise hope provides the space in which we can see the goodness as well as the suffering of others, and where we hold all in equal regard.

The fifth Edge State is *engagement* in our work, which gives a sense of purpose and meaning to our lives, particularly if our work serves others. But overwork, a toxic workplace, and an experience of the lack of efficacy can lead to burnout, which can cause physical and psychological collapse. Conventional hope often leads to burnout. A feeling of futility is also a cause of burnout. Wise hope prevents burnout, and fuels and inspires healthy engagement.

Like a doctor who diagnoses an illness before recommending a treatment, I felt compelled to explore the healthy and destructive sides of altruism, empathy, integrity, respect, and engagement. Along the way, I was surprised to learn that even in their degraded forms, Edge States can teach and strengthen us, just as bone and muscle are strengthened when exposed to stress, or, if broken or torn, can heal in the right circumstances and become stronger for having been injured.

In other words, losing our footing and sliding down the slope of harm need not be a terminal catastrophe. Being caught in the grip of unrealistic hope or abject futility need not be the worst thing in the world. There is humility, perspective, wisdom, and wise hope that can be gained from our greatest difficulties.

In her book *The Sovereignty of Good* (1970), Iris Murdoch defined humility as a "selfless respect for reality." She writes that "our picture of ourselves has become too grand." This I discovered from sitting at the bedside of dying people and being with other caregivers. Doing close work with those who were dying and those who were giving care showed me the costs of suffering for caregiver as well as patient. Since that time, I have learned from teachers, lawyers, CEOs, human rights workers, and parents that they can experience the same. I was then reminded of something profoundly important and yet completely obvious: that the way out of the storm of suffering, the way back to freedom on the high edge of strength and courage is through the power of compassion born of wise hope. This is why I took a deep dive into trying to understand the dual nature of Edge States are and how they can shape our lives and the life of the world.

Sitting with a dying person or a dying planet, we show up; we do the best we can; we rely on altruism, empathy, integrity, respect, engagement, and most importantly compassion and wise hope, even though these powerful human virtues can be challenged. Without these virtues, we cease to really live. Etty Hillesum, who died in Auschwitz in November 1943, said: "Ultimately, we have just one moral duty: to reclaim large areas of peace in ourselves, more and more peace, and to reflect it toward others. And the more peace there is in us, the more peace there will also be in our troubled world." We all know that indifference kills. In service to peace, in service to nonviolence, in service to life, we live by vow: we have the courage to stand at the edge, and we live in the embrace of wise hope.

bell hooks

Toward a Worldwide Culture of Love
2006

A T A CONFERENCE on women and Buddhism that took place in spring last year, I was upset because most of the speakers were giving their talks in this serene, beautiful chapel, a place evoking a sense of the divine, a sacred place for the word to be spoken and heard, yet my talk was to take place on a Friday night in an unappealing, cavernous auditorium. Lamenting my exclusion from the realm of the sacred, I complained that I was exiled because I was not seen as a "real" Buddhist—no long time with a teacher, no journey to India or Tibet, never present at important retreats—definitely someone engaged in buddhadharma without credentials. The two companions who had joined me at the conference listened with compassion to my whining. Why did I have to speak in a huge auditorium? Why did I have to speak on a Friday night? Yes, I told them, lots of people might want to hear bell hooks speak on feminist theory and cultural criticism, but that's not the same as a talk about Buddhism.

Yet when the time came, the seats were filled. And it was all about Buddhism. It was a truly awesome night. Sacred presence was there, a spirit of love and compassion like spring mist covered us, and loving-kindness embraced me and my words. This is always the measure of mindful practice—whether we can create the conditions for love and peace in circumstances that are difficult, whether we can stop resisting and surrender, working with what we have, where we are.

Fundamentally, the practice of love begins with acceptance—the recognition that wherever we are is the appropriate place to practice, that the present moment is the appropriate time. But for so many of us our longing to love and be loved has always been about a time to come, a space in the future when it will just happen, when our hungry hearts will finally be fed, when we will find love.

More than thirty years ago, when l first began to think about Buddhism, there was little or no talk about Buddhism and love. Being a Buddhist was akin to being a leftist; it was all about the intellect, the philosophical mind. It was faith for the thinking "man" and love was nowhere to be found in the popular Buddhist literature at that time. D. T. Suzuki's collection on Buddhism published in the late forties and throughout the fifties had nothing to say about love. Shunryu Suzuki's *Zen Mind, Beginner's Mind* was the Buddhist manifesto of the early seventies, and it did not speak to us of love.

Even though Christmas Humphreys would tell readers in his fifties publication *Buddhism: An Introduction and Guide* that "Buddhism is as much a religion of love as any on Earth," Westerners looking to Buddhism in those days were not looking for love. In fact Humphreys was talking back to folks who had designated Buddhism a "cold religion." To prove that love was important to Buddhists, he quoted from the *Itivuttaka*: "All the means that can be used as bases for right action are not worth the sixteenth part of the emancipation of the heart through love. This takes all others up into itself, outshining them in glory." Yet twenty years after this publication, there was still little talk of Buddhism and love. In circles where an individual would dare to speak of love, they would be told that Buddhists were more concerned with the issue of compassion. It was as though love was just not a relevant, serious subject for Buddhists.

During the turbulent sixties and seventies, the topic of love made its way to the political forefront. Peace activists were telling us to "make love not war." And the great preacher Martin Luther King, Jr., elevated the call to love from the hidden longing of the solitary heart to a public cry. He proclaimed love to be the only effective way to end injustice and bring peace, declaring that, "Sooner or later all the people of the world will have to discover a way to live together in peace. . . . If this is to be achieved, man must evolve for all human conflict a method which rejects revenge, aggression, and retaliation. The foundation of such a method is love."

There could not have been a more perfect historical Dharma moment for spiritual leaders to speak out on the issue of love. No doubt divine providence was at work in the universe when Martin Luther King, Jr., and a little-known Vietnamese Buddhist monk named Thich Nhat Hanh found themselves walking the same path—walking toward one another—engaged in a practice of love. Young men whose hearts were awakening, they created in mystical moments of sacred encounter a symbolic sangha.

They affirmed one another's work. In the loneliness of the midnight hour, King would fall on his knees and ask himself the question, "How can I say I worship a god of love and support war?" Thich Nhat Hanh, knowing by heart all the bonds of human connection that war severs, challenged the world to think peace, declaring in the wake of the Vietnam War that he "thought it was quite plain that if you have to choose between Buddhism and peace, then you must choose peace." Linking Buddhism with social engagement, Thich Nhat Hanh's work attracted Westerners (myself included) precisely because he offered a spiritual vision of the universe that promoted working for peace and justice.

In *Essential Buddhism: A Complete Guide to Beliefs and Practices*, Jack Maguire sees Buddhism's emphasis on nonviolence as one of the central features that attracts Westerners. He writes: "Already large numbers of people concerned about such violence have been drawn to Buddhism as a spiritual path that addresses the problem directly. Besides offering them a means of committing themselves more actively to the cause of universal peace, it gives them a context for becoming more intimate with others who are like-minded. It therefore helps restore their hope that people can live together in harmony."

Significantly, Buddhism began to attract many more Western followers because it linked the struggle for world peace with the desire of each individual to be engaged in meaningful spiritual practice. Coming out of a time when it had been cool for smart people to be agnostic or atheist, people wanted permission to seek spiritual connection.

Introducing the collection of essays entitled *Engaged Buddhism in the West*, editor Christopher Queen calls attention to the fact that socially engaged Buddhism "has emerged in the context of a global conversation on human rights, distributive justice, and social progress. . . . As a style of ethical practice engaged Buddhism may be seen as a new paradigm of Buddhist liberation." In the late eighties and nineties, Thich Nhat Hanh's teachings on engaged Buddhist practice spoke directly to concerned citizens in the United States who had been working on behalf of peace and justice, especially for an end to domination based on race, gender, and sexual practice, but who had begun to feel hopelessness and despair. The assassination of visionary leaders, the inability to end racism and create a just society, the failure of contemporary feminism, which, rather than healing the split between men and women, actually led to further gender warfare—all of this engendered a collective feeling of hopelessness. Buddhist teachers addressed this suffering directly.

Chögyam Trungpa Rinpoche was one of the first Buddhist teachers in the West offering the insight that this profound hopelessness could be the groundwork for spiritual practice. Certainly I came to Buddhism searching for a way out of suffering and despair. Thich Nhat Hanh spoke to my struggle to connect spiritual practice with social engagement. Yet at the time, his Buddhism often seemed rigid, and like many other seekers I turned to the teachings of Trungpa Rinpoche to confront the longings of my heart and find a way to embrace a passionate life. For many Western seekers, the feeling that we had failed to create a culture of peace and justice led us back to an introspective search of our intimate relations, which more often than not were messy and full of strife, suffering, and pain. How could any of us truly believe that we could create world peace when we could not make peace in our intimate relationships with family, partners, friends, and neighbors?

Responding to this collective anguish of spirit, visionary teachers (like King, Thich Nhat Hanh, the Dalai Lama, Sharon Salzberg) were moved by spiritual necessity to speak more directly about the practice of love. Proclaiming transformation in his consciousness engendered by a focus on love, Thich Nhat Hanh declared in the poem "The Fruit of Awareness Is Ripe": *when I knew how to love, the doors of my heart opened wide before the wind. / Reality was calling out for revolution.* That spirit of revolution, that call to practice transformative love, captured my critical imagination and merged with my longing to find a loving partner.

When lecturing on ending domination around the world, listening to the despair and hopelessness, I asked individuals who were hopeful to talk about what force in their life pushed them to make a profound transformation, moving them from a will to dominate toward a will to be compassionate. The stories I heard were all about love. That sense of love as a transformative power was also present in the narratives of individuals working to create loving personal relationships. Writing about metta, "love" or "loving-kindness," as the first of the brahmaviharas, the heavenly abodes, Sharon Salzberg reminds us in her insightful book *Lovingkindness: The Revolutionary Art of Happiness*, that, "In cultivating love, we remember one of the most powerful truths the Buddha taught ... that the forces in the mind that bring suffering are able to temporarily hold down the positive forces such as love or wisdom, but they can never destroy them.... Love can uproot fear or anger or guilt, because it is a greater power. Love can go anywhere. Nothing can obstruct it." Clearly, at the end of the nineties, an awakening of heart was taking place in our nation, our concern with the issue of love was evident in the growing body of literature on the subject.

Because of the awareness that love and domination cannot coexist, there is a collective call for everyone to place learning how to love on their emotional and/or spiritual agenda. We have witnessed the way in which movements for justice that denounce dominator culture, yet have an underlying commitment to corrupt uses of power, do not really create fundamental changes in our societal structure. When radical activists have not made a core break with dominator thinking (imperialist, white supremacist, capitalist patriarchy), there is no union of theory and practice, and real change is not sustained. That's why cultivating the mind of love is so crucial. When love is the ground of our being, a love ethic shapes our participation in politics.

To work for peace and justice we begin with the individual practice of love, because it is there that we can experience first-hand love's transformative power. Attending to the damaging impact of abuse in many of our childhoods helps us cultivate the mind of love. Abuse is always about lovelessness, and if we grow into our adult years without knowing how to love, how then can we create social movements that will end domination, exploitation, and oppression? John Welwood shares the insight in *Perfect Love, Imperfect Relationships*, that many of us carry a "wound of the heart" that emerged in childhood conditioning, creating "a disconnection from the loving openness that is our nature." He explains: "This universal wound shows up in the body as emptiness, anxiety, trauma, or depression, and in relationships as the mood of unlove. . . . On the collective level, this deep wound in the human psyche leads to a world wracked by struggle, stress, and dissension. . . . The greatest ills on the planet—war, poverty, economic injustice, ecological degradation—all stem from our inability to trust one another, honor differences, engage in respectful dialogue, and reach mutual understanding." Welwood links individual failure to learn how to love in childhood with larger social ills; however, even those who are fortunate to love and be loved in childhood grow to maturity in a culture of domination that devalues love.

Being loving can actually lead one to be more at odds with mainstream culture. Even though, as Riane Eisler explains in *The Power of Partnership*, our "first lessons about human relations are not learned in workplaces, businesses, or even schools, but in parent–child and other relations," those habits of being are not formed in isolation. The larger culture in our nation shapes how we relate. Any child born in a hospital first experiences life in a place where private and public merge. The interplay of these two realities will be constant in our lives. It is precisely because the dictates of dominator culture structure our lives that it is so difficult for love to prevail.

When I began, years ago now, to focus on the power of love as a healing force, no one really disagreed with me. Yet what they continue to accept in their daily life is lovelessness, because doing the work of love requires resisting the status quo. In Thich Nhat Hanh's most recent treatise on the subject, *True Love: A Practice for Awakening the Heart*, he reminds us that "to love, in the context of Buddhism, is above all to be there." He then raises the question of whether or not we have time for love. Right now, there is such a profound collective cultural awareness that we need to practice love if we are to heal ourselves and the planet. The task awaiting us is to move from awareness to action. The practice of love requires that we make time, that we embrace change.

Fundamentally, to begin the practice of love we must slow down and be still enough to bear witness in the present moment. If we accept that love is a combination of care, commitment, knowledge, responsibility, respect, and trust, we can then be guided by this understanding. We can use these skillful means as a map in our daily life to determine right action. When we cultivate the mind of love, we are, as Sharon Salzberg says, "cultivating the good," and that means "recovering the incandescent power of love that is present as a potential in all of us" and using "the tools of spiritual practice to sustain our real, moment-to-moment experience of that vision." To be transformed by the practice of love is to be born again, to experience spiritual renewal. What I witness daily is the longing for that renewal and the fear that our lives will be changed utterly if we choose love. That fear paralyzes. It leaves us stuck in the place of suffering.

When we commit to love in our daily life, habits are shattered. We are necessarily working to end domination. Because we no longer are playing by the safe rules of the status quo, rules that if we obey guarantee us a specific outcome, love moves us to a new ground of being. This movement is what most people fear. If we are to galvanize the collective longing for spiritual well-being that is found in the practice of love, we must be more willing to identify the forms that longing will take in daily life. Folks need to know the ways we change and are changed when we love. It is only by bearing concrete witness to love's transformative power in our daily lives that we can assure those who are fearful that commitment to love will be redemptive, a way to experience salvation.

Lots of people listen and affirm the words of visionary teachers who speak on the necessity of love. Yet they feel in their everyday lives that they simply do not know how to link theory and practice. When Thich Nhat Hanh tells in *Transformation and Healing* that "understanding is the very foundation of love and compassion," that "if love and compassion are in our hearts, every thought, word, and deed can bring about a miracle," we are moved. We may even feel a powerful surge of awareness and possibility.

Then we go home and find ourselves uncertain about how to realize true love. I remember talking deeply with Thich Nhat Hanh about a love relationship in which I felt I was suffering. In his presence I was ashamed to confess the depths of my anguish and the intensity of my anger toward the man in my life. Speaking with such tenderness he told me, "Hold on to your anger and use it as compost for your garden." Listening to these wise words I felt as though a thousand rays of light were shining throughout my being. I was certain I could go home, let my light shine, and everything would be better; I would find the promised happy ending. The reality was that communication was still difficult. Finding ways to express true love required vigilance, patience, a will to let go, and the creative use of the imagination to invent new ways of relating. Thich Nhat Hanh had told me to see the practice of love in this tumultuous relationship as spiritual practice, to find in the mind of love a way to understanding, forgiveness, and peace. Of course this was all work. Just as cultivating a garden requires turning over the ground, pulling weeds, planting, and watering, doing the work of love is all about taking action.

Whenever anyone asks me how they can begin the practice of love I tell them giving is the place to start. In *The Return of the Prodigal Son*, Henri Nouwen offers this testimony: "Every time I take a step in the direction of generosity I know that I am moving from fear to love." Salzberg sees giving as a way to purify the mind: "Giving is an inward state, a generosity of the spirit that extends to ourselves as well as to others." Through giving we develop the mind of gratitude. Giving enables us to experience the fullness of abundance—not only the abundance we have, but the abundance in sharing. In sharing all that we have we become more. We awaken the heart of love.

Dominator thinking and practice relies for its maintenance on the constant production of a feeling of lack, of the need to grasp. Giving love offers us a way to end this suffering—loving ourselves, extending that love to everything beyond the self, we experience wholeness. We are healed. The Buddha taught that we can create a love so strong that, as Salzberg states, our "minds become like a pure, flowing river that cannot be burned." Such love is the foundation of spiritual awakening.

If we are to create a worldwide culture of love, then we need enlightened teachers to guide us. We need concrete strategies for practicing love in the midst of domination. Imagine all that would change for the better if every community in our nation had a center (a sangha) that would focus on the practice of love, of loving-kindness. All the great religious traditions share the belief that love is our reason for being. This shared understanding of love helps connect Buddhist traditions with Christian practice. Those coming to Buddhism from Christian traditions appreciate the work that Thich Nhat Hanh has done to create a bridge connecting these spiritual paths. In *Living Buddha, Living Christ* he offers a vision of inclusiveness, reminding us that both Jesus and Buddha are doors we can walk through to find true love. He explains: "In Buddhism such a special door is deeply appreciated because that door allows us to enter the realm of mindfulness, loving-kindness, peace, and joy." Sharing the truism that there are many doors of teaching, he states: "Each of us, by our practice and our loving-kindness, is capable of opening new Dharma doors."

All of us who work toward creating a culture of love seek to share a real body of teaching that can reach everyone where we are. That was the lesson I learned at the conference last May—to be broad, to extend the circle of love beyond boundaries, bringing together people from different backgrounds and traditions, and feeling together the way love connects us.

MATTHIEU RICARD

Wisdom and Compassion at the Service of Others 2016

B UDDHIST TEXTS OFTEN state that wisdom and compassion are the two wings of the bird that takes us to enlightenment. Without compassion, wisdom is sterile, and without
wisdom, compassion is blind. As the great Buddhist master
Shantideva wrote:

All the joy the world contains
Has come through wishing happiness for others.
All the misery the world contains
Has come from wanting pleasure for oneself.[1]

A nineteenth-century Tibetan master, Shabkar, also wrote:

With compassion, the root of Dharma is planted,
Without compassion, the root of Dharma is rotten.[2]

---

1 Shantideva, Padmakara Translation Group, trans., *The Way of the Bodhisattva*
(Boston: Shambhala Publications, 2006).
2 Matthieu Ricard and Padmakara Translation Group, trans., *The Life of Shabkar:*
The Autobiography of a Tibetan Yogin. (Boston: Shambhala Publications, 2001).

Buddhism teaches that there are three attitudes that we can have toward beings: the attitude of a king, who establishes his own power before taking care of his subjects; the attitude of the ferryman, who reaches the farther shore at the same time as his passengers; and the attitude of the shepherd, who walks behind his flock and ensures that all his charges are safe before taking care of himself. A true Bodhisattva is like the shepherd. He or she is ready to renounce nirvana, or Buddhahood, in order to stay in samsara to help sentient beings.

In order to significantly help others, it is essential to build a stable inner practice that fosters essential qualities such as wisdom, inner freedom, inner strength, resilience, emotional balance, and selflessness. All human shortcomings can be addressed through training of the mind.

To be at the service of others is doubtless one of the most essential ways to have a meaningful life. However, too often we hear of charitable endeavors and humanitarian projects that are meant to accomplish good being derailed by clashes of ego, biases, greed, or even worse corruption. Likewise, we should not stop at helping only human beings.

Buddhism is quite unique in recognizing that all beings, including the eight million animal species that are our co-citizens on this Earth, are endowed not only with consciousness, but also with buddha-nature. It is clear that all beings, no matter what their level of intelligence is, share one common aspiration: to avoid suffering. Since we are all in favor of morality and justice, it is obvious that it is immoral and unjust to inflict unnecessary suffering and death on any sentient beings. This sums up the reason why we should, in our modern world, change our attitude toward other species.

It is estimated that around 100 billion *Homo sapiens* have lived on Earth since our species appeared. Only 12,000 years ago there were only two to five million humans on earth! Now, this is the number of animals we kill every *two months* for our so-called "needs." This is a lot of animals and a lot of deaths! We kill sixty billion land animals and 1000 billion (one trillion) sea animals yearly.

Everybody loses. The animals of course, but we humans are losers too. This mass killing and its corollary—the excessive consumption of meat in wealthy countries—perpetuates hunger in the world, increases the world's ecological imbalances, and is even harmful to human health.

- A thousand million tons of grain (soy, wheat, corn) that could be used to feed a billion people in the developing countries where they are produced are used every year to feed livestock used for meat production in the developed countries.

- Animal breeding contributes 15 percent of the greenhouse gas emissions linked to human activities, putting it in second place after construction and before transport.

- According to studies conducted by the European Prospective Investigation into Cancer and Nutrition, the United Nations' report on human development, and a meta-analysis of over three hundred scientific publications carried out by the World Health Organization (WHO), regular consumption of meat increases the incidence of cancer and coronary diseases.

From the point of view of Buddhism, it is out of the question *to use human intelligence for the purpose of exploiting other beings.*

In the *Lankavatara Sutra,* we read:

Alas, what sort of virtue do these beings practice? They
fill their bellies with the flesh of animals, thus spreading
fear among the beasts who live in the air, in the water,
and on the earth! Practitioners of the Way should
abstain from meat, because eating it is a source of terror
for beings.

When someone enters the Buddhist path, she says the following sentence: "In taking the Dharma as refuge, I promise not
to harm any being." It is clear that this promise also applies to animals. We may assume that a Buddhist rejects the idea, maintained
by the monotheistic religions, that man was brought into being
to occupy the summit of creation and other creatures were made
to satisfy his needs, to feed, and amuse him. In contrast to this, a
Buddhist takes the view that all beings have the fundamental right
to exist and not to suffer.

A being that is called "sentient" is a living organism capable
of distinguishing between well-being and pain and between different ways of being treated; that is, between conditions that are
either favorable or harmful for its survival. It is also capable of
reacting in an appropriate fashion, meaning that it is capable of
avoiding or moving away from anything that might put an end
to its existence and of seeking out whatever might be favorable
to its existence.

In the case of the most rudimentary organisms, such reactions
obviously do not reflect thought-out activity or a subjective experience of well-being or suffering, but nevertheless they are part
of a *continuity* in which a gradual growth in complexity leads to
the development of a nervous system that first permits perception

of sensations of pain and then the subjective awareness of pain. Acknowledging the existence of such continuity should lead us to see value in all forms of life and to respect them.

All Buddhists are not vegetarians, and Buddhist texts do not unanimously condemn the consumption of meat. Certain sutras of the Great Vehicle, the Mahayana, however, do so unequivocally. An example is the *Lankavatara Sutra*, which states:

> So as not to become a source of terror, bodhisattvas established in benevolence should not eat food containing meat.... Meat is food for wild beasts; it is unfitting to eat it.... People kill animals for profit and exchange goods for the meat. One person kills, another person buys—both are at fault.

Similarly, in the *Great Parinirvana Sutra*, the Buddha says: "Eating meat destroys great compassion" and advises his disciples to avoid the consumption of meat "just as they would avoid the flesh of their own children." Numerous Tibetan masters also condemn consumption of the flesh of animals.

Fifty years after the death of the Buddha, Emperor Ashoka, who embraced Buddhism and vegetarianism, promulgated several edicts calling for animals to be treated kindly. Most notably, he had precepts engraved on a stone pillar enjoining his subjects to treat animals with kindness and forbidding animal sacrifices throughout his territory.[1]

---

1 Ashoka's edict number five, against the killing of animals, is engraved on one of the nineteen surviving Ashokan pillars located at Feroze Shah Kotla in Delhi. This pillar was transported from outside the city in the fourteenth century by Firoze Shah Tughlaq to his new capital Firozabad. Only a few remnants can be found in Old Delhi. Thank you to Gérard Busquet for this information.

Chinese and Vietnamese Buddhists are strictly vegetarian. Many Tibetans live on high plateaus, vast plains that are unsuitable for anything but raising herds of yaks, goats, or sheep. Renouncing eating meat in such conditions would have meant, until recently, living purely on butter, yogurt (in the summer) and *tsampa*, the traditional Tibetan dish made from roasted barley flour. These conditions have led the inhabitants of these plains, nomads for the most part, to live off their herds. Moreover, most Tibetans are very fond of meat.

In spite of this, they are quite aware of the immoral aspect of their behavior and attempt to compensate for it by only killing the number of animals strictly necessary for their survival. In exile, in India or Nepal, more and more Tibetan monasteries have stopped authorizing the use of meat in the meals prepared in their kitchens.

For the Buddhist in general, to be vegetarian or vegan (especially in industrialized countries) is a means of manifesting his or her compassion toward animals. In contrast to Hindu vegetarians, for Buddhists meat is not impure in itself. The motivation not to eat meat is based on justice, morality, and compassion.

Most of us are fond of animals, but our compassion stops at the edge of our plate. This egoistic activity of ours is not only morally debatable, it's unreasonable from any point of view. This unreasonable approach is based on a lack of respect for other life forms, a lack of respect resulting from ignorance, pride, egoism, or ideology. As far as animals are concerned, a lack of respect caused by ignorance consists, in particular, in not recognizing that they feel emotions and are sensitive to pain. It is also a matter of ignoring the continuum that binds all species of animals into one whole. When, as is now the case, there is adequate scientific data to substantiate this, it becomes a denial of reality if we choose to ignore it.

Lack of respect resulting from pride comes from imagining that our superiority in certain areas gives us the right of life and death over animals. Lack of respect based on egoism results in using animals as though they were mere instruments for satisfying our desires or for promoting our financial interests. Finally, lack of respect through ideology is justifying our instrumentalization of animals on the basis of religious dogmas, philosophical theories, or cultural traditions.

Our attitude toward animals calls into question our entire ethical outlook and is evidence of how fragile it is. This ethical outlook of ours is what governs how we behave toward each other. That is why it is essential for us to accord animals an intrinsic value, to have consideration for them, and to take account of their legitimate aspirations. If we exclude all nonhuman beings from our ethical system, that system becomes shaky.

It seems that if we were merely to reach out and extend to animals the golden rule that we usually reserve for humans—do not do to others what you would not have them do to you—both humans and animals would benefit.[1] It is clear, however, that being concerned with the fate of animals does not in the least diminish

---

1 The golden rule—do not do to others what you would not have them do to you—is found in all the great religions and cultures. If in the "religions of the book" this rule concerns only humans, this is not the case in other religions and cultures. As early as the fourth to third centuries BCE, the Hindu text, Mahabharata, tells us: "This is the highest point of duty: do not do to others what you would not wish them to do to you." Buddhism poses the question, "How could I inflict on others what is painful to me?" (Udana-Varga 5:18). Jainism affirms: "Every man should treat all creatures as he would wish to be treated" (Sutrakritanga 1.11.33). Confucianism declares: "What you do not wish for yourself, do not impose upon others." Judaism teaches: "Thou shalt not avenge, nor bear any grudge against the children of thy people, but thou shalt love thy neighbor as thyself" (Leviticus 19:18). Jesus urges us: "Love thy neighbor as thyself" (Matthew 22:36–40). In the sixth to seventh century, Muhammad said: "None of you truly believes until he wishes for his brother what he wishes for himself" (Hadith 13 of Imam al-Nawawi). The Taoists, Zoroastrians, ancient Egyptians, Sikhs, Native Americans, and many other cultures also have forms of this rule. Source: Wikipedia article "Golden Rule."

the need to be concerned with the destiny of humans—quite the contrary: both of these concerns are derived from a sense of altruism and are not, with the exception of a few cases, in direct competition with each other.

So we can do a lot better than we have been doing. Real altruism and compassion should know no bounds. Compassion relates to all suffering and is directed toward all who suffer. Someone who is moved by genuine compassion is not capable of inflicting suffering on other sentient beings.

Omnivores do their best to make vegans and vegetarians look ridiculous or dangerous, especially those who have adopted their diets for moral reasons (they are not subjected to reproach if they do it on their doctor's orders). Two English sociologists made a study of how the British media portrays vegans: 5 percent of media portrayed them positively, 20 percent were neutral, and 75 percent were negative. According to the two sociologists, this negative portrayal "makes it possible to reassure omnivore readers concerning the normality of their ethical choice and, by association, the normality of their personality in contrast to the abnormality of the vegans."[1]

It seems that people resent vegetarians and vegans because they represent a living reminder of their moral incoherence. Most of us would find it revolting to have to slit the throat of an animal every day with our own hands, but we are ready to condone the killing of animals, the abusive treatment they are subject to, as well as the ecological disaster caused by industrial breeding and

---

1 Matthew Cole and Karen Morgan, "Vegaphobia: Derogatory Discourses of Veganism and the Reproduction of Speciesism in UK National Newspapers," *British Journal of Sociology* 62, no. 1 (2011): 142. According to M. Gibert, *Voir son steak comme un animal mort: Véganisme et psychologie morale* (Montreal: Lux Éditeur, 2015), 134–35.

fishing just because "everybody does it." We cannot go on treating the world and its contents like a huge supermarket.

How have major changes in attitude come about in society, even when those changes at first appeared improbable and unrealistic? How has it happened that things that were completely taken for granted came to be seen as unacceptable? The way it works is that, right at the beginning, a few individuals become aware of a particular situation that is morally indefensible. They come to the conclusion that the status quo cannot be maintained without compromising the ethical values that they respect.

At first isolated and ignored, these pioneers end up pooling their efforts and becoming activists who upset habitual outlooks and bring about a revolution in ideas. At that point they tend to be mocked and reviled. But little by little, other people who were shy at first come to believe that the pioneers are right in what they are doing, and they begin to sympathize with their cause. When the number of those in favor of the new approach reaches a critical mass, public opinion begins to swing in their direction. Gandhi summarized this process as follows: "At first they ignore you, then they laugh at you, then they fight you, and then you win." Let us think of the abolition of slavery, of the defense of human rights, of female suffrage, and any number of other breakthroughs.

Cultures can evolve. In the course of generations, individuals and cultures never cease to influence each other. Individuals who grow up in a new social environment become different just by acquiring new habit patterns that transform their way of being. They then contribute in turn to the further evolution of their society, and so it goes on.

Today, at least in the West, not only slavery but also racism, sexism, and homophobia (even though they remain endemic in our societies) are theoretically disapproved of by the majority of people. Soon the same could happen, let us hope, to our attitude toward animals. As philosopher Martin Gibert sums it up: "The basic argument is simple. If it is possible to live without inflicting unnecessary suffering on animals, then that's what we ought to do."[1]

According to a study conducted in Australia, the reasons given for continuing to eat meat, in spite of all the arguments, are eating pleasure (78 percent—"I like it, period!"), reluctance to change habitual patterns (58 percent), the idea that humans were made to eat meat (44 percent), the fact that one's family eats it (43 percent), and a lack of information on vegetarian and vegan diets (42 percent).[2]

Except for populations that cannot survive except through hunting and fishing, it seems to me impossible to put forward a valid reason—based on morality, justice, and kindness or on necessity as opposed to appetite, habit, dogma, ideology, conformism, profit, or lack of information—that justifies eating, clothing oneself with, or seeking entertainment at the price of the suffering and death of other sentient beings.

It is clear that the way we eat and our use of products derived through animal suffering go against the values that are upheld by a society that never ceases to boast of the progress it has made in the realm of human rights, women's rights, the rights of children, and the rights of minorities and the oppressed. How can we see ourselves as manifesting equality, fraternity, and liberty when we subject, exploit, imprison, and massacre our neighbor, whether this neighbor is a person of a different skin color, walks on four

---

1　Gibert, *Voir son steak comme un animal mort*, 9–10.
2　Emma Lea and Anthony Worsley, "Benefits and Barriers to the Consumption of a Vegetarian Diet in Australia," *Public Health Nutrition* 6, no. 5 (2003): 505–11. Cited in Gibert, *Voir son steak comme un animal mort*, 184.

legs, is covered with hair, has to live in the water, or has other characteristics we do not have?

Clearly it is time to extend the notion of "neighbor" to other life forms. If we were to understand and feel thoroughly and fully that in truth animals and ourselves are fellow citizens of the world, rather than see animals as some subcategory of living beings, we could no longer permit ourselves to treat them as we do.

A growing number of us no longer are content with a conservative ethic regarding the behavior of humans toward their fellow beings. Many of us now feel that benevolence toward all beings is no longer an optional addendum to our ethics but an essential part of it. It is incumbent upon us to continue to promote the achievement of impartial justice and compassion toward all sentient beings.[3] Kindness is not an obligation; it is the noblest expression of human nature.

---

3 "L'homme et la souffrance des animaux" [Humans and the Suffering of Animals], drawn from the "Sermon du 3ᵉ Dimanche de l'Avent" [Sermon on the third Sunday of Advent] [1908] and "La protection des animaux et les philosophes" [The Protection of Animals and the Philosophers] [1936], *Cahiers de l'association française des Amis d'Albert Schweitzer* [Journal of the French Association of Friends of Albert Schweitzer] 30 (Spring 1974): 3–13. Cited in Jeangène Vilmer, *Anthologie d'éthique animale,* 233–34.

Hope for the Future
1988

I WANT TO speak with you about the importance of kindness and compassion. When I speak about this, I regard myself not as a Buddhist, not as the Dalai Lama, not even as a Tibetan, but as one human being, and I hope that you will think of yourself as a human being rather than just an American, or a Westerner, or a member of a particular group. These things are secondary. If you and I interact as human beings, we can reach this basic level. If I say, "I am a monk; I am a Buddhist," these are, in comparison to my nature as a human being, temporary. To be human is basic. Once you are born as a human being, that cannot change until your death. Other characteristics—whether you are educated or uneducated, rich or poor—are secondary.

Today we face many problems. Some are essentially created by ourselves, based on divisions due to ideology, religion, race, economic status, and other factors. Because of this, the time has come for us to think on a deeper level, on the human being level, and from that level to respect and appreciate the sameness of ourselves and others as human beings. We must build closer relationships of mutual trust, understanding, respect, and help, regardless of differences in culture, philosophy, religion, or faith.

After all, all human beings are made of flesh, bones, and blood, wanting happiness, and not wanting suffering. We all have an equal right to be happy, and it is important to realize our sameness as human beings. We all belong to one human family. We quarrel with each other, but that is due to secondary reasons, and all of this arguing, cheating, and suppressing each other is of no use.

Unfortunately, for many centuries, human beings have used all sorts of methods to suppress and hurt one another. Terrible things have been done. We have caused more problems, more suffering, and more mistrust, and created more hatred and more divisions.

Today the world is becoming smaller and smaller. Economically and from many other viewpoints, the different areas of the world are becoming closer and much more interdependent. Because of this, international summits often take place; problems in one remote place are connected with global crises. The situation itself expresses the fact that it is now necessary to think more on a human level rather than on the basis of the matters which divide us. Therefore, I am speaking to you as just a human being, and I earnestly hope that you are also reading with the thought, "I am a human being, and I am here reading the words of another human being."

All of us want happiness. In cities, on farms, even in remote villages, everyone is quite busy. What is the purpose? Everyone is trying to create happiness. To do so is right. However, it is very important to follow a correct method in seeking happiness. Too much involvement with superficialities will not solve the larger problems.

There are all about us many crises, many fears. Through highly developed science and technology, we have reached a very advanced level of material progress, both useful and necessary. Yet if you compare the external progress with our internal progress, it is quite clear that our internal progress falls short. In many countries, crises—terrorism, murders, and so on—are chronic. People complain about the decline in morality and the rise in criminal activity. Although in external matters we are highly developed and continue to progress, at the same time we neglect our inner development.

In ancient times, if there was war, the effect was limited. Today, because of external material progress, the potential for destruction is beyond imagination. When I visited Hiroshima, though I knew something about the nuclear explosion there, I found it very difficult to see it with my own eyes and to meet with people who actually suffered at the moment of the bombing. I was deeply moved. A terrible weapon was used. Though we might regard someone as an enemy, on a deeper level an enemy is also a human being, also wants happiness, also has the right to be happy. Looking at Hiroshima and thinking about this, at that moment I became even more convinced that anger and hatred cannot solve problems.

Anger cannot be overcome by anger. If a person shows anger to you and you respond with anger, the result is a disaster. In contrast, if you control anger and show the opposite attitude— compassion, tolerance, patience—then not only do you yourself remain in peace, but the other person's anger will gradually diminish. World problems also cannot be challenged by anger or hatred. They must be faced with compassion, love, and true kindness. Even with all the terrible weapons we have, the weapons themselves cannot start a war. The button to trigger them is under a human finger, which moves by thought, not under its own power. The responsibility rests in thought.

If you look deeply into such things, the blueprint is found within—in the mind—out of which actions come. Thus, first controlling the mind is very important. I am not talking about controlling the mind in the sense of deep meditation, but rather in the sense of cultivating less anger, more respect for others' rights, more concern for other people, more clear realization of the sameness of human beings. This attitude may not solve problems immediately, but we have to try. We have to begin promoting this understanding through magazines and through television. Rather than just advertising to make money for ourselves, we need to use these media for something more meaningful, more seriously directed toward the welfare of humankind. Not money alone. Money is necessary, but the actual purpose of money is for human beings. Sometimes we forget human beings and become concerned just about money. This is illogical.

After all, we all want happiness, and no one will disagree with the fact that with anger, peace is impossible. With kindness and love, peace of mind can be achieved. No one wants mental unrest, but because of ignorance, depression, and so on, these things occur. Bad attitudes arise from the power of ignorance, not of their own accord.

Through anger we lose one of the best human qualities—the power of judgment. We have a good brain, allowing us to judge what is right and what is wrong, not only in terms of today's concerns, but considering ten, twenty, or even a hundred years into the future. Without any precognition, we can use our normal common sense to determine if something is right or wrong. We can decide that if we do such and such, it will lead to such and such an effect. However, once our mind is occupied by anger, we lose this power of judgment. Once lost, it is very sad—physically you are a human being but mentally you are not complete. Given that we have this physical human form, we must safeguard our mental capacity of judgment. For that, we cannot take out insurance. The insurance company is within ourselves: self-discipline, self-awareness, and clear realization of the shortcomings of anger and the positive effects of kindness. Thinking about this again and again, we can become convinced of it; and then with self-awareness, we can control the mind.

For instance, at present you may be a person who, due to small things, gets quickly and easily irritated. With clear understanding and awareness, that can be controlled. If you usually remain angry about ten minutes, try to reduce it to eight minutes. Next week make it five minutes and next month two minutes. Then make it zero. This is the way to develop and train our minds.

This is my feeling and also the sort of practice I myself do. It is quite clear that everyone needs peace of mind; the question is how to achieve it. Through anger we cannot. Through kindness, through love, through compassion, we can achieve peace of mind. The result will be a peaceful family—happiness between parents and children; fewer quarrels between husband and wife; no worries about divorce. Extended to the national level, this attitude can bring unity, harmony, and cooperation with genuine motivation. On the international level, mutual trust, mutual respect, and friendly and frank discussions can lead to joint efforts to solve world problems. All these are possible.

But first we must change within ourselves. Our national leaders try their best to solve our problems, but when one problem is solved, another crops up. Trying to solve that, there is another somewhere else. The time has come to try a different approach. Of course, it is very difficult to achieve a worldwide movement of peace of mind, but it is the only alternative. If there were an easier and more practical method, that would be better, but there is none. If through weapons we could achieve real, lasting peace, all right. Let all factories be turned into weapons factories. Spend every dollar for that, if that will achieve definite, lasting peace. But it is impossible.

Weapons do not remain stockpiled. Once a weapon is developed, sooner or later someone will use it. Someone might feel that if we do not use it, millions of dollars will be wasted, so somehow we should use it—drop a bomb to try it out. The result is that innocent people get killed. A friend told me that in Beirut there is a businessman who deals in weapons solely to make money. Because of him, many poor people in the streets get killed—ten or fifteen, or a hundred every day. This is due to lack of human understanding, lack of mutual respect and trust, not acting on a basis of kindness and love.

Therefore, although attempting to bring about peace through internal transformation is difficult, it is the only way to achieve a lasting world peace. Even if it is not achieved during my own lifetime, that is all right. More human beings will come—the next generation and the one after that—and progress can continue. I feel that despite the practical difficulties and the fact that this is regarded as an unrealistic view, it is worthwhile to make the attempt. So wherever I go, I express this, and I am encouraged that people from many different walks of life receive it well.

Each of us has responsibility for all humankind. It is time for us to think of other people as true brothers and sisters and to be concerned with their welfare, with lessening their suffering. Even if you cannot sacrifice your own benefit entirely, you should not forget the concerns of others. We should think more about the future and the benefit of all humanity.

If you try to subdue your selfish motives—anger, and so forth—and develop more kindness, more compassion for others, ultimately you will benefit more than you would otherwise. So sometimes I say that the wise selfish person should practice this way. Foolish selfish persons always think of themselves, and the results are negative. But a wise, selfish person thinks of others, helps others as much as he or she can, and receives good results.

This is my simple religion. There is no need for complicated philosophies, not even for temples. Our own brain, our own heart is our temple. The philosophy is kindness.

Collective Awakening and the Five Mindfulness Trainings 2009

E ACH WINTER IN Plum Village we have a three-month retreat. There are about 250 people, monastics and laypeople, practicing together for ninety days. We get up very early in the morning and we practice joyfully as a spiritual family. We listen to Dharma talks, we practice walking meditation, we practice eating in mindfulness, we practice cooking, cleaning, doing everything in mindfulness. We want to practice so that every moment of our daily life can be a peaceful moment, can be a nourishing moment, can be a happy moment. We are trying our best. And we create a very powerful kind of energy with our collective practice. Practicing the three-month retreat is our simple and modest way to contribute to collective awakening. We should wake up ourselves before we can help other people to wake up. That is our principle.

Right now, our technology is good enough to substitute the fossil fuels we are using with renewable sources of energy. We can make use of the water, the air, and the sunshine, and completely replace gasoline and coal by 2030 if we are strong enough, if we are united enough. But we need leadership. And the leadership we need is not only political. We need spiritual leadership as well.

We have a lot of fear, violence, and anger in us. We are using a lot of money in order to manufacture weapons. The big powers are still creating a lot of weapons: in the United States of America, in Great Britain, in France. That is a very important source of income for these powers. Why do people in other countries need to buy weapons? Because they have fear. They want to protect themselves.

Fear is something we should remove, we should transform, together with anger. Terrorists have a lot of violence and fear. But anti-terrorists also have a lot of fear and anger. That is why political leadership is not enough. We need spiritual leadership to tell us how to recognize the poison of violence, the poison of anger, the poison of fear in us so that we can transform them.

The Five Mindfulness Trainings are the kind of spiritual practice that can bring about true happiness, true love, and that can protect life, restore communication, and bring about the healing of the planet, and of every one of us on Earth.

The Five Mindfulness Trainings represent the Buddhist vision for a global spirituality: a global ethic. They are a concrete expression of the Buddha's teachings on the Four Noble Truths and the Noble Eightfold Path, the path of right understanding and true love, which leads to healing, transformation, and happiness for ourselves and for the world. To practice the Five Mindfulness Trainings is to cultivate the insight of interbeing. This is Right View, which can remove all discrimination, intolerance, anger, fear, and despair. If we live according to the Five Mindfulness Trainings, we are already on the path of a bodhisattva. Knowing we are on that path, we are not lost in confusion about our life in the present, in preoccupation with the past, or in fears about the future.

When we practice the mindfulness trainings, we make a commitment to refrain from behaviors that harm ourselves and others.

We commit to not killing, not stealing, not engaging in sexual misconduct, not speaking falsely, and to abstaining from intoxicants. The first training is to protect life, to decrease violence in oneself, in the family, and in society. The second training is to practice social justice, generosity, not stealing, and not exploiting other living beings. The third training is the practice of responsible sexual behavior in order to protect individuals, couples, families, and children. The fourth training is the practice of deep listening and loving speech in order to restore communication and bring reconciliation. The fifth training is to practice mindful consumption, not bringing toxins into our body and mind, not consuming TV programs, magazines, films, and so on, that may contain poisons, such as violence, craving, and hatred. The practice of mindful consumption is the practice of protecting ourselves, our families, our society, and our communities.

These Trainings have come from our understanding of the Eightfold Path. For example, the root of suffering is not only that people kill. The killing happens because we have a wrong perception, a wrong view. If we see wrongly, we may be ready to kill. But if we see clearly and have Right View, we have neither the ability nor desire to kill. With Right View, we see clearly that whatever we want to kill is part of us; it is like our own family member, and we lose our ability to harm it.

The Five Mindfulness Trainings are offered without dogma or religion. Everybody can use them as an ethics for their life without becoming Buddhist or becoming part of any tradition or faith. You are just yourself, but you try to make a beautiful life by following these ethics.

The Five Mindfulness Trainings are not commandments; they don't come from an external god. They come from our own wisdom and insight. The insight they contain is the outcome of our practice of mindfulness and concentration.

The trainings can be a joy, not something we *have* to do. It's like when we refrain from polluting the planet or we refrain from eating too much meat, we don't feel that we're suffering because of it. In fact, we feel that we're very lucky to be able to consume and to live in such a way that makes a future for the planet a real possibility. If with your practice of the Five Mindfulness Trainings, you feel that your understanding, loving kindness, and compassion have become bigger, then you can share your practice with others and in that way we can make things better.

The Five Mindfulness Trainings

1. Reverence for Life

Aware of the suffering caused by the destruction of life, I am committed to cultivating the insight of interbeing and compassion and learning ways to protect the lives of people, animals, plants, and minerals. I am determined not to kill, not to let others kill, and not to support any act of killing in the world, in my thinking, or in my way of life. Seeing that harmful actions arise from anger, fear, greed, and intolerance, which in turn come from dualistic and discriminative thinking, I will cultivate openness, nondiscrimination, and nonattachment to views in order to transform violence, fanaticism, and dogmatism in myself and in the world.

2. True Happiness

Aware of the suffering caused by exploitation, social injustice, stealing, and oppression, I am committed to practicing generosity in my thinking, speaking, and acting. I am determined not to steal and not to possess anything that should belong to others; and I will share my time, energy, and material resources with those who are in need. I will practice looking deeply to see that the happiness and suffering of others are not separate from my own happiness and suffering; that true happiness is not possible without understanding and compassion; and that running after wealth, fame, power, and sensual pleasures can bring much suffering and despair. I am aware that happiness depends on my mental attitude and not on external conditions, and that I can live happily in the present moment simply by remembering that I already have more than enough conditions to be happy. I am committed to practicing Right Livelihood so that I can help reduce the suffering of living beings on Earth and reverse the process of climate change.

3. True Love

Aware of the suffering caused by sexual misconduct, I am committed to cultivating responsibility and learning ways to protect the safety and integrity of individuals, couples, families, and society. Knowing that sexual desire is not love, and that sexual activity motivated by craving always harms myself as well as others, I am determined not to engage in sexual relations without true love and a deep, long-term commitment made known to my family and friends. I will do everything in my power to protect children from sexual abuse and to prevent couples and families from being broken by sexual misconduct. Seeing that body and mind are one, I am committed to learning appropriate ways to take care of my sexual energy and cultivating loving kindness, compassion, joy, and inclusiveness—which are the four basic elements of true love—for my greater happiness and the greater happiness of others. Practicing true love, we know that we will continue beautifully into the future.

4. Loving Speech and Deep Listening

Aware of the suffering caused by unmindful speech and the inability to listen to others, I am committed to cultivating loving speech and compassionate listening in order to relieve suffering and to promote reconciliation and peace in myself and among other people, ethnic and religious groups, and nations. Knowing that words can create happiness or suffering, I am committed to speaking truthfully, using words that inspire confidence, joy, and hope. When anger is manifesting in me, I am determined not to speak. I will practice mindful breathing in order to recognize and to look deeply into my anger. I know that the roots of anger can be found in my wrong perceptions and lack of understanding of the suffering in myself and in the other person. I will speak and listen in a way that can help myself and the other person to transform suffering and see the way out of difficult situations. I am determined not to spread news that I do not know to be certain and not to utter words that can cause division or discord. I will practice Right Diligence to nourish my capacity for understanding, love, joy, and inclusiveness, and gradually transform anger, violence, and fear that lie deep in my consciousness.

5. Nourishment and Healing

Aware of the suffering caused by unmindful consumption, I am committed to cultivating good health, both physical and mental, for myself, my family, and my society by practicing mindful eating, drinking, and consuming. I will practice looking deeply into how I consume the Four Kinds of Nutriments, namely edible foods, sense impressions, volition, and consciousness. I am determined not to gamble, or to use alcohol, drugs, or any other products which contain toxins, such as certain websites, electronic games, TV programs, films, magazines, books, and conversations. I will practice coming back to the present moment to be in touch with the refreshing, healing, and nourishing elements in me and around me, not letting regrets and sorrow drag me back into the past nor letting anxieties, fear, or craving pull me out of the present moment. I am determined not to try to cover up loneliness, anxiety, or other suffering by losing myself in consumption. I will contemplate interbeing and consume in a way that preserves peace, joy, and well-being in my body and consciousness, and in the collective body and consciousness of my family, my society, and the Earth.

....

The Five Mindfulness Trainings Come from Our Practice

When we study and practice the Five Mindfulness Trainings, we are aware that they are the fruit of our meditation. They are born from our mindfulness and concentration. They represent our insight. We need to practice them daily with a lot of joy.

We know that killing has been going on in many places in the world due to fanaticism, narrowness, and wrong thinking. If we just say that killing is not good, that doesn't help very much. But if we know how to help the person who is about to kill to get the insight of interbeing, to remove fanaticism and narrowness, then naturally that person will stop killing.

Interbeing and the First Mindfulness Training

War is a product of misunderstanding and wrong perceptions. We have wrong perceptions about ourselves and about other people. And from those wrong perceptions arise a lot of anger and fear. In order to end wars, we should try to help each other remove our wrong perceptions.

The cause of violence, the cause of war and wrong perceptions is also our attachment to our views. We believe that our view about the truth is the only correct view, and that we should destroy other kinds of views. And that leads to fanaticism, intolerance, and war. That is why the First Mindfulness Training encourages us to look deeply in order to change our way of thinking. We have to look deeply in order to see the interconnectedness of everything and release our dualistic thinking. Once we can see the interconnectedness of everything, we will be able to understand the views of others.

People are killing each other, and it's because they don't have the insight of interbeing. They don't see that the person they're killing is themselves. If we just advise people not to kill, that may not be enough. We have to inspire them. We have to help them to understand that killing someone is killing yourself. If you're inhabited by the insight of interbeing, you *know* that killing someone is killing yourself. The first mindfulness training, not to kill, always to protect life, should not be just a commandment, someone telling you that it's a good thing to do. But you have to understand *why* you should not kill. If you can touch the insight of interbeing, and you are free from double grasping—the illusion that subject and object are separate from each other—then you see very clearly that killing the other is to kill yourself.

A person who is free from all views, a person who is capable of seeing the interbeing nature of everything, will never have the desire to kill. The practice of the First Mindfulness Training nourishes our compassion. Compassion benefits us and makes us happy. Without compassion we cannot relate to the world and to other living beings. Communication is impossible. That's why cultivating compassion is crucial. It will bring well-being to us and to the world. It is a training; we need to train ourselves to be able to help compassion grow day by day.

There were moments during the Vietnam War that many of us were very close to despair. The war was going on and we did not see any sign that it would end. Every day, every night, people died, and the country was being destroyed by bombs and chemicals. The young people came to me and asked, "Thay, is there any hope that the war will end soon?" In that moment, we did not see any hope. We were very close to despair, because the war went on and on for a long time. So when people ask you a question like that, you need to breathe in and out several times. After having breathed in and out several times, I told the young people, "The Buddha told us that things are impermanent. The war is also impermanent. It should end some time."

But the problem is: are we doing anything to help end the war? If we allow ourselves to be overwhelmed by the feeling of despair or anger, we can't help. We can even fuel the war and make it intensify or last longer. So the question is whether we can do something for peace, whether we can *be* something for peace.

When you produce a thought of compassion, of loving kindness, or of understanding, that is peace. When you do something to help the victims of war, the children and adults, to suffer less, and when you bring food for refugee children, these are the kinds of actions that can help relieve a situation of suffering. So in that difficult situation, it's crucial for you to find a way to be peace, a way to practice peace. Even if you can do it only in a very limited way, it will help you survive. It helps you nourish hope. It's very important not to allow ourselves to be carried away by the feeling of despair. We should learn how to bring peace into our bodies, to our minds, so we're able to give rise to thoughts of compassion, words of compassion, and acts of compassion in our daily lives. That will inspire many people, and it will help them not be drowned in the ocean of despair. Our thinking and acting show that the First Mindfulness Training is possible. If we have some peace within ourselves, in our way of thinking, speaking, and acting, we'll be able to influence people and inspire them to go in the same direction. Little by little, we can improve the situation.

Generosity and the Second Mindfulness Training

The second mindfulness training is about generosity, not stealing, not harming the environment, not being greedy. It's about our ability to be happy with a minimum of conditions. This is very important. The second mindfulness training is about true happiness. If people are not able to practice this training, it's because they have too much desire. If you have too much desire, you don't have time to live your life, to love, and to experience healing and transformation. You burn yourself with the fire of desire. This training should be a bell of mindfulness for people who work too hard. There are many such people in our world. They may be powerful. They may be very successful in their enterprises. But they suffer; they don't really live their lives; they are sucked into their work.

We cultivate compassion by looking deeply to understand the suffering inside us and around us. You don't have to be rich to help people. In fact, if you're too wealthy you *can't* help people. Some people invest all their time and energy in maintaining their wealth; they don't even have time to take care of themselves and their family, so how can they help others? Being wealthy is not a good condition for spiritual life. It is possible to live simply and to be happy. When you transform yourself into a bodhisattva, you have a lot of power—not the power of fame and money, but the power that helps you to be free and enables you to help and bring relief to many people.

With awakening, we no longer think that we need more power, more wealth, more sex, or more fame in order to be happy. If we want to save our planet, we need to have a new way, a new view of happiness. And with that collective awakening we can stop the course of destruction of our society and of the Earth.

Every one of us has an idea of how to be happy. We have our own view of happiness. It is because of that view that we have sacrificed our time. We have run after objects of our desire. We have destroyed our body and our mind to a very great extent. And that is why it's very important to have a new view about happiness. The Buddha said that, "Well, happiness is simple. If you go home to the present moment, you realize that you have the conditions to be happy right here and right now." All the wonders of life are in you and around you.

That is why in Plum Village we practice the Fifth Mantra: "This is already a moment of happiness." Before sitting meditation, we recite the mantra, before sharing lunch or dinner, we share the mantra. Before working together in the field or in the vegetable garden, we practice the mantra. And happiness can come right away. So easy. So simple. "This is a moment of happiness." Yes, we are very lucky. We are still alive. And our planet is beautiful. We have to really be there in the present moment to live deeply in that moment. We can get nourishment and healing in the here and the now. And we have to release the kind of craving, anger, and hate that has destroyed much of us and much of the world.

When we practice walking meditation, for instance, we focus our attention on our in-breath and out-breath. And every time we breathe in we can take one step, or two steps, or three steps. We are fully aware of the contact between our foot and the ground. We walk as if we kiss the Earth with our foot. Because we are entirely in the present moment, every step we make brings us home deeply in the present moment. With every step we touch all the wonders of life that are in us and around us. That's very nourishing, very healing both for us and the Earth.

We have done injustice to the Earth. We have done a lot of damage to the Earth. And walking like that, kissing the Earth with every step, we heal our self and we heal the Earth. And this practice is not only for Buddhists. Everyone can do it: Muslims, Christians, Jews, Communists. We can all enjoy walking like that. And every step like that can bring solidity, freedom, peace, and joy. That is why I recommend that we practice walking meditation every day.

The Third Mindfulness Training and Love

If we really love others, we will try to protect ourselves and protect others, and sexual misconduct will not happen. Sexual misconduct usually comes from violence, fear, anger, and craving. It is not about sex or love. If true love and understanding are there, anger and violence decrease, and we do not act out of fear.

We have many kinds of energies in us, including the energies of anger, violence, and craving. Compassion is also a very big energy. If you allow the energy of compassion to take over, you will spend *all* your twenty-four hours doing things that will profit people.

We all have sexual energy. The ways we eat, play, and spend our time are big factors in how we handle our sexual energy. The way we serve, the way we spend our leisure time, the way we pass our time when we're with others has a lot to do with it. This is an art. We shouldn't suppress any kind of energy in us, including sexual energy. But we need to be intelligent in the way we handle this energy. There are good kinds of energy, and there are energies that can disturb us. Mindfulness, concentration, and the time we spend together with other practitioners can help us tremendously. We should smile to our own energies and know that we have the capacity to handle them. "My dear energy, I know you are there. I am here for you. I will learn how to help and to handle you. Together we can be in peace. And you can help me also. You are energy, and it's possible to transform one energy into another, like the wind can be transformed into electricity." So sexual energy can be transformed into the energy of compassion and acts of compassion. We only have to learn how to transform it. With a community, a Sangha, it's possible to learn. The way we eat, drink, and manage our leisure time; the way we work together; and the way we serve, will determine our success.

The Fourth Mindfulness Training and the Power of Communication

We have organized groups of Palestinians and Israelis to come to spend time in Plum Village for many years. At the beginning of each retreat, the two groups are suspicious of each other and have trouble looking at each other. Both groups have suffered a lot, and they have a belief that their suffering has been caused by the other side. We give each side plenty of time apart from each other to practice and a lot of support in using the practices of deep listening and loving speech.

One side uses loving speech, and one side uses compassionate listening, and the outcome is wonderful. While listening, you recognize that those on the other side have suffered almost exactly the same way as you have. Before that, we thought that only our side had suffered in that way. But now we see they have suffered exactly the same things—fear, anger, suspicion, and so on. So you begin to see them as human beings, like you. And when you begin to see them as human beings who suffer, the intention to punish is no longer there, and you begin to look at them with the eyes of compassion. You may even be motivated by the desire to say something or do something so they can suffer less. That is the transformation you experience during the time you practice compassionate listening. When you look at them now, you suffer much less, because you've been able to see the suffering in them, and you see them as human beings like you. When they see your eyes, they feel that you are looking at them with love and not with suspicion, fear, or anger anymore. So transformation takes place on both sides. And you know that you will also have a chance to speak out, maybe next week. And you will tell them about your suffering, and they will listen. This practice of compassionate listening and loving speech is very important to liberate us from our fear, anger, hatred, and so on. And it has the power to restore communication.

In the beginning we may notice that others have many wrong perceptions. It's because they have suffered so much. That's why in their way of speaking there's still some bitterness, accusation, and so on. But because we're practicing mindfulness of compassion, we don't interrupt them, and we allow them to speak out so they suffer less. And the outcome is that we recognize them as living beings who have a lot of suffering. And so we suffer less, and we no longer have the intention to punish them. We have the intention to help. We say that we can provide them with information that can help them to see that it's not our intention to make them suffer. And we know that on our side there is also fear and suspicion that makes us difficult for them. If we have a difficult relationship with our partner, or with our parents and family members, or even with someone from a group we think has hurt us and our family, it's always possible to restore communication and to reconcile by practicing compassionate listening and loving speech.

There are those who are capable of using loving speech in the political circle. President Barack Obama is capable of loving speech. I think the wars in Afghanistan and in Iraq can be ended with the practice of deep listening and loving speech. We don't have to send more troops. The Taliban are human beings like us, and they also love their country, their people, their nation. And we can talk to them. I think President Obama can invite them to the White House, invite them to dinner, to do walking meditation together, and share with them the difficulties of America, and ask them to help, and offer help to solve the problems in Afghanistan. And they can talk about global warming, the danger that our planet is facing. We need our leaders to be together in such a way. To spend time together as friends, the way we do in Plum Village. We cook together, we clean together, we walk together, we sit together. We let the other know about our suffering, our difficulties. We listen to their suffering, their difficulties.

I think a peace conference should be organized like that. People come, they have to spend a few weeks living together and sharing together in a very informal way, and establish real human relationship and understanding of each other, especially the difficulties and the suffering. If we do that, our peace negotiation will be successful.

With the practice of the fourth mindfulness training, we can restore communication in our family and bring back happiness. With the practice of deep listening and loving speech we can bring warring parties together. I think spiritual leaders have to help political leaders in this respect. They have to work hand in hand. We need a lot of patience, compassion, in order to solve problems like Iran, Afghanistan, and so on. President Obama can go to Iran as a guest and stay a few weeks with the President of Iran. And they should eat together, walk together, share together their suffering, their difficulties—because President Obama has a lot of difficulties also. And as two human beings living on the Earth, they will understand each other and they can release the fear, the anger.

We need our political leaders to practice this kind of spirituality. And we don't need to be a member of a religion in order to do so. It's possible to have spirituality without religion. The way we drink our tea can be very spiritual. We drink our tea in such a way that we become alive, that the world shines, that happiness becomes possible in the here and the now. You don't need a god, you don't need a religion in order to do that.

The Ethical and Spiritual Aspects of the Fifth Mindfulness Training

Suppose you practice the fifth training and you've stopped drinking alcohol or using drugs. But you're suffering because you still *have the desire* to drink alcohol or use drugs. You're following the guideline, the precept, but you haven't yet really seen the value of it, the insight, and the spiritual dimension. You still refrain, because you know that it's good for your health to do so, but you suffer. It is possible to enjoy refraining from consuming things that are toxic for body and mind, just as it's possible to enjoy being vegetarian. If you're happy eating vegetarian food, you feel lucky to eat only vegetables and not cause suffering to other living beings. There is joy, there is insight, and there is compassion and spirituality in your eating. Eating becomes a very spiritual thing. There is no barrier dividing the ethical and the spiritual—they are one.

In Buddhism we speak of four sources of nutriment. Edible food is only one source, the first kind of nutriment we consume.

Sensory impressions are the second source of consumption. What we view, like television programs; what we read, like magazines; what we listen to, like radio and music, are objects of our consumption. With mindfulness we know how to consume only the items that can bring about peace and well-being into our body and our mind.

The third source of nutriment is called volition. It means your deepest desire, your deepest aspiration. Our desire is a kind of food. If you have a good desire, like the desire to preserve our planet, the desire to help people suffer less, the desire to bring safety to children and others from abuse. That is a good kind of desire. And each of us should have a strong desire in us in order for us to be truly alive. If you have no desire in yourself, you are not very alive. This is called volition, the deepest aspiration that each of us could have.

So let us look deeply into ourselves to identify our deepest desire. If that desire is wholesome, like the desire to help protect the Earth, to help end war, and to help other people to transform and to be happy, that is a good desire. But the desire to run after more fame, more sex, more power, more wealth may not be healthy.

Our deep desire should be nourished, because it gives us vitality, it is a source of joy. You will give up your efforts to help the world if you don't have the support.

The fourth source of nutriment is the collective consciousness. If you live in a bad environment, your ideal, your beginner's mind, your good intention, will be gone very quickly. That is why it's very important to choose a place, a community, a neighborhood where people are producing together the energy of loving kindness, the energy of peace, the energy of brotherhood and sisterhood. If you live in such a community, your good desire will be protected and nourished.

If you allow yourself to be in a crowd that is very angry, or filled with craving, or that has a lot of discrimination and despair, you will consume that energy in the collective consciousness, and you will destroy yourself. That is why environment is another kind of food. As practitioners, we have to create the kind of environment that can help provide us with the wholesome energy of brotherhood, sisterhood, hope, peace, and happiness.

We should try to create as many of these kinds of communities as possible in the world. Spiritual and religious teachers have the duty to create these communities, living in a way that can produce the energy of mindfulness, concentration, and insight, to generate the energy of brotherhood, sisterhood, and happiness in the here and the now.

We don't have to consume much in order to be happy. If we understand the teaching of the four nutriments, we will know how to nourish ourselves and our community, and how to protect our environment.

Happiness and well-being are key to a global ethic. We practice the Five Mindfulness Trainings because we see that they increase our well-being and ease our suffering. And there is no distinction between our own suffering and the suffering of the world. We act ethically because we're motivated by the insight we have into interbeing and nondiscrimination. Our insight causes our thoughts, speech, and physical actions to manifest in a way that brings well-being to the world and to ourselves. We act this way not because we think we have to or are told to, but because of our own insight. Therefore our actions only bring about more well-being.

We need a collective awakening. Many of us, all over the world, are trying to bring that about. If we have a collective awakening, everything will be fine. With a collective awakening, we will live together in such a way that we'll be able to save the planet and to make a future possible for our children and their children.

◌

Robert Aitken
Robert Aitken was one of the most prominent, influential, and highly esteemed Zen masters in the last fifty years. He was of seminal importance in shaping the expression of modern American Zen and, as one of the original founders of the Buddhist Peace Fellowship, was also a leading social activist advocating for social justice of all varieties. He is the author of numerous books on Zen Buddhism, including *The Dragon Who Never Sleeps.* He died in 2010.

Venerable Bhikkhu Bodhi
Ven. Bhikkhu Bodhi is an American Buddhist monk from New York City, born in 1944. He currently lives and teaches at Chuang Yen Monastery in Carmel, New York. Ven. Bodhi has many important publications to his credit, either as author, translator, or editor. These include *The Middle Length Discourses of the Buddha* (Majjhima Nikaya, 1995), *The Connected Discourses of the Buddha* (Samyutta Nikaya, 2000), and *The Numerical Discourses of the Buddha* (Anguttara Nikaya, 2012). In 2008, together with several of his students, Ven. Bodhi founded Buddhist Global Relief, a nonprofit supporting hunger relief, sustainable agriculture, and education in countries suffering from chronic poverty and malnutrition.

His Holiness The Dalai Lama
His Holiness the Fourteenth Dalai Lama, born Tenzin Gyatso, is the spiritual leader of the Tibetan people. He frequently

describes himself as a simple Buddhist monk. In his capacity
as a spiritual and political leader, he has traveled to more than
sixty-two countries on six continents and met with presidents,
popes, and leading scientists to foster dialogue and create a
better world. In recognition of his tireless work for the nonviolent liberation of Tibet, the Dalai Lama was awarded the Nobel
Peace Prize in 1989. In 2012, he relinquished political authority
in his exile government and turned it over to democratically
elected representatives. His Holiness frequently states that his
life is guided by three major commitments: the promotion of
basic human values or secular ethics in the interest of human
happiness, the fostering of interreligious harmony, and securing
the welfare of the Tibetan people, focusing on the survival of
their identity, culture, and religion. His efforts to foster dialogue
among leaders of the world's faiths envision a future where people of different beliefs can share the planet in harmony.

Brother Phap Dung

Brother Phap Dung (pronounced "Fap Yung") is a Vietnamese-
American who emigrated to the United States in 1979 during
the so called "second wave" refugee exodus from his homeland.
He grew up in Southern California and trained and worked
as an architect before becoming a monk in 1998. Thich Nhat
Hanh appointed him abbot of Deer Park Monastery in Southern
California, which he led for nine years. He is now a senior
Dharma Teacher in the international Plum Village Community
of Engaged Buddhism, actively involved in bringing mindfulness
into education, ecology, business, and politics, and to the next
generation. He is inspired by meditation as a method of examining and cultivating the mind, individually and collectively, and by
building community as a way to heal and develop society.

Maha Ghosananda

Samdech Preah Maha Ghosananda was a meditation master and an international peacemaker. Often referred to as the "Gandhi of Cambodia," he was nominated for the Nobel Peace Prize three times. He is the author of *Step by Step*, among other publications. He continued his peace work until his death in 2007.

Roshi Joan Halifax

Roshi Joan Halifax, PhD, is a Buddhist teacher, Zen priest, anthropologist, and pioneer in the field of end-of-life care. She is founder, abbot, and head teacher of Upaya Institute and Zen Center in Santa Fe, New Mexico.

Sister Jina van Hengel

Sister Chan Dieu Nghiem (also known as Sister True Wonder or simply "Sister Jina") ordained in Japan in 1985 and joined the Plum Village community in 1990, as one of Thich Nhat Hanh's first Western monastic disciples. Sister True Wonder is of Dutch and Irish descent, fluent in five languages and an accomplished yoga teacher. A senior Dharma Teacher and dearly beloved Abbess in Thich Nhat Hanh's Plum Village Monastery in France for sixteen years, she has been a leader in cultivating fourfold sangha across Europe. Sister True Wonder is also an avid mountain-hiker and bird-watcher, and enjoys deep relaxation and folk dancing. Her gentle, insightful teachings have inspired generations of practitioners around the world.

bell hooks

bell hooks is an acclaimed intellectual, feminist theorist, cultural critic, artist, and writer. Born Gloria Jean Watkins in Hopkinsville, Kentucky, bell hooks adopted the pen name of her maternal great-grandmother, a woman known for speaking her mind. bell hooks has authored over three dozen books and has published works that span several genres, including cultural criticism, personal memoirs, poetry collections, and children's books. Her writings cover topics of gender, race, class, spirituality, teaching, and the significance of media in contemporary culture.

Mushim Patricia Ikeda

Mushim Patricia Ikeda has become widely known for her down-to-earth, humorous, and penetrating approach to Dharma and social transformation. Mushim is currently a socially engaged Buddhist teacher, mindfulness meditation teacher, social justice activist, author, and diversity and inclusion facilitator based in Oakland, California. She teaches primarily at the East Bay Meditation Center in downtown Oakland, where she also served on the board of directors, known as the Leadership Sangha, for seven years. She now works on EBMC's staff as the community coordinator.

Charles Johnson

Charles Johnson is an American scholar and the author of novels, short stories, screenplays, and essays, most of which have a philosophical orientation. Johnson has directly addressed the issues of black life in America in novels such as *Dreamer* and *Middle Passage*. *Middle Passage* won the U.S. National Book Award for Fiction in 1990, making Johnson the second black American male writer to receive this prize after Ralph Ellison in 1953. Johnson received a MacArthur Fellowship or "Genius Grant" in 1998. He is also the recipient of National Endowment for the Arts and Guggenheim Fellowships and many other prizes, such as a 2002 Academy Award in Literature from the American Academy of Arts and Letters. He was inducted into the American Academy of Arts and Sciences, and his most recent award is the 2013 Humanities Washington Award for creating and contributing for fifteen years a new, original short story to a literary event called "Bedtime Stories," which since 1998 has raised a million dollars for the literacy programs of the nonprofit organization Humanities Washington.

Sister Chan Khong

Sister Chan Khong (Cao Ngoc Phuong) was born in a village on the Mekong River Delta in 1938. She has devoted her life to the development and practice of nonviolence grounded in the Buddhist precepts of non-killing and compassionate action, and began studying and volunteering with Thich Nhat Hanh in 1959, helping him found the School of Youth for Social Service in Vietnam in 1964. Sister Chan Khong was in the first group to ordain with Thich Nhat Hanh's new bodhisattva precepts of the Order of Interbeing in 1966, and received monastic ordination in 1988. She is today Thich Nhat Hanh's most senior disciple and a leader in the international Plum Village Community of Engaged Buddhism. Sister Chan Khong has authored several books, including *Learning True Love* and *Beginning Anew: Four Steps to Restoring Communication*. The transformative practice of deep relaxation and guided prostrations which she has developed have brought healing and insight to thousands of people around the world. Thich Nhat Hanh has said: "Many of my students are my teachers, and Sister Chan Khong is one of the foremost among these."

Jack Kornfield

Jack Kornfield trained as a Buddhist monk in the monasteries of Thailand, India, and Burma. He has taught meditation internationally since 1974. After graduating from Dartmouth College in Asian Studies in 1967, he joined the Peace Corps and worked on tropical medicine teams in the Mekong River valley. He met and studied as a monk under the Thai Buddhist master Ven. Ajahn Chah, as well as the Ven. Mahasi Sayadaw of Burma. Returning to the United States, Kornfield cofounded the Insight Meditation Society in Barre, Massachusetts, with fellow meditation teachers Sharon Salzberg and Joseph Goldstein and the Spirit Rock Center in Woodacre, California. Over the years, Jack Kornfield has taught in centers and universities worldwide, led International Buddhist Teacher meetings, and worked with many of the great teachers of our time. He holds a PhD in clinical psychology and is a father, husband, and activist.

Kenneth Kraft

Kenneth Kraft was a professor of Buddhist studies and author of several books. Kraft received a BA from Harvard University in 1971, followed by an MA in Asian language and cultures from the University of Michigan in 1978, and a PhD in East Asian Studies from Princeton in 1984. Throughout his work, Kraft focused on Buddhism, delving into the budding field of socially engaged Buddhism in the 1980s. Kraft taught at the University of Pennsylvania, Swarthmore College, and Lehigh University, and served as a visiting professor at Stanford. He served on the boards of the Buddhist Peace Fellowship, the Journal of Buddhist Ethics, the Rochester Zen Center, the Forum on Religion and Ecology at Yale, and the World Faiths Development Dialogue. He died in 2018 in Haverford, Pennsylvania.

Sister Annabel Laity

Sister Annabel Laity (Chan Duc, True Virtue) was born in England, and studied Classics and Sanskrit before going to India to study and practice with Tibetan nuns. She has been a disciple of Thich Nhat Hanh since 1986. In 1988, in India, she became the first Western European woman to be ordained as a nun by Thich Nhat Hanh. Sister Annabel was director of practice at Plum Village for many years. She travels widely, leading meditation retreats and inspiring many with her unique teaching style throughout the world. In 2000, she became the first Western European nun to teach Buddhist Dharma in Thailand, and is currently head of practice at the European Institute of Applied Buddhism in Germany. Her autobiography, *True Virtue: The Journey of an English Buddhist Nun,* was published in 2019.

Joanna Macy

Joanna Macy is a scholar of Buddhism, general systems theory, and deep ecology. She is known in many countries for her workshops and trainings to empower creative, sustained social action. Her books include *Thinking Like a Mountain: Toward a Council of All Beings,* coauthored with John Seed and others, *Mutual Causality in Buddhism and General Systems Theory: The Dharma of Natural Systems,* and Parallax Press's *World as Lover, World as Self.*

Zenju Earthlyn Manuel

Rev. Zenju Earthlyn Manuel, PhD, a Soto Zen priest, was born to parents who migrated from rural Louisiana and settled in Los Angeles, where she was raised with her two sisters. She is the author of *The Way of Tenderness: Awakening Through Race, Sexuality and Gender* and *Tell Me Something about Buddhism*; the compiler and editor of the award-winning *Seeds for a Boundless*

Life: Zen Teachings from the Heart, by Zenkei Blanche Hartman; and the contributing author to many books, including *The Hidden Lamp: Stories from Twenty-Five Years of Awakened Women.*

Cheri Maples

Cheri Maples was ordained as a Dharma Teacher by Zen Master Thich Nhat Hanh. She was also a private consultant and trainer. Cheri Maples worked in the criminal justice profession for twenty-five years as a police officer, the head of probation and parole, and an assistant attorney general in Wisconsin. She also had extensive experience as a community organizer and a social justice advocate. She incorporated all these experiences into her understanding and teaching of the dharma and her practice of Engaged Buddhism until her death in 2017.

Peter Matthiessen

Peter Matthiessen was an American novelist, naturalist, wilderness writer, Zen teacher, and CIA agent. A cofounder of the literary magazine *The Paris Review,* he is the only writer to have won the National Book Award in both fiction and nonfiction. He was also a prominent environmental activist. Matthiessen's nonfiction, notably *The Snow Leopard,* featured nature and travel He died on April 5, 2014, three days before publication of his final book, the memoir *In Paradise.*

Bill McKibben

Bill McKibben is an author and environmentalist who in 2014 was awarded the Right Livelihood Prize, sometimes called the "alternative Nobel." His 1989 book *The End of Nature* is regarded as the first book for a general audience about climate change, and has appeared in twenty-four languages; he has gone on to write a dozen more books. He is a founder of 350.org, the first planet-wide, grassroots climate change movement, which has organized 20,000 rallies around the world in every country save North Korea, spearheaded the resistance to the Keystone Pipeline, and launched the fast-growing fossil fuel divestment movement.

Thich Nhat Hanh

Thich Nhat Hanh, who coined the term "Engaged Buddhism" in the 1960s, is one of the most revered and influential teachers in the world today. Born in Vietnam in 1926, he has been a Zen Buddhist monk since the age of sixteen. Over seven decades of teaching, he has published over 100 titles on meditation, mindfulness, and Engaged Buddhism, as well as poems, children's stories, and commentaries on ancient Buddhist texts. Since his exile from Vietnam in 1966, he has been a pioneer in bringing Buddhism to the West, founding six monasteries and dozens of practice centers in the United States, Asia, and Europe, as well as over 1,500 local mindfulness practice communities. He has built a thriving community of over 700 monks and nuns worldwide, who, together with his tens of thousands of lay students, apply his teachings on mindfulness, peace-making, and community-building in schools, workplaces, prisons, politics, and businesses throughout the world.

Matthieu Ricard

Matthieu Ricard received a PhD in molecular genetics from the Pasteur Institute in 1972 before departing his native France to study Buddhism in the Himalayas, eventually becoming a monk of the Shechen Tennyi Dargyeling Monastery in Nepal.

Renowned also as a photographer and translator, he is the author of numerous books, including *Altruism: The Power of Compassion to Change Yourself and Your World, Happiness: A Guide to Developing Life's Most Important Skill,* and, with his father, the late Jean-François Revel, *The Monk and the Philosopher: A Father and Son Discuss the Meaning of Life.* He dedicates all the income of his work to two hundred humanitarian projects run in the Himalaya by the organization he founded, Karuna-Shechen.

Sulak Sivaraksa

Sulak Sivaraksa, a leading Thai dissident, is founder of the International Network of Engaged Buddhism. He has been a visiting professor at UC Berkeley, University of Hawaii, Cornell University, and Swarthmore College. He is author of *Seeds of Peace: A Buddhist Vision for Renewing Society.* He won the Right Livelihood Award in 1995.

Gary Snyder

Gary Snyder was born in San Francisco on May 8, 1930. His first book, *Riprap,* published in 1959, has become a classic in American poetry, and he has published more than a dozen collections of poetry and prose. *Practice of the Wild* is one of the most influential books about the environment of the last fifty years. His recently completed long poem, *Mountains and Rivers without End,* is broadly recognized as one of the greatest long poems in American literature, and his last book of poems, *Danger on Peaks,* was a finalist for the National Book Critics Circle Award. He was awarded the Bollingen Prize for poetry in 1997. He also has the distinction of being the first American to receive the Buddhism Transmission Award from the Bukkyo Dendo Kyokai Foundation.

Robert A. F. Thurman

Robert A.F. Thurman is the Jey Tsong Khapa Professor of Indo-Tibetan Buddhist Studies in the department of religion at Columbia University, president of Tibet House US, a nonprofit organization dedicated to the preservation and promotion of Tibetan civilization, and president of the American Institute of Buddhist Studies, a nonprofit affiliated with the Center for Buddhist Studies at Columbia University and dedicated to the publication of translations of important artistic and scientific treatises from the Tibetan Tengyur. Thurman is known as a talented popularizer of the Buddha's teachings. He is a riveting speaker and an author of many books on Tibet, Buddhism, art, politics, and culture.

Larry Yang

Larry Yang teaches meditation retreats nationally and has a special interest in creating access to the Dharma for diverse multicultural communities. Larry has practiced extensively in Burma and Thailand, with a six-month period of ordination as a Buddhist monk under the guidance of meditation master Ajahn Tong. Larry is one of the core teachers and leaders of the East Bay Meditation Center and is on the Spirit Rock Teachers Council. He is one of the coordinating teachers of the Spirit Rock Teacher Training program and their Community Dharma Leader program. He lives in San Francisco.

SOURCES

Part I—Being Peace

Thich Nhat Hanh, "Suffering Is Not Enough," *Being Peace* (Berkeley, CA: Parallax Press, 1987), 3–9.

The Dalai Lama, "Cultivating Altruism," *Worlds in Harmony* (Berkeley, CA: Parallax Press, 1992), 3–10.

Charles Johnson, "Be Peace Embodied," reprinted by permission of *Lion's Roar*, July 1, 2004.

Maha Ghosananda, "Letting Go of Suffering," *Step by Step* (Berkeley, CA: Parallax Press, 1991). Meditation selections from the text.

Jack Kornfield, "Spiritual Practice and Social Action," in Fred Eppsteiner, ed., *The Path of Compassion* (Berkeley, CA: Parallax Press, 1988), 24–30.

Bill McKibben, "Enoughness" was first published in *Resurgence & Ecologist Magazine,* issue 299 March/April 2005. Reprinted by permission. All rights to this article are reserved to The Resurgence Trust.

Part II—Touching Peace

Thich Nhat Hanh, "Life Is a Miracle," *Touching Peace* (Berkeley, CA: Parallax Press, 1992), 1–9.

Robert Aitken, "The Dragon Who Never Sleeps," *The Dragon Who Never Sleeps* (Berkeley, CA: Parallax Press, 1992), xiii–xxii and selected verses from the text. Poems originally published in fine-press limited edition (Monterey, KY: Gray Zeitz, Larkspur Press, 1990).

"Walking Meditation" is from *The Long Road Turns to Joy* (Berkeley, CA: Parallax Press, 1996), meditation selections from the text.

Larry Yang, "In the Moments of Non-Awakening," reprinted by permission from *Buddhadharma*, Spring 2019.

Thich Nhat Hanh, "The Good News," *A Joyful Path* (Berkeley, CA: Parallax Press, 1994), 1.

Part III—Compassion in Action

Thich Nhat Hanh, "Love in Action," *Love in Action* (Berkeley, CA: Parallax Press, 1993), 39–47.

Kenneth Kraft, "Engaged Buddhism," in Fred Eppsteiner, ed., *The Path of Compassion* (Berkeley, CA: Parallax Press, 1988), xi–xviii.

Sulak Sivaraksa, "Buddhism in a World of Change," in Eppsteiner, *The Path of Compassion*, 9–18.

Robert F. Thurman, "Nagarjuna's Guidelines for Buddhist Social Action," in Eppsteiner, *The Path of Compassion*, 120–21 and 130–44.

Thich Nhat Hanh, "Please Call Me by My True Names," in Eppsteiner, *The Path of Compassion*, 31–39.

Sister Chan Khong, "Days and Months," *Learning True Love* (Berkeley, CA: Parallax Press, 1993), 96–108.

Gary Snyder, "Buddhism and the Possibilities of a Planetary Culture," in Eppsteiner, *The Path of Compassion*, 82–85.

The Dalai Lama, "Genuine Compassion," *Worlds in Harmony* (Berkeley, CA: Parallax Press, 1992), 131–39.

Part IV—The Greening of the Self

Thich Nhat Hanh, "The Bells of Mindfulness," *The World We Have* (Berkeley, CA: Parallax Press, 2004), 1–5.

Bhikkhu Bodhi "Reflections on the Fire Sermon," originally published in *Parabola* magazine, Volume 37 Number 1, Spring 2012 (parabola.org).

Peter Matthiessen, "Watering the Seed of Mindfulness," *A Joyful Path*, 66–69.

Thich Nhat Hanh "The Sun My Heart," *Love in Action*, 127–38.

Brother Phap Dung, "Reflections on the Paris Climate Conference" is reprinted with permission from the Plum Village website, plumvillage.org. Sister Hien Nghiem also contributed to this piece.

Joanna Macy, "The Greening of the Self," *World As Lover, World As Self* (Berkeley, CA: Parallax Press, 1991), 183–92.

Part V—Community

Thich Nhat Hanh, "Community as a Resource," *A Joyful Path*, 5–22.

Mushim Patricia Ikeda, "I Vow Not to Burn Out" is reprinted with permission of *Lion's Roar* (2017).

Sister Annabel Laity, "The Six Principles of Harmony," revised from the original version of the essay in *A Joyful Path*, 87–90.

Zenju Earthlyn Manuel, "Where the Heart Lives," excerpted from *Sanctuary* (Boston: Wisdom Publications, 2018). Reprinted by permission from Wisdom Publications.

Sister Jina van Hengel, "Precious Jewel," *A Joyful Path*, 91–92.

Cheri Maples, "Mindfulness and the Police," *The Mindfulness Bell*, Issue 74 Winter/Spring 2017, article based on a talk given on June 15, 2016, in New Hamlet, Plum Village.

Part VI—For a Future to Be Possible

Thich Nhat Hanh, "Why We Need a Global Ethic," from *Good Citizens* (Berkeley, CA: Parallax Press, 2012), 2–6, with additional material on Applied Buddhism.

Roshi Joan Halifax, "Hope at the Edge," original material for this collection.

bell hooks, "Toward a Worldwide Culture of Love," is reprinted by permission of *Lion's Roar* (2006).

Matthieu Ricard, "Wisdom and Compassion at the Service of Others," *A Plea for the Animals* (Boulder, CO: Shambhala, 2016).

The Dalai Lama, "Hope for the Future," Fred Eppsteiner, ed., *The Path of Compassion* (Berkeley, CA: Parallax Press, 1988), 3–8.

Thich Nhat Hanh, "Collective Awakening and the Five Mindfulness Trainings," *Good Citizens*, 103–117, with additional material from Thich Nhat Hanh's speech to the World Parliament of Religions in 2009.

Monastics and visitors practice Engaged Buddhism, Applied Buddhism, and the art of mindful living in the tradition of Thich Nhat Hanh at our mindfulness practice centers around the world. To reach any of these communities, or for more information about how individuals, couples, and families can join in a retreat, please contact:

Plum Village Monastery
Dieulivol, France
plumvillage.org

Blue Cliff Monastery
Pine Bush, NY, USA
bluecliffmonastery.org

Deer Park Monastery
Escondido, CA, USA
deerparkmonastery.org

Magnolia Grove Monastery
Batesville, MS, USA
magnoliagrovemonastery.org

Asian Institute of Applied Buddhism
Lantau Island, Hong Kong
pvfhk.org

Thailand Plum Village
Bangkok, Thailand
plumvillage.org/tag/thailand/

Maison de l'Inspir
Noisy-le-Grand, France
maisondelinspir.org/

Stream Entering Monastery
Victoria, Australia
nhapluu.org

European Institute of
Applied Buddhism
Waldbröl, Germany
eiab.eu

Healing Spring Monastery
Verdelot, France
healingspringmonastery.org

The Mindfulness Bell, a journal of the art of mindful living in the tradition of Thich Nhat Hanh, is published three times a year by our community. To subscribe or to see the worldwide directory of Sanghas or local mindfulness groups, visit mindfulnessbell.org.

The Thich Nhat Hanh Foundation supports Thich Nhat Hanh's peace work and mindfulness teachings around the world. For more information on how you can help, or to subscribe to a monthly newsletter with teachings, retreat listings, and other information to nourish your mindfulness practice, visit the foundation at tnhf.org.

**PARALLAX
PRESS**

Parallax Press, a nonprofit publisher founded by Zen
Master Thich Nhat Hanh, publishes books and media
on the art of mindful living and Engaged Buddhism. We
are committed to offering teachings that help transform
suffering and injustice. Our aspiration is to contribute
to collective insight and awakening, bringing about a
more joyful, healthy, and compassionate society.

For a copy of the catalog, please contact:

Parallax Press
P.O. Box 7355
Berkeley, CA 94707
parallax.org